To my nameless companion.

Wherever you are, whatever you are doing,
I have to believe you made it as a better wizard than me.

LINEAGE
The Art of Stalking

(part two)

by
Robert Abelar

Book Six
in the 'LINEAGE: The Legacy of Don Juan & Carlos Castaneda' series.

Contents

The Song of Warriorship.

"… I am a collapsed pin-point potential, riding the crest of a wave.

I am entirely empty, being an inverted bubble within the *Great Flux* – reflecting nothing but universal compassion.

Death blows the *Great Wave* ever-forward, providing for me purpose and poise – being my most trusted advisor as to my lack of time.

The illusion of separation grows from the *tonal* collapsing the wealth of the *Great Flux*. This, is the source of all my strife.

Discontent is only deserved as much as I cling to my *self-importance*. Assuming *personal responsibility* is my release, whereby I now see that suffering was the seed of compassion all along.

Singing, for knowing the biggest challenges award my greatest resilience – my opportunity to more radiantly shine.

Forever at ease, knowing I can *stop the world* at any time, in order to see the beauty infused within the *infinite now*. This, is where true *power* lays.

Born of the *Great Mother*, I am steadfast in knowing I am always nurtured, always supported and always have home beneath my feet. My core being is safe and untouchable with the *Great Mother*, as I know its true indestructibility.

In the *infinite now*, I forego all phantoms. There, the *myth of the self* cannot haunt me, for the weave of the story only stretches behind and before me, never where I am.

With gratitude as my talisman, I humbly recognise the great gift of *The Eagle* – in allowing me one chance to refine my awareness in this glorious lifetime, to offer my-self, and to be audacious enough to bow past at the moment my old friend releases me.

I am a collapsed pin-point potential, riding the crest of a wave…"

1

Home(lessness).

(aka: The Inevitable Disintegration of Self)

Robert… Robert Abelar. That had been his name. He had been someone I once knew. Or, had I? It was all so unclear now.

The name haunted about the mind, like a curious dream half-forgotten – a mental echo that you somehow feel is supposed to be important, but in all honesty, you just do not have the energy or simple motivation to recall.

He had been a funny man, had Robert. Serious. Painfully-cognitive. Obsessed with martial arts and so-called self-developmental practices. Utterly egotistical. A curiously isolated creature, with few ties, yet not suffering with loneliness because of it. After all, it was the world of people that had always represented the biggest cause-of-strife for him. And yet, it had also been the same world he was drawn back to again-and-again. It was almost inevitable that the world of people would break Robert.

And that, is precisely what happened.

He had thrown his hat in with a group of sorcerers. How he had hated that term!

For the first time in his life, he had felt connected… guided… like he belonged. Something had just felt intrinsically 'right' about being amongst such peerless individuals – regardless how odd or challenging it had felt at times.

He had done all sorts of weird and bizarre things. He had done literally-unthinkable things. He then went and did the one unthinkable thing he did not believe he was ever capable of, to the person he valued most in the world.

That one act – to his mentor, guide and friend – had finally shattered the mind he had striven to hold together for decades. He finally fell apart, and became no more. Perversely, he had almost welcomed it – finally absolving him of the *personal responsibility* of keeping it all together. It had been such an unparalleled relief; just to let it all go after so long.

As the last vestiges of self disintegrated and finally broke asunder, I had walked away from the rest of the group – unable to face what had been done.

I am not quite sure what happened to Robert after that.

And that, is where I had found myself. Homeless… without purpose, history or belonging. I was whatever was left when the *personal myth* is destroyed.

It almost seems inevitable now. Growing up in a dysfunctional family, Robert had been chronically used to imminent homelessness. Too many times as a child, his mother had rushed in to wake him and his brothers – all sleeping in the same crowded room. Waking-up to his mother in indecipherable wails once more, the child Robert understood that was the signal to pack his limited belongings, and flee the house as quickly as possible yet again.

At one point, the family had found themselves living in a squalid bedsit – the one room serving as lounge, laundry-room, dining area and bedroom for all four of the family members. The remainder of the family had sought similar accommodation elsewhere, on the other side of the city.

Not understanding at such an early age, the child Robert had found himself too many times sharing communal bathrooms with strange old men, society's drop-outs, ex-cons, and curious characters of unnerving personality. Even in the naivety of his youth, Robert had known that they should not smell of alcohol at that time of the morning, nor look at his young body in quite that way. Yet child-Robert always remained painfully polite, even when his skin crawled for no discernable reason.

The shared family room had ice on the inside of the cracked windows each morning, fighting for space alongside the mushrooms. The chip-board wallpaper sloughed-off in great weeping-fluffy sheets, as water openly ran down the mildewed walls. A constant breeze flitted through the bricks. It was where the young Robert had first learned the benefits of sleeping in his outdoor jacket.

Robert's father only heavily smoked in a vain attempt of coping. It lent the room an ethereal haze, as the thick blue-grey smog fought to blot-out the reality of puffy mould growing from within the sofa – the place his two sons called a shared bed – which had previously been over-used by so many of society's struggling. The long-faded material was scarred with the burn-marks from so many others similarly trying to cope.

Of course, the one-room bedsit had not been the only experience. For example, there was also the time Robert's mother had begged a friend to allow them to camp in her lounge. Even at a young age, Robert had been keenly embarrassed to watch his mother beg her friend for accommodation – being so vulnerable and dependent on that rainy doorstep, without any mature security or self-promoting back-up plan; their worldly belongings unceremoniously stuffed within waterlogged trash bags.

When his mother's friend begrudgingly consented, Robert felt each day the unwelcome burden of his presence. He had angered that his mother had made no show to ingratiate herself to her Samaritan friend – not cleaning a single dish, or providing any further gesture of gratitude, such as smoking outside.

Perhaps she had been too embarrassed to. He could always feel that ghost of constant humiliation enshrouding his mother like a suffocating aura. Her simply ignoring things, seemed to be her go-to coping strategy. Yet life always managed to force its presence upon her, with the family lurching to yet the next crisis. The young Robert mused that life always seemed to be hammering at his mother's door; yet like the landlords demanding rent, and the bailiffs insisting on collection, she always pretended as though she did not hear.

Maybe her smoking forty-a-day, was also her way of blanking-out the spectre of shame, with her own ritualistic spell-casting haze. It only left it to the younger Robert to make appeasing gestures to their benefactor's begrudging hospitality, as he tidied their boots, washed the dishes, and vacuumed. Often, he felt like he was trying to erase any sense of their shameful intrusion – never feeling able to scrub deeply enough.

Child Robert had desperately wanted to go as invisible and unseen as possible. This was not only to avoid his mother's unpredictable temper, but also for respite from the pity-full stares of the host's own quizzical children – who stood gawking at the dishevelled, smelly, down-and-out family, with open resentment at the intrusion. It was there, under the unbearable scrutiny of his young peers, that Robert developed a burning desire to become insubstantial and unseen. If only he could just vanish.

The agreement between his mother and friend, had been that each household assume responsibility for feeding themselves. As the friend sat around the dining room table, sharing a sumptuous three-course meal with her children and husband, Robert was all too painfully self-conscious to the discrepancy. His mother camped-out next door on the living room floor, could only ration-out candy-bars amongst her own scruffy brood, with the reprimand that they should be more openly grateful. The home-cooked demonstration of love wafting in from the next room, mocked the young salivating Robert as to the insufficiency of his store-brand candy-meal.

More than anything, it was the distinct smell of their refugee camp that had most shamed the child-Robert. He had been raised in a familiar environment constantly saturated with cigarette smoke, dog excrement and stale booze. Whenever guests had called, young Robert had always felt mortified by the insufficiently-washed underwear – showcasing interred yellowed-discharge and long-ingrained skid-marks – constantly drying across the fireplace. The musty-ness of the failed laundry, only added to the overall stank of the home.

Conversely, the home of his mother's friend weirdly smelled… *clean*. That felt like mind-boggling magic to the child-Robert! He had been enthralled how the house constantly emanated the aroma of furniture polish, fresh linen and laundry detergent, which he considered the epitome of affluence. One day, he promised himself, he would have that too… no matter how ridiculously over-ambitious and unachievable it felt.

Being ever one-step-away from homelessness, was something Robert had grown up with. It was perhaps why he never truly feared it, nor developed any real attachments of 'home' later as an adult. 'Home' was not something either of his parents had been able to keep for very long. Home, was just somewhere you inevitably had to move on from, at some surprising time or another – when the illusions of safety and security where cruelly yanked away from under you yet again.

No, what Robert had grown to fear much more, was likely that of his father's legacy: the prospect of incarceration – of being denied freedom, or at the very least, the ability to flee.

Being obliged to live alongside strangers you would never choose to. Being made to keep someone else's routine. Being forced to accept someone else's judgment. Being *helpless. That* was what had truly plagued the darker parts of Robert's psyche. Compared to that, homelessness had never been something to dread.

As an adult, finding the group of… sorcerers?… agents of freedom?… friends? Whatever term they could be considered, it had truly felt like Robert's first real homecoming.

They tested and tried him in totally new ways. Yet, he had experienced a profound belonging and trust with the other members, even when pushed to bizarre and incomprehensible extremes. He had known that their challenges of him were not of personal gain or incompetence, but rather truly well-meant for his betterment. For the first time in his life, rather than experience shame or resentment, he had been truly grateful.

Yet, that world of sorcery – or as Robert's group preferred to call it, *the art of freedom* – had challenged him in other ways (or, was it exactly the same ways?). It had pushed him on mercilessly. In all fairness, they had warned him.

Whether it was his chaotic childhood, or his later dealings with an unusual group of 'seekers', perhaps it had always been inevitable that Robert would finally break. Maybe as an entity, he had always been entirely unsustainable. Not even the best of men can hide from fate, no matter how far or fast they run… no matter how hard they may train.

Robert's father had suffered a mental breakdown at one stage – abandoning the family, moving back to the coddling arms of his own over-bearing mother. It had repercussions, in years-and-years of acrimonious divorce proceedings. Robert's mother had openly and repeatedly bad-mouthed and belittled her husband for his unfortunate mental decline. Yet, even the young Robert acknowledged how it was somewhat ironic, that she too went on to suffer several nervous breakdowns.

Being brought back from the hospital once again – after having left Robert and his siblings alone to somehow figure-out another living arrangement – he could only watch his broken mother constantly twitching away from her most-recent psychological break. As his mother helplessly sat covered in a pathetic mound of her own cigarette ash, the child Robert had resented his incapable parents. He grew to fear and despise helplessness, much more so than homelessness.

A particularly stark memory of another of his mother's breakdowns, had been the image of his native grandmother walking in – tabard donned, rolling her sleeves up, and getting on with the school lunches, ironing and laundry. With remnants of war-time pragmatism, she corralled the children to help – not allowing anyone, including herself, the luxury of moaning.

It had been that matriarchal grandmother who had first instilled within Robert, that you did what the situation *needed*, not what you *wanted*. It was to be unknowingly enforced years later, within martial arts training. Unbeknownst to Robert, he had started learning to tackle *self-importance* – and *assume personal responsibility* – from an unusually early age.

Before school one day, his grandmother had instructed the young Robert to go reassure his broken mother that he loved her. It had been such a routine day – and such a simple request – but a life-changing moment for his young psyche, which would ripple-out for years to come.

20

Robert had an unforgiving teaching moment, whereby he had stood over the sleeping form of his trembling mother. Surrounded by cigarette buts and his mother's nervous whisperings, he had not felt love. No, it was anger that consumed his being – at how helpless his mother was, and how helpless she made those around her.

He knew he *should* say, 'I love you Mom'. But even at that young age, he just could not – and never did again. It choked him, unable to pass his lips. He could offer no refuge or solace to the shattered being of his mother. He crossly wondered why it was even his young responsibility to be care-giver and reassurer.

Instead of offering assurances, child-Robert had hidden in the closet, until sufficient time had silently passed, whereby he felt it had been long enough to meet his grandmother's expectations. He had then stealthy tip-toed down the stairs, and disappeared into the city for the next twelve hours – losing himself in the noise; desperately searching for, and trying to escape, he knew not.

Yet from that morning onwards, he carried the constant guilt, as to how much of a monster he must be, for not being able to express… or feel… simple love for his own mother – the person who had given him being. That, only drove him more zealously over the coming decades – always moving him from home to home, in order to escape the monster he always assumed he was.

These experiences – of watching his primary caregivers lose a hold on their very sense of self – being incapable of even speech, let alone the ability to care for themselves or their children – had keenly burnt into Robert's memory, forming a significant part of his *personal history*. He had grown into a man, who on some level assumed that due to his psychological and genetic heritage, understood that it was merely statistically inevitable that he too was harbouring the seed for a full mental collapse at some stage. After all, it had to be inborn somewhere, nestling within the fibres of his neurological inheritance.

It was part of the reason Robert had always felt it was none of his business ever being (self) confident in anything – as the conclusion felt almost pre-written. At some point, he would break too. The 'self-illusion' would shatter. What had been the point of pretending otherwise?

It was partly what had fuelled him to gratitude – being thankful for each preciously self-aware moment before the inevitable. He truly appreciated the lucid moments before the monster finally broke free.

He had never felt quite unconvinced that the group had intentionally played on this – his innate sense of uncertainty and predestined doom. Perhaps he had been raised as a prime candidate for cult-hood after all.

Robert had always questioned if he was more vulnerable and naïve than he cared to admit. It was another legacy of his upbringing – the stark examples provided by his caregivers, as to how lacking in self-awareness they repeatedly chose to be.

Over the course of their unusual association, Robert's beloved Chinese instructor – Meili – had given him a series of koan-like riddles, as an on-going meditative exercise. The idea was to utilise the 'unsolvable' riddles, to purposefully deconstruct the usual mental narrative. That, was dangerous for someone like him… or more accurately, for someone with that dubiously-constructed sense of self, built upon such unreliable psychological foundations.

Ever trying to please others and ingratiate himself – like the perennial guest forever squatting on the floor of greater people – Robert had sat, meditated, pondered and struggled to answer each of Meili's 'mind mines', (or, 'nexi') as she nicknamed them.

"Where is now?"

"If I were to pour you tea, who would receive it?"

"What is the nature of all things?"

"Who is dreaming?"

"If I were to draw my blade, what is the truth of the matter?"

These, were just a few of the 'mind mines' that haunted and aggravated Robert's adult mind over the course of his (re)training. After numerous mistakes, rejected answers, and so many hours sat on his damned *zafu* cushion, he had replied to each one, to his little master's smiling acceptance.

"Good," she would flatly reply, without looking up from her tomato plants. And then, he would simply be given another excruciating riddle.

Yet, in the years of their association, there had been one 'mind mine' that Robert had never answered to Meili's satisfaction.

"What, is your real name?"

It had deeply frustrated Robert. As part of his dysfunctional upbringing, he had his own name changed as a young child, by his unmeaningfully-wayward parents. Even the eventual new name (Robert) had not stuck – as the family only went on to use a nickname for the remainder of his childhood (Bo-Bo, later Bobby).

With his half-siblings being adopted – then changing their surnames yet again as adults (as well as that of their own children, perpetuating the cycle) – with his mother marrying several times, and Robert befriending several people in university who had changed their own names (as part of gender-reaffirmation), it was little wonder he found the concept of names to be less solid than most others appeared to. It was another unsettling echo of his *personal history*, leaving him less sure of himself and the world.

His world had grown into a quagmire of smoke and mirrors – not the concrete absolute, which everyone else appeared safely harboured within. His very sense of self had been as solid and irrefutable to him, as much as the possibility of changing one's name for only a few bucks.

After the grown Robert had finally walked away from his family, and threw his hat in with the group, he had gone on to legally change his own surname under law, to 'Abelar' – to reflect his purported mark as a 'stalker'. It was at that point, that Meili had pushed him to answer the new 'mind mine.'

"What, is your real name?" she had relentlessly pursued him with. It had fiercely burned within him, much more so than the physical protest within his legs, from the increasingly impossible squatting positions the tiny instructor had also imposed upon him.

Robert had gone to Amsterdam with his fellow trainees, with this one burning question in-mind. No matter how he answered – no matter what name he gave – it was always rebuffed by the cherished little Asian herbalist.

"The monkey chatters at his reflection in the pond, and think himself so clever!" came her typical reproach to his latest answer.

It stood to reason, that Meili had known of Robert's *personal history*, and was intentionally picking at a particularly festered psychic scab. This one, was uniquely effective at unravelling the threads of his being.

Robert had gone to Amsterdam under the misguided wish of a lighthearted vacation. Instead, he had been charged with yet another taxing training opportunity. He had found the truly bizarre, and worse, the truly terrifying. Alongside his two cohorts – Elizabeth and Josephina – they had been pitted against three apprentices of a counter organisation of sorcerers. The trial had not been without cost.

His most cherished instructor – Florinda – was the one person he had felt bonded with the most throughout the entire course of his life. Yet, Robert had gone on to do the unthinkable to her – pushing her over the edge of the abyss, into the stark darkness of the void. He had crossed a threshold he had never considered himself capable. The consequence of his lashing-out at his beloved teacher, had echoed-out with a greater force than the sickening 'crack' that had filled the dark basement.

It had been utterly unthinkable. And, it had finally broken him.

"What, is your real name?"

Right up until the last vestiges of his self disintegrated, Robert had not known. But, I did.

I was homeless, as had always seemed inevitable. It is funny how that truly delighted me. Rather than being scared or defeated, fully accepting it made me lighthearted and liberated, more than Robert ever had been – finally releasing a decades-long possession of anxiety and dis-ease. I was now born of freedom.

In a strange way, I took comfort from the *flow of power* – how it rippled through decades of circumstance and discourse, to bloom and manifest just as it was always meant to. I was part of something bigger than myself. I at last belonged to something that ceaselessly provided for me, even when I failed to recognise it, or no matter how lost I became along the way.

I finally succumbed. I finally stepped forth without care or burden.

I was not homeless because I had nowhere to rest or belong. I was homeless simply because the central pin fastening my personal narrative had finally, and completely, come undone.

"What, is your real name?"

I was homeless. I was nameless. I was truly no-one.

2

Practical Matters of the Everyday World.

(aka: Doings of the Tonal)

Robert had been a stubbornly dichotomous creature – thinking in terms of 'this' or 'that', or somewhat idiotically of the 'normal world' versus the 'sorcerer's world'. Being unburdened of the entrapments of modern thinking… or even, just thinking… I was free of such limitations.

Walking away from the airport after Robert's return from Amsterdam, I could instantly appreciate that the world was not so neatly compartmentalised. Whereas Robert had been so remarkably blinded by his education and so-called intellect (his anxiety-fuelled desperation of clinging, bolstered by the *self-importance* of intellectualisation), I now saw with clear eyes that the world of sorcery flowed right in, around and through the everyday world. Despite Robert's life-long ignorance, it always had. It was astoundingly beautiful, now that I was no longer that constant one-step removed from it.

What that counterintuitively meant, is that I ignored the pragmatic and as-equally-real demands of the everyday 'real' world, to my own detriment. In my new, unburdened state – whilst there was a real pull to the abstracts of the realm of sorcery – I knew that my survival also meant paying equal consideration to more down-to-earth matters. Balance in all things, as an old pipe-smoking hippy had often reproached the violently-dichotomous Robert.

Whilst Robert had never been homeless as an independent adult, some part of me now appeared to automatically know the rules of making it work. Perhaps, it was Robert's childhood legacy lingering? Yet, I knew it was the result of my new mind-state… or more accurately, the lack of mind-state… and my newly granted perceptual fluidity. I simply *knew* how to immediately proceed, because now I could *see*.

Gone, was the world of shoulds, shouldn'ts, wants, can'ts, of *this or that*. Arbitrary classification was a shadow-dream of Robert's. Now, I dealt in simple *is-ness*.

As the airport had shaken with the collapse of the last vestiges of his habitual mind, Robert had handed his belongings to his cohort, Elizabeth. With comprehending and imploring tears in her eyes, she had reluctantly taken his wallet, phone and luggage. Yet, he could no longer hear her pleas, from the gulf of impassable distance that separated them by the hair's-breath of a broken mind.

The only thing I had walked away with – actually, of the most value – was a small carry-on bag, which contained the likes of a wash-bag, and a small change-of-clothes, such as extra pair of socks and underwear, alongside a second shirt.

Otherwise, the only clothes I had to wear, were the jeans I wore, the light jacket, and my boots. Thankfully, denim jeans are a life-saver for anyone living on the streets, not only being comfortable and insulating, but mostly, durable.

Somehow, the new rules to survive by came to me like city sounds on the wind.

First-and-foremost, I knew to remain within the city. As Robert had proven too many times, he had been raised as a uniquely urban-dweller – being entirely unaccustomed to the countryside, unlike his burly Ninjutsu instructor, Jon-Paul.

Yet, it was more than practical concern. In my new state of *seeing*, a core part of me intrinsically knew that the *powers* that coursed through the world, would cut me down in an instant, should I attempt to live in the wilds.

No – *power* dictated that I was to stay and thrive within the city. There was purpose there for some reason, even if I could not see to all ends. The urban jungle was simply the 'right' place for me to be, by dictates of balancing myself within the *flow of power*.

In reality, in my more harmonious state of perceptual synergy, I had no personal issue with remaining city-bound. Utterly gone, where the vestiges of reasonableness and rationality that Robert had pigheadedly championed for so long.

The cheap distinctions of 'urban' and 'rural' had vanished. I now saw an energetic environment, and its energetic occupants. The sharp-suited businesspeople herded around their city coffee-shops, like docile gazelle at their watering-holes, each quietly stalked by unseen *powers* much greater and threatening than they ever realised.

Within the unique energetic conflux of the urban jungle, is where I felt I needed to be. So simply, it was the duty of my own warriorship to acquiesce to that, and make it work.

To do so, I had to adhere to unspoken rules. These were not arbitrary rules of the mind, but again, commandments of *power*.

The first rule of staying in the city, just made practical sense. After all, even on the fringes of society, the cityscape remains replete with easily-accessible abundance. Being a modern manifestation of waste and over-provision (indulgence), the city could still richly provide, even to those with reduced social status.

I had quickly sourced additional supplies to the limited belongings I had walked away with. It turned-out that provision was all around me; I just had to let go, and trust. That, would have been near-impossible for Robert, who had learned not to trust even himself.

Now, I did not neurotically need to know the intricacies and doings of all around me, in order to fashion confidence, via the illusion of control. Instead, I merely positioned myself within the *Great Flux, listened to the shadow of my own death as my most trusted advisor,* and had faith in my *personal power* to move me. Words do not do it justice; but the lived experienced was everything.

"Confidence is for average men, doing average things, forever seeking to average everything out, so that it is known, familiar and safe," Robert's tiny Chinese instructor had once told him. "The true confidence of a warrior, is the humbleness he get from *letting go*, and giving himself over to *power*. He know the *Great Mother* always under his feet! He know he always has gesture with *death!* He know, that in releasing his fearful grasp of everything, that he was safe and at home all along!"

Despite having the least worldly possessions and social status, that feeling of overflowing abundance, now permeated every aspect of my being. In my abandonment, I was fuller than Robert had ever been; yet, it was not with ideas, as he had been. I was now bursting of emptiness.

One of the most bountiful sources for supplies, was the local railway system. The things people would leave behind on a daily basis, was truly astounding. Umbrellas, jackets, food, and even a brand-new quilt, where just some of the items the urban-dwellers habitually left behind on their hectic migrations.

The trick to reaping such rewards – which included utilising the heat, shelter and toilets of the train carriages – was in using the heavily subsidised (and thus, less well-used and less-monitored) urban branch lines. As the major source of revenue was on the fancier commuter and shopping routes, these were much more policed by railway personnel, and thus big interchange stations best avoided. Instead, it was the infrequent local lines – with sporadic traffic (best avoided at peak-times, but open-pickings out-of-hours) that reaped greater rewards at reduced risk. This included choosing smaller stations with no automated barriers, no CCTV and no staffing at the inter-urban stops.

Conversely, camouflaging myself within the din and hedonism of travelling soccer fans, reaped particularly bountiful rewards on game days. On these occasions, the trains were too busy to effectively police, and the fans too inebriated and celebratory, to take too much care of their waste and belongings. They would leave so much behind in their pursuit of escapism.

This, lead on to the second important rule – knowing just when, where and how to capitalise on opportunity. For instance, too many times did I see people leave the likes of laptops, mobile phones and wallets on the trains. These, I did not touch.

This is where the unique make-up of my none-mind manifested. I did not refrain from taking such items because of any moralistic reasoning. Morality was merely the ugly construct of discourse, the judicial system, academia and mind… all too crude and inorganic. 'Morality' had the distinct, artificial scent of civilisation about it.

Rather, I was now existing in terms of *power*; and that, was more of an unstructured feeling, or organic placement, than of words or petty reason.

Some part of me – a level beyond rationality and reason – intrinsically *knew* that such financially-lucrative objects like laptops, held an inherent detriment. If I purposefully coveted the likes of money or pawnable goods, I would only hemorrhage *personal power*, and fail in whatever this new life was.

Just like leaving the city for the isolation of the countryside was tempting, I ultimately knew that taking anyone else's credit cards or electronic goods, would only lead to doom.

Such easy pickings were the lure of malevolent spirits. It was enough, whereby helping myself to someone's purse, would only open one of my energetic meridians, to allow in an *ally*. Thus, I accepted only those pragmatic gifts that *power* put in my way via beneficial *omens*.

In his arrogantly-rigid reasoning, Robert had always been highly skeptical of such trickeries, as he considered them. Yet here I now was, listening to the squawks of birds, the honk of a taxi, and the hum of an overhead power-cable – all uniquely timed within the *Great Flux*, to let me *know* when it was safe to proceed… what was safe to harvest. The city was bountiful with such *affirmations*, if one chose to listen.

It was all so hilariously simple! All it had needed was for Robert to let go of his decades-long obsession with rationality and reasonableness. No wonder he had been so tired, spending so many of his inner resources anxiously grasping onto everything. All along, he had only needed to truly relax for once, and the world would harmoniously provide!

Once I realised that the floor of my abode was the very dirt beneath my feet, then my home suddenly becomes planet-wide! My feeling of being grounded and just where I needed to be, engulfed every atom of my being.

Of course Robert had been so lost! Whilst he did not subscribe to traditional trappings of westernised life, he still stubbornly insisted on reason, labels, categorisations… that somehow, everything had to make sense. He aggressively clung.

Now, I realised there was more reassurance by leaning into the chaos, and not desperately trying to explain it away. Recoginising there was vastly more to the universe that we did *not* know, than we ever did, impregnated the *great unknown* with magical possibility. The great din of the city, was no longer given the *power* to be assumed as 'right' or 'normal'.

The third rule was one of the most important: that no-matter what I did, I was to avoid other people, and go unseen. The trick, was to lose myself in plain sight, within the throngs of the city's zombie inhabitants.

The type of people to avoid, were *all* people. To this end, I knew I needed to be well-groomed and presentable enough to avoid looking like a homeless person. This, was to make sure I did not make those city-dwellers around me uncomfortable, thus drawing attention to myself via turning any self-reflection on their *internal dialogue*. I knew enough, that their *tonals* would lash-out in (self)destructive ways, if the light of their attention were ever to be drawn to true self-reflection. My invisibility was as much to protect everyone else, as myself.

Clearly, avoiding the attentions of the authorities was paramount. The primary focus of the police was not in truly helping the homeless, but in moving them on – again, with the priority to avoid any uncomfortable self-reflection forced upon the city's compliant tax-paying masses.

Too many times, I saw other homeless people being harassed and herded-on by the police. It was largely not because of anything they were doing, but simply rather where they chose to flaunt their existence. They were an intolerable offence to civilised society's delicate sense of self.

Being homeless in the busy retail sector of the city center was not ideal. There, you were too visible to the average urbanite, and too much of an uncomfortable reminder. The police corralled you – not for anything like a shelter or support – but merely to herd the destitute to the less obvious camps of homeless elsewhere in the city. Out of sight, and out of mind.

Some street-dwellers made use of this. After all, a night in a dry police cell was not too bad, especially on a stormy or colder day. Likewise, the prospect of imprisonment did not hold the same threat to a homeless person – with nothing to lose, and everything to gain, such as food, a comfortable bed, shelter, drug-rehabilitation programs, and quite importantly, imposed routine and structure etc. Subsequently, I would often witness a homeless counterpart become theatrically hostile with the police, easily cajoling them into the provision of temporary accommodation.

As much as avoiding the general masses and authorities was understood to be crucial, so too was avoiding my fellow homeless. There was no refuge or belonging in the abundance of the city's nomads.

Robert in his naivety, would have assumed that an understanding – of a connective thread of compassion – would bind the homeless together in common struggle. It was with unclouded eyes, how I saw that one of the biggest threats to the homeless, was their own kind.

Most people living on the streets only had a handful of worldly possessions. After all, you had to be able to carry whatever you had with you, in a nomadic lifestyle. As such, these handful of objects were possessively guarded – literally being the deciding factor between life-and-death. Shoes or rucksacks thus had far more real-world value than any new banker's state-of-the-art car, or doctor's skiing paraphernalia. Consequently, such belongings were the primary target for other opportunistic street-dwellers.

Too often, the homeless are considered as 'lazy' or 'without truly trying'. The reality is, that the majority of them are in such dire circumstance because of very real and very persistent reason. Homelessness is the unfortunate – and to those lucky enough to afford the luxury of judgement, unsightly – side-effect, not the underlying problem in itself.

Alcohol and drug use were rife amongst the unhoused tribes. Yet, I could *see* that such addictions were also not the cause, but a contributing factor and heart-breaking symptom. Rather, the primary stench of lingering trauma hung about the homeless much more than anything else.

Too often, I could *see* the vast spans of their *personal histories* leeching the *power* right out of my fellow vagrants. Childhood physical, sexual and emotional abuse imbued nomadic people, well into their fifties, sixties and beyond; entire lives threaded in pain.

The shadows of their wounded childhood psyches plagued them everywhere, like haunting wraiths hounding them for their very lifeforce. The voices of their long-deceased parents and abusers still called after them, decades afterwards – taunting from within the crammed hollow-spaces of their fractured psyches, which they still carried around, unable to relinquish even in homelessness. The possessive ghouls of self-judgment and shattered self-esteem allowed no respite, even when disenchanted from home and belonging. The temporary relief offered by the *false-allies* of booze and drugs, only offered shallow release from *personal history*.

Sure, you could take such a person off the streets, and put them into a rehabilitation program. Indeed, many of them were given financial assistance of the state, even getting the likes of food vouchers and free temporary hotel accommodation. Charities would hand-out new shoes and blankets, and offer places on drug-programmes. Well-meaning Samaritans would toss them a few coins, in exchange for alleviation of their own guilt and fear – an entire world of suffering only separated by a nice suit, or some top-spec headphones.

This, was part of the problem when viewing homelessness – as many people like Robert would see the so-called advantages, and subsequently criticise the vagrant for not readily capitalising on them. Too many people, see the homeless as 'choosing' to be homeless, and thus somehow being worthy of their lower station in life.

"Try harder, like the rest of us!" was a common retort I would often see hurled at those vagrants begging for loose change.

The problem is, that once a person comes out of a two-week rehabilitation residency, or is forced to leave the temporary over-night shelter, their *personal history* floods right back over them like a possessing ghost. They may have even been without booze or drugs for a month, but when left unsupported to face the recurrent myth of their 'self', the old, debilitating ways soon rob even the best of us of *power*. The *spirits* clustered about the exists of the shelters like hungry ghosts.

After the latest bout of rehabilitation, I would observe a fellow nomad forced back onto the streets – only days or hours later, slumped within the release of their old, *false-allies*. No, the mythical-strands woven of trauma, threaded into *personal history*, were much trickier to *see*, let alone untangle.

In his new-found middle-class, westernised sensibilities, the matured Robert had attended too many dinner parties, whereby his equally affluent friends would debate trendy issues – such as homelessness. His friends would cite disgust, chastising in self-congratulatory tones that, "if the bums can afford a mobile phone or cigarettes, they can afford somewhere to live!" Robert's dining companions conveniently failed to understand the simple reasoning that a mobile phone was much easier to afford, than a house.

Silently, Robert would feel embarrassed, recalling how even at their most destitute times, his parents always found a way to fund their nicotine addictions. No… his fortunate dinner-party friends always conveniently failed to take into account the one troublesome factor that seemed to taint life: the distinct, trademark reek of human fallibility. It was never to be underestimated, in his eyes (especially when one or another of the guests would politely excuse themselves, visiting the restroom to purge after eating, or to text their mistress – always thinking themselves discreet and savvy, despite being as plainly flawed as any homeless person).

Too often, Robert would listen to his suburban dinner hosts rail as to how they do not give to the homeless, scoffing that they, "only waste it on drink and drugs."

Robert had kept his observations to himself, as to how often he had witnessed those same friends have 'a bad day in work', and reflexively open a bottle of wine on their immediate return home. Some, even self-medicated on the weekends with a little LCD, or pepped themselves up for office corporate gatherings, via a little cocaine. It was all too conveniently forgotten, in the medicating self-narrative their *tonals* spun.

When faced with sexual abuse from family members, life-long undiagnosed mental health complications, or any number of truly traumatic life-experiences – such as inadvertently finding yourself homeless – it was little wonder to my new eyes, that anyone would immediately seek to purposefully block-out the harsh realities of such things. It was how the stubbornly persistent self-deceits of their *tonals* coped.

Sometimes, it was not even that complicated. The harsh reality was that purposefully bringing about unconsciousness, was often more bearable than dealing with the cold.

Given the vulnerability of being homeless – especially to the clandestine 'raids' of other vagrants – it was crucial to maintain a proper schedule, as this makes you less vulnerable. Move and attend to ablutions during the nighttime if possible. And, moving your body during the colder time of day keeps your core temperature up too.

It was also the reason that many homeless chose to sleep both in the daytime (when it is warmer), as well as in public spaces. Caring for one's larger reputation is a luxury few homeless can afford to prioritize. Rather, in sleeping in the likes of a busy commercial through-fare, it means you are constantly observed by the crowds, and thus less vulnerable whilst asleep. Of course, that is, until the police moved you on.

I could always tell the newcomers to the scene, recognising their increased vulnerability – especially if teenagers. Other urban-nomads would feign grandiose acceptance and camaraderie, granting the connection and empathy the newcomer desperately needed at such an intensely vulnerable time. They would only wake up to find their shoes gone, or what little money they had, stolen. The newcomers soon learned harsh lessons of humanity; their own ghosts of trauma, only rankling their chains that much louder when released of the shackles of 'civilisation'.

The misguided suburbanites trying to 'help' the homeless, was another set of people to avoid. This, was especially so of religious-type do-gooders.

On several occasions, I witnessed church-goers waking up those trying to sleep in a shop doorway or in a bus shelter. This had a detrimental effect, in disturbing the much-needed sleep of the individual during safer periods. Trying to function at your best – just trying to make your best decisions – when suffering from broken sleep-patterns, was a challenge in itself. After all, being constantly vigilant, threatened by eviction, forever uncomfortable, cold, wet, hyper-alert to mugging, or hounded by well-meant interruption – it all posed a major problem when navigating homelessness, as even the most sophisticated urbanite does not think best when their cognitive functions are impaired by endless exhaustion.

Church-going interlopers would offer food or clean clothes, but only in exchange for a sermon on the teachings of the bible. Such words were of little useful currency to the street-dweller, only costing precious time. Rather, the teachings comforted the preacher much more so than the recipient. The desperate conscription of the *tonal* was perversely relentless in its obsessive recruitment, and its greater addiction to feeding *self-importance*.

In view of these factors, I immediately became a solitary creature – moving alone, trying above all else to go unseen. This included not uttering a single word. It was not a vow of silence or conscious decision. Rather, something in my new state-of-being was utterly without speech. It was though I had become exhausted of words. It felt natural… right, somehow.

In dressing smart-enough to avoid the attention of the urban-dwellers, I also had to avoid appearing too well-groomed to arouse the attention of the swathes of fellow street-dwellers too. The trick was to strike that ever-fine balance of middle-ground.

My day consisted of balancing two primary tasks: that of continued self-developmental practices (albeit, by that stage, they were not consciously-undertaken tasks, merely a fundamental expression-of-being), yet still attending to practical matters. However, just what was 'practical' and what was 'self-developmental' had become curiously blurred.

Robert, would have been utterly disgusted – and ashamed – of eating food from the trash. Yet, I learned all-too-quickly, that the level of abundance and waste in the city is such, that an obscene quantity of food is unnecessarily discarded every day.

Public water-fountains were an easy source of hydration. Eating from bins became relatively simple to decode: you did not eat food directly from the trash, but it was okay to consume the leftovers from still within the polystyrene and plastic containers.

Too many malls and supermarkets now had locks on their dumpsters, to prevent the homeless from raiding the (grossly plentiful) amounts of perfectly-edible food, daily tossed into the garbage. The trick was in finding those grocery stores that did not ascribe to such practices (usually, local-run organisations) or those who did not pay for their over-worked staff to care enough about the upkeep of such bureaucratic tasks, spun a hundred miles away.

The madness of it all made me laugh aloud one day. I had found an unlocked dumpster sporting a written disclaimer, towards liability should anyone partake of the contents. Even homelessness had succumbed to the ghouls of officiousness and litigation!

It remained, that finding a dumpster of perfectly fine food was a delight! As always, it only depended on maintaining the right schedule, and avoiding detection. To this end, the retailing areas were an endless treasure-trove of sustenance. On occasion, it was easier to let the city's birds point-out a bountiful stash of food, who would then squark offendedly-away when approached. After all, the crows had much keener eyes than I ever did.

Robert's instructors had always made fun of his eating habits. Being the youngest of five children, from a poor family with limited meals, he had developed into an adult who wolfed-down his food. It was a long-unexamined impulse to eat what you could, as quickly as you could, lest you go to bed hungry. His Chinese instructor had tried to train him out of this unmindful habit, by forcing him to eat with chopsticks.

"Ancestors save me!" she had sighed in exasperation, when finding Robert had only learned to use the chopsticks more proficiently and rapidly to devour his food.

What my new self delighted to discover, was just how little I actually needed to eat in order to survive. In comparison to the expensive protein-shakes, organic produce, fine whiskeys, luxury cheeses, and trendy farmer-market goods Robert routinely over-consumed, I found myself eating only morsels in comparison.

What truly thrilled me, was that in my deprived state, it was like I were only tasting food for the first time! Even the tiniest parcel of food scavenged out of the trash, tasted amazingly good. Each mouthful was enough – a composition of truly astounding sensory stimulation, bursting with joy and gratitude!

In the deluge of his quick-paced, over-stimulating consumption, Robert had been practically blind in not only his appreciation of taste, texture and satiation, but in every other bodily sense too.

The only co-existing rule to my new manner of eating, was that I refrain from the likes of refined sugars, processed meats, or anything saturated with trans-fats, palm-oils and preservatives etc.

Robert had always scoffed at anybody monitoring their intake in such a way – teasing his friends as to their gluten-free or carb-free faddy diets. He had even taken a weird pride in demonstrating that he could eat anything he wanted.

But again, my now not partaking of such artificial ingestants, was not a moralistic or cognitive choice. I now *saw* how such over-processed substances poisoned the *luminous body*. Yet, it was little to do with the effects of chemical interaction; more so as an amalgamation of the warped *intentional* investment woven into such goods. Feeling much more energised and pliable from eating natural or organic foods, it was easier than Robert had assumed to seek proper sustenance within the wasteful abundance of the city.

Self-care, hygiene and health were also of high priority. After all, when solely reliant on your immediate self without medical support, you cannot afford to get sick or damaged. You cannot afford to stop, and opt-out of such nomadic existence.

The realisation came that modern concepts of hygiene were not as concrete or unforgiving as they first appeared. There was no need to wash several times a day, as the cosmetics companies advertised. There was no biological demand to imbue clothing and surroundings with multiple layers of protective antibacterial chemicals, as big-pharma would have us believe. Millions of years of evolution had granted us a remarkably robust immune system, which meant there was proportionality little risk of me becoming seriously ill, through consuming the left-over food that another person had tried and discarded. I now had a faith in my own body, which Robert had never enjoyed.

Self-care also meant figuring-out the best ways of attending to your personal care unseen (again not only for your own self-preservation of going unmolested, but primarily as to not cause an increase of attention to the detriment of by-standers). The local train and bus stations were usually too busy to allow you to go unnoticed. However, certain public facilities were worth paying the token admission fee, in order to use the sinks, toilets and dryers. If you could afford a small investment via some loose coins found on the street, then it could reap bigger rewards, in allowing you to wash the 'social passport' of your face, or invaluable items like socks.

Maintaining a constant migration, I quickly learned that one of the biggest unspoken assets to a homeless person, is their feet. After all, one of the crucial factors to surviving on the streets, is to keep moving. And to do that, you need healthy feet.

One of the tricks to promoting mobility, was to cut a few inches off my jeans. The last thing I needed was for the jeans to get wet, soak up the water, in-turn waterlogging my socks, and thus increasing the risk of foot infections.

Having unskillfully hacked my way with a discarded pair of blunt scissors, I made sure my newly-tailored jeans were hemmed with some industrial glue I had also found. Again, it was all about prioritising a certain 'unnoticeable' appearance – whereby even the likes of a rough hem could draw attention to my homeless status.

Avoiding the wet was a large part of vagrant pragmatism, especially during much-needed – albeit vulnerable – periods of sleep. Here, anything like cardboard or plastic bags would serve well, acting as insulation and damp-proofing. Keeping the body away from the ground was paramount to maintaining good health.

It was not always what was over your head that was the main concern, but your interaction between your body and the earth. "The cold and damp rise. It enter up, through sole of foot; through the earth, not the air," Robert's old Chinese instructor had baffled him with, "the rising damp make you sick." Now, I was living the reality of that teaching.

My last rule of homelessness, was one of the most pragmatic, yet contradictorily, one stemming directly from sorcery: I was not to capitalise on any of the city's services intended for vagrants. I was not to use food banks, shelters, soup kitchens, charities or hand-outs.

There was practical reason for this. For instance: even Robert had routinely noticed how often the ambulances and police were stationed outside of the homeless shelters. He also noticed the gangs that organized themselves outside, self-policing any new unfortunate who happened to naïvely find their way there. Too often, these well-intentioned places were too dangerous and hostile to individuals, who would often find themselves intimidated, hustled, robbed or worse.

More importantly to my new state-of-being, was simply the *intention* surrounding my potential use of such charitable services. My own existence was not the result of harsh or unfair life circumstances, or even dubious lifestyle choices. Rather, my fall from description, had been the result of sorcery. As such, to approach my new life on anything other than those terms, would be my downfall.

Like the matter of my taking left wallets or phones, my refusal to seek charitable support concerned what some would consider as 'karma'. The group had described it to Robert, as the *mirrored wings of the Eagle* – consisting of perfectly polished silver feathers – casting back the light of *intent*, given off by each individual *balloon of awareness*. As the primeval forebearer of the universe, the *Eagle* encompassed all of existence within its wings. In each talon, it held the two complimentary halves of being: the *tonal* and the *nagual*. With this giving arise to form – via the separation of the substance of *awareness* – the delicate light cast of each being's *assemblage point*, was in some fashion reflected back to their *balloon of awareness*.

This journey back of an individual's *intent*, could be immediate, or take longer to manifest. In some instances, it was said to take lifetimes to traverse back to the point of origin on the *sheet of awareness* – whereby another individual may have since formed. How quickly or not intent traversed the fluidic mediums of the *tonal* and *nagual*, all depended on that individual's initial command, of how potently the *intent* was originally manifested.

This had nothing to do with an omnipotent, sentient god-like deity judging humanity from up-on-high. Robert had been taught that the whims and wants of humanity held no substance of appeal for the *Eagle*, other than tenderising the underlying form of awareness for food, for it to consume at the point of death.

To this end, the reflection back of *intent*, was a thoroughly personal affair, without moralistic value-judgement. *The Eagle's embrace* – or 'latent manifestation', as John sometimes called it – was a natural balancing consequence of *personal intent*, and the fruition of its seeds.

I simply knew that if I were to personally seek benefit from the services specifically provided to those suffering the *tonal's* onslaught, the *mirrored wings of the Eagle* would reflect back such dubious intention, to manifest in a natural counterbalance.

I could not be offended or aggrieved by such limitation. There was a natural accepted that I could not bewail or claim of poor fortune, at the not being able to seek charitable or state-funded help. That would only be the *self-importance* of the *tonal* rearing its ugly head, and an unsustainable *indulgence*. Rather, I accepted it all as part of the natural balance innate to a luminous understanding. I was quite happy attending to my lot as a homeless person, content not to challenge the natural order with warped intention.

In attending to many of the gritty realities of homelessness – especially living as a *warrior* – it involved sustaining that impossibly-thin balance of maintaining routines, all whilst not maintaining routines. It meant personifying the *principles of stalking*.

To this end, there were five chief 'sites' that I frequented – albeit making a decision to constantly move between them in nomadic fashion, as need, circumstance and opportunity dictated.

The first site, was the rooftop of a city-centre store. It had not much in the way of amenities. However, it was one of the few city-centre locales which I had found to have an unsecured fire-escape, granting access to the roof. There, it was quiet and isolated.

Primarily, the chief benefit to the store-roof, was an overhanging air-conditioning vent, which blew-out warm air 24-hours a day. This not only allowed me to sleep in relative warmth (being more important, should my clothes happened to have gotten damp), but also to dry my alternative pair of socks or underpants, should I have had opportunity to wash them.

The second site, was a public garden. It had been developed into the side of a steep cliff, overlooking the water. The problem was, that – despite being nicely landscaped into a Japanese-themed garden – the steps were so numerous and steep to traverse, that seldom did any members of the public utilise the space. The local residents were largely of an aging population, thus they did not have the physical capabilities to navigate so many steep stairs. The garden was a typical testament of the city – as living manifestation of something deliberated by someone behind a desk, but poorly executed in reality.

The thing that tipped me off to this garden's discreet and underutilised nature, were the number of men I saw using the site for clandestine sexual activities. Capitalising on this, I could see that such ('straight'-identifying, married) men were more nervous of public attention than I was. As such, my presence in the Japanese gardens usually scared such skittish creatures off.

Again, there were unique pros-and-cons to the Japanese sanctuary. It consisted of a lovely little set of cascading waterfalls and individual, isolated gardens, clinging to the cliffs like layered blooms of fungi. Surrounded with an abundance of flowers, there were statues trickling clear water into an array of lily-covered ponds, being inter-connected by little curved bridges. The lack of koi fish let me know that the gardens were not regularly inspected by the city's wardens – taking too many resources to properly maintain.

Whereas the Japanese gardens did not have hot air to warm me, the landscape was peaceful and quiet, and even had a stone seated shelter (without any 'anti-homeless' designs) to protect me from the elements. And, the majority of the city's homeless did not typically venture out this far from the city centre, lest they rouse the attention and wrath of the local older residents. The aged locals perched like gargoyles, quicker to call the police from behind twitching curtains, feeling a false abundance of time to be meddlesomely-vigilant.

The third *place of power*, was an industrial site located towards the city docks. Resources – like trashcans and water fountains – were considerably fewer out in the industrialised sector. So again, few of the city's homeless ventured out so far.

Yet, it was through an act of explorative *seeing*, that I had found a unique site. There was an older section of the dockyard, which was under dwindling use. Rows-upon-rows of powerlines, cables, conduits and pipes ran for miles. The area was a tangle of by-gone industry. It had been allowed to fall into disuse and disrepair, being financially cheaper than maintaining or dismantling the infrastructure.

Amongst the rust and grime, there was a large air-duct or exhaust-vent, which rose out of the ground through a raised platform, turned ninety-degrees at a meter's height, then ran off into the distance.

For some, the pipe would not make for ideal sleeping. Whatever exhaust or chemical the duct was carrying away, there was a constant *thrum-thrum-thrum* of tireless mechanised effort.

Yet to me, sleeping under the pipe was soothing… like nestling next to a giant's heart-beat. Moreso, the duct gave off warmth. With the concrete platform being raised off the ground, it was also dry. And even if it snowed or rained, the colossal pipe overhead not only provided warmth and a noise-cancelling shelter, but prevented me from getting wet. In good conditions, I could also drape my newly-washed jeans or blanket out across the top of the conduit, to dry as I slept.

35

With the historical dockyard industry winding-down, this end of the site was seldom checked by security. Whilst having a forlorn and neglected feeling, the site provided isolation and warmth. It almost felt organic, within its rusted complexity.

The fourth site I had happened across quite by chance. There was a part of the more modernised city, which was unusually placed between suburbia and the industrial quarter. In what had historically been poorer, nineteenth-century housing – cheaply thrown-up for dock workers – in the post-modern age, that neighbourhood had been taken over by wealthier homeowners. The quaint charm of the old, had been destroyed, and aggressively paved-over with the steel-and-glass indulgences of the new.

Whereas the rich capital-working elite lived closer to their professional sources-of-income, elsewhere they owned second (or third) homes in such unique cities. They were luxurious new-builds in an isolated part of the city, serving as platforms for easier vacation access to more trendy parts of the country, or to the airport for their plethora of foreign vacations.

The construction of these expensive homes had forced many locals into more impoverished areas. Not a single one of the properties were owned by any native city-born, being vastly outside of their price range. The displaced local residents had come to resentfully call the isolated neighbourhood, 'millionaire's lane'.

There was one row of modern, large (luxurious) houses, which backed onto a small woodland. The trees ensured the rich owners did not have to either look upon the unsightly uniformed rows of poorer housing below, nor be sullied by the envious gaze of the city's masses.

In one particular property, situated on the end of the row, the owner had commissioned a little private studio at the rear boundary of his garden. From a place of *seeing*, I could tell that the rich, male owner of the property, had constructed the private sub-dwelling as an escape to his overbearing wife. He had built the small, self-contained building almost into the trees themselves, which provided ideal cover when approaching the rear of the property. Wholly irrespective to affluence and education, resentment had been magically soaked within the very foundations and mortar of the new-build – and this mal-intent cloaked my own presence much more than the trees.

Inside, there was a sink, toilet, and a sofa-come-storage unit. The owner clearly was into surfing and watersports, as so there was an outside shower – which also allowed him to wash-down his pedigree dogs too. Whilst showering in the nighttime of winter was not ideal, it remained an invaluable facility to both wash myself and my clothes (sometimes, at the same time).

The benefit of 'millionaire's lane', was that only two of the homes were permanently occupied. The rest, were vacation homes, and thus not used during the majority of the year.

Even had any of the houses been temporarily occupied, the nature of these rich-folk dwellings was such that they did not know each other, nor cared to. Rather, they had been each built with large walls, to protect the inside possessions and privacy, as only the more affluent are reflexively habituated to do. It was not a neighbourhood per se, but a collection of isolated displays of insular wealth.

Realising that the main house was regularly attended by both paid neighbourhood associations and a domestic cleaner, the much-smaller abode on the edge of the woods was routinely overlooked, being considered more as a shed or outhouse (albeit, in the owner's understanding of 'basic necessities', it was relatively luxurious). The smaller, ancillary abode was routinely overlooked, because its value was.

I figured the owner of the property must have routinely vacated the property, and forgotten to secure the sub-structure. As long as I left it clean and precisely as I found it – foregoing the use of lights and underfloor heating (as well as leaving his stash of marijuana and Vicodin untouched) – then it was an ideal place of rest and shelter, even if it were admittedly a little off the beaten track, situated midway between the dockyard and the city centre.

These sites, I felt as *places of power*. Beyond the last vestiges of my reasoning mind, my *energy body* felt them as safe places – as sites with an intrinsic flow of *power* that was beneficial to my own unique energy configuration. In each one, I could rest unperturbed, gaining an inexplicably beneficial level of recuperation in a relatively short space of time.

The last of the five sites, was the most re-energising of the *power spots*. This, was an old church located right within the city centre. It was partially falling down, being ringed-off by fencing and warning signs. Unable to offer easy commercial reward, the church was instead commonly used by the city's drug-addicts and ne'er do wells. They congregated in uneasy sermons, to lose themselves to the Holy Spirit offering absolution from within a needle.

From a place of *seeing*, I could tell the site had been deconsecrated. It no longer held that brand of *intention*. Yet, *power* remained, being much older than the church itself. I wondered if it accounted for the church's original construction of hundreds of years before, and now the inexplicable pull to the city's needy.

Normally, this site – located within the hustle and bustle of the immediate city centre, as well as frequented by so many of society's drop outs (and thus, occasional police checks) – would not be ideal. The constant din of the city reverberated around the church, being the crashing, tumultuous waves pounding ceaselessly against a beaconing lighthouse.

Yet, it was when exploring the abandoned building for the first time, that I noticed its advantage. In a semi-collapsed section of the lower tower opposite the pulpit, there was a pile of beams and rubble towards one corner. In navigating these, and utilising a series of upper-body movements and agility, I was able to pull myself up through a rough hole in the ceiling, to the first floor. From there, the aged stairs were largely intact, allowing me to access to the remains of the belltower.

To any visiting vagrant, they only utilised the spacious shelter of the ground floor – having no wish, reliance-of-health or luxury-of-risk, to try a seemingly dangerous climb. Primarily, the typical visitor only desired to temporarily use the main sanctuary of the church, in order to shoot-up in peace, before moving on – rather than using it as a legitimate place to rest.

Raising myself up into the belltower, the sudden absence of graffiti, cigarette lighters and broken glass advertised that it was a safe-space to stay. There, on a floor of rotten wood and dust, I would have the best night's sleep of all.

One of the reasons I tended to frequent the church as much as possible, was the result of a curious phenomenon. I would lay my cardboard down on the dusty, wooden floor of the belltower. The din of the surrounding city would echo around what was left of the stone walls, lulling me into immediate sleep – the sounds of traffic, crowds and roadworks like an urban chorus of angels singing me into otherness.

Each time I slept on the *power spot* of the church, I always had the same dream. I would find myself disembodied, floating miles above the earth. A great warm globe of copper sun would send out an encompassing, mellow light. The gentle curve of the earth's darkened horizon arched across my entire visual field, sloping enough to let me understand just how high I was within the outer edges of the atmosphere.

Below, the earth at first appeared densely black. However, golden ribbons of pleasing light ran like veins through the blackness – great rivers reflecting the hue of the setting sun. Above – as black as the earth below – the orange-copper horizon gave way to the infinite darkness of space. An ocean of twinkling stars pierced the void. I could not distinguish if it were the gaze of the stars I could feel, or the scrutiny of infinity itself.

Looking down across the globe, I felt peaceful and at ease. Yet, I noticed strange patterns of the same golden light, tickling across the vastness of the dark landscape below. My first thought, was that the ripples of light, appeared to run like the patterns of the wind across the top of a corn field. There was something organic and unpredictably complex to the movement of gentle amber waves.

As I became more familiar with the dreams – learning to muster my attention and focus in on the details – I saw how, what I had at first taken to be great, sweeping dark continents, were actually an infinite, global collection of individual trees. An entire world filled with the shadowy trees of sunset (or, was it sunrise?).

I came to understand the dream as interpretative – a way for my *tonal* to semi-collapse the wider sensitivities of the *nagual*. An intrinsic *knowing* came to me, beyond the doubts and fragilities of the thinking mind. The thought-leaves coated the bare branches of being, creating a rich, organic foliage.

The world I floated above, was the collective of humanity. Each one of its trees, making up the uniform dark mass far below, were individual people. Each branch, each leaf and even each shoot, were the thoughts, opinions, labels, feelings and constructs, which collectively contributed to the individual manifestations of 'self'.

As the invisible winds of *intent* ran across the human tree-landscape, it caressed individual leaves. As the branches and limbs swayed to the gentle touch of *intent*, human thought and feeling glowed into existence, before eventually passing and fading away, running on to manifest in the next tree, ad infinitum.

Seen from so far above, the wider ripples of *intent* ignited beautiful patterns of awareness across the forest of humanity. The copper light infused me with compassion, as I realised how alone, separated and painfully isolated each tree felt – being distracted by the beauty and intensity with which their own individual leaves temporarily glowed, stroked by the fleeting movement of the winds of *intent*.

"If only they could look from high above, and *see*," I thought to myself. "They would understand how much more beautiful and alike they are in their inter-organic collectivity!"

Seen from so high up, the trees were more alike than not. They each glowed with the same inner light at the touch of *intent*. Yet equally, each failed to see just how delicate, precious and all-too-fleeting that caress was, as the light waves rippled on and across the great dark sea. The glow of manifest thought and feeling was only fleetingly temporary. Yet, each tree suffered, in being distracted by, and addicted to, that passing radiance, each failing to *see* how utterly illusionary form and being were.

There remained one element to the beautiful world-scape dream, that I could not understand. I understood the huge energy-store of the sun to represent the source of all things: the *Eagle*. The forest of trees was clearly humanity, with their thoughts and feelings as leaves. The wind was the *intent*. I even knew the remote pinpricks of stars to represent the distant glow of *assemblage*, of alternative forms of life elsewhere in the universe.

Yet, there was one star that stood-out from the infinite rest. Whilst looking no brighter than the other celestial phenomena, it felt brighter – more potent perhaps, as though its distant rays touched me somehow. Whereas all of the other stars were white, this solitary point of light had the slightest colouration to it – a delicate hue that taunted a whisp of memory from me, as though I should be on the verge of recalling its significance.

I felt that I should know that star. Yet, I could not recall just why I should know its position and formation, all of the way out into the *great unknown*. It quietly called to me, shining delicately out with its strange tinge on the very edge of *infinity*.

Whilst having no conscious intention of doing so, I would experience this same dream – bursting with equal parts pitying remorse and connective compassion – over-and-over. I would begin basking in humanity's collective existence, and end with confusion over my quasi-feelings towards that one tinted star.

It was as I came to focus-in on that one frustratingly incomprehensible element of the dream, that I would suddenly start awake. Each time I did, I would come to feeling energised and refreshed... always wakening sat within the full-lotus position (of which, Robert had never been flexible enough to do). Laying myself down in the rubble of the remaining belltower, I would lie horizontal each night... and each morning find myself sitting upright, having experienced the same dream.

There was something there...

Something about that singular bright pin-prick within the sky, shining so pointedly, felt important. Something elusive tugged at the comfort of my mind, though I could not recall just what. Was it something Robert would have known?

I felt it needed decoding somehow. There was meaning or purpose within its symbology.

Known to many older cultures as two separate objects, the 'morning star' and the 'evening star' are in fact the same planet, Venus. To the Romans, she was the goddess of love and beauty – being the third-brightest celestial object in the sky, second only to the sun and moon. The nineteenth century French astronomer – Nicolas Camille Flammarion – also called Venus, the 'shepherd's star'. That felt right, yet I had no idea as to why.

John had once told Robert over honeycomb tea and sweet oatcakes, how the Mesoamerica cultures had many names for Venus: 'Nok Ek', 'Quetzalcoatl', 'Xux Ek', and in some societies, it was associated to god-figure of 'Kukulcan'.

Through the chuffs of his pipe, he had explained that in ancient Toltec civilisation, the shamans were responsible for charting the celestial movements of this strange, shining star – as it appeared mysteriously born from the light of the sun, only to be devoured by darkness each day.

The Toltecs considered it no coincidence that Venus disappeared beneath the horizon for a period of eight-days – which they considered a teaching to the eight central bands of awareness, which are only capable of sustaining sentient life within the universe. '*The Serpent's Eye*' they had called this unique pocket of centralised reality.

Furthermore, with its cyclical pattern of four, the bright-star of Venus became known amongst certain lineages for its significance to *four-pronged Naguals*, the leaders of sorcerers, with unique energetic properties.

With Venus rising in the east, and setting in the west like the sun, the Toltecs held it to be a living demonstration of the duality of the *Eagle* – of the innate symmetry of the universe, stemming from the interplay of the *tonal* and the *nagual*, which the great bird holds in each talon. Venus, to the *seers of old*, was considered the planet-star containing the secrets of death and resurrection. It was the living celestial manifestation of the recycling force of the *Eagle*.

Waking up with clear memories of that unique dream-state, there was a strange feeling left of melancholy and profound beauty. Yet, the only worthwhile response I could offer, was to lower myself down into the convenience of immediacy, of the city's centre, in order to attend to whatever pragmatic needs I had.

Whatever that poignant prick of light represented in the psycho-celestial constellations of my dream-states, it was inaccessible to my waking mind. All I could do, was therefore to live the sober and streamlined life of a warrior.

Without rational volition, I was naturally living by the *seven principles of stalking*. In actively moving between sites, I was daily choosing my battleground. In carrying only what I truly needed for survival, I was discarding all that was unnecessary. This, included letting go of all of Robert's old clutter, such as his sense of self, and his addiction for meaning.

In utilising an uncharacteristic perceptual focus, I was moving through the daily requirements of life with an unprecedented efficiency. After all, with so much balanced on such a dubious precipice – such as my continued core wellbeing reliant on the cleanliness of a pair of socks – I had little choice but to adopt a certain cold pragmatism. Every choice, and every turn of the road, imbued life with an importance that did not allow for the old indulgence of self. I felt infinitely lighter and happier for it, unburdened by much of the psychic weight Robert had unknowingly carried.

With the old constructs of Robert fallen away, I had also relaxed to embody the fourth principle of stalking. I moved with a deep sense of ease and joy, being overjoyed by the simplest flower or scuttling bug. The old habitual anxiety was gone, and with it, all of the fears that Robert had clung-to in perversely self-bolstering tension. Without clinging to the self-masturbatory delusion of ideas, opinions and *self-importance*, my new eyes were free to *see*.

Retreating from any given site or situation was also easily allowed by the absence of self. It was why adopting a semi-nomadic existence was crucial, as it allowed me a fluidity and responsivity, whereby no-one could locate me at any given time. If the police, church-goers or other homeless arrived, it was simply time to move on, without hesitation of deliberation. I became a feather on the wind, which could not be tethered.

Compressing time in accordance with the sixth rule of stalking, was not even an effort. With the last vestiges of mind gone, so too were ideas of temporality. I had no idea what day of the week or month it was. Such taken-for-granted falsities held no advantage for me anymore. Instead, I lived between fluidic states of time, which could be compressed into an eternity or immediacy, as *power* dictated. The organic – rather than artificial – flow of time, was almost tactile in its new organic sensuality.

And last, was the seventh principle of stalking: of never pushing myself to the front. This too, came naturally enough. Everything about my new existence meant I was living almost as a ghost, moving unseen between the city's endless inhabitants.

In Robert's training, the burly ex-forces instructor, and the old hippy couple, had tried to teach him two crucial tools of *warriorship:* to become both *accessible and inaccessible to power*, and to *become a hunter*. Robert had been an idiot; always trying to rationally interpret and reason-out such teachings.

Now, without the tension of mind, I embodied such *knowledge*. It was because I lived within *power* itself. I opened myself to the *Great Flux*, and it moved me without meeting resistance. It was one of those contradictory teachings, which had too often frustrated Robert: the principle of *wu wei* – of accomplishment without trying. To his group, they had called it *the art of not-doing*.

In practical terms, I intrinsically knew that I could not rely on the services or supports offered to the city's needy. Food banks, charity hand-outs and state-funded services were all unavailable to me.

I was one of them, but not of them. I was attached to no-one.

My independence and isolation are not to be mistaken as the effects of guilt or personal ethics. From my unique standing from within the *flow of power*, I was assured by the *spirit* itself, that should I try to seek free housing or visit a soup-kitchen, that *power* would cut me down in an instant. It would manifest as illness, ill-fated happenstance or violence etc.

This core *knowing* did not stem from an artificial place of crude thought or self-bolstering morality. In my new synergistic living, it was accepted as the proper manifestation of natural *balance*.

The white-haired old witch had always taught Robert to think in terms of 'reward and cost' – of an endless, ageless transaction, inherent to all energetic environments. I now *saw* that as more truthful than Robert ever had – *knowing* I could not test the *powers* with *indulgence*, as it would only be a costly offence to the *spirit*.

As such, as I was living right within the busy doings of the city and its endless array of residents – yet very much alone, almost a million miles away from civilisation.

For the very first time in my life, I was the living embodiment of a *stalker*... despite having entirely dropped the name 'Abelar'.

3

Abstracts of the Sorcerer's World.

(aka: Not-Doings of the Nagual)

Even in homelessness, day-to-day life still required a degree of pragmatism – in many ways, much more so than fashion choices, vacation spots, social status and urban décor etc. Matters of hygiene, cleanliness, safety and sustenance became more important than ever.

And yet, I was no typical vagrant.

As Robert's burly ex-Army instructor had repeatedly cautioned him, when the time came, his transition into the world of sorcery would be like his suppressed temperament… violent and stark in its undisciplined extreme.

With the breaking of mind, I was no longer held by usual constraints and perceptions. As predicted, I had jumped fully into an alternative 'magical' world. I was living in the realm of the abstract, as Jon-Paul would have put it.

The world of sorcery – for want of a better short-hand – formed an equal part of my daily being. Yet, as Florinda had also warned Robert, I could not commit myself to sorcery practices with my entirety, just as much as I could no longer fully commit to the daily world.

Balance in all things. It was a warning echoing around the last memories of mind, as if a manifest lesson of a previous lifetime. How many other incarnations of Robert had failed to heed its caution and advise?

Yet living between worlds was more than the recollections of a previous existence. I now dealt with… perceived in… lived by… terms of *power*. It was the reality that now flowed about me.

With the last rational and 'civilised' fragments of my mind gone, I was free to experience *power* – the flow of energy throughout all things; the living, breathing *Great Flux* of the *Eagle's emanations*. It was not poetic metaphor, but a new real-lived capacity of existence.

Of course, Robert had been utterly blind. *Power* had always been right in front of him, yet he still vainly searched – the quest itself deluding him. He only had to drop everything he carried, in order to *see*. So simple, yet for him, so utterly and recurrently impossible.

The enchantments of the *Black Magicians* had prevented Robert from any true synergistic use of his senses. The spells were the unspoken, unacknowledged and pervading rules of 'civilised' society, of which each member was an unwitting dark contributor. The words, assumptions, expectations and beliefs of an entire civilization – emanating back from within the historical collective psyche – cumulating in a set of invisible constructs and binding agreements of the *tonal*, robbing humankind of its magical potential. Necromancy: the dark art of constantly reanimating a dead a past, separating one from the immediacy of the infinite now, via a gulf of impassible narrative.

The agreements of the past were almost holographic in their structured insubstantiality. Yet, they had been no less implacably binding for their lack of tangible form.

Robert had choked on the sleeping-curse of the *Black Magicians*. He had drowned in the ocean of narrative, and it had filled him from the inside out. Under the self-aggrandising enthrall of the *tonal*, he had been one of the blackest magicians.

Yet now, I was free of that. I no longer honoured the old agreements, to which Robert had been unconsensually groomed since conception.

Now, I could deal with the world on an energetic level, in terms of sorcery... as a *seer*. Whereas Robert's old teachers would have perhaps been disappointed with the violence-of-progress, in parting ways with Robert, I had made the leap from idiot to *seer*, in one daring manoeuvre. Bypassing the traditional steps of *warriorship*, *sorcerer* and *man of knowledge*, I had jumped to a full-blown *seer* – able to perceive the wider energetic majesty of reality (and non-reality).

The absurdity and naturalness of it titillated me.

Of course, there was danger in the evolution too. To perceive the *flow of power* directly, lent just as much as an addictive temptation as the 'real' world, as cast by the *Black Magicians*. The magical allure of experiencing the *nagual* was if anything, even more spell-binding.

As such, I knew on a reliable energetic level, that my success in my new found life as nobody, meant neither prioritising the *tonal* or the *nagual*, nor balancing them... but constantly trying to walk *between* them, caring or committing to neither. I traversed the dual realms of the *Eagle*, like the city-scape I occupied.

As much as my days consisted of finding food, warmth and shelter, so too did the magical world of sorcery seamlessly bleed into my perceptual reality, without resistance or effort. Gone, was the painful craving to understand. I knew it was the effect of the shrinking of my *tonal*, being the natural consequence of my fractured, non-normative mind-state. So, I did not suffer the experiences as Robert would have – not beating myself up with the how's and why's of it all. I merely went along with my new perceptual reality.

It started off small. Robert, had been meticulously preened. As part of that disguise, he had a particular personal foible concerning nasal hair – whereby he had been distinctly repulsed by any sight of hair protruding from anyone's nose. As such, he went to unusual lengths to ensure this was not something he himself suffered with – becoming acutely self-aware as to the minutest signs of growth. As soon as he felt any suspect tickle, he would pull out the tweezer's to aggressively de-weed his nasal passages.

Now, without the benefit of mirrors, tweezers or electric shavers, I could feel my nasal hair tickling inside my nostril. Robert would have been infuriated and mortified. Yet now, I found the sparkle of raw sensation to be utterly delightful!

It was not the schism between approaches or perceptions that amused me. What Robert had thought or done was absolutely of no concern to me anymore. Rather, the sheer delight came from a more direct experience of the base physical sensation – of feeling the little hair tickle the inside of my nose. It was utterly wonderous, like I was only experiencing physical sensation for the very first time!

This, was how my life now was. I took delight, laughing aloud to myself in genuine, abandoned mirth, at the simplest of sensory experiences. Life was now pregnant with so much raw beauty and an unfiltered wonder-of-being.

The running of water over my hands captivated me, especially the interplay of light over the liquid surface. I could get lost for considerable time, pursuing the question: just what was the sensation of liquid water running over my skin – where was the pure sensation of fluid (was I even capable of truly experiencing that?), and where did it cross-over with the boundary of the *internal dialogue?* The hold of the description of water fell back, and I was left to revel in the unquestioned, unknowable reality of the direct experience. *Infinity* itself lay at the boundary of that playful liquid.

The digestion of the merest morsel of food, was utterly enchanting – at its changing textures and symphonic explosion of tastes. Even toileting – something Robert had for decades ignored as a necessary-but-banal chore – now represented something remarkably titillating. The inner movements of the digestion system distracted and amused me for hours. How utterly bizarre and wonderful!

It was as though seeing the world with the eyes of a new-born. This, extended beyond myself, to the outside world – even though I no longer drew such distinctions between myself and the world, between 'inside' and 'outside'.

Sitting in full-lotus within the Japanese gardens, I could spend hours mesmerised by my surroundings. The intermixing smell of the lilies, hydrangea and azaleas played-out like a delightful musical composition. The supple squeak of their dewy petals slowly unfolding, creaking like comfortable old leather. There was structured knowledge written within their scents, of which Robert had been wholly oblivious.

I would become fixated to the creak of the bamboo shoots, as they imperceptibly grew thirty feet away. The fat bees entertained me with their own knowledge, transmitted through dance rather than words; the buzz of their impossible wings, was a sheer joy.

The little sparrows frolicking in dirt-baths were endlessly entertaining to me. What great blessing I had, to be manifest in this particular energetic matrix – whereby nature had spent millions of years expertly evolving such a delightful little fellow. I was so fortunate!

Robert had been terrified of frogs – to the point of a legitimate phobia. Now sitting at the edge of the trickling pond, I was transfixed by the visiting amphibians. Their plump bodies, and the manner in which they expertly extended their slender legs, enchanted me. Once, they would have sent Robert recoiling at the mere sight. How silly and brilliant the frog was!

The merest falling of a single sycamore seed from above, transmitted an entire universe of feeling, information and experience. I saw the uniquely-designed pod twirl and dance in its downward journey. I felt it in my chest. I experienced its same sensation of movement and enacting potential, as if I were the tiny seed myself. Seed. Me. There was no such distinction.

Florinda had been entirely right, in that other lifetime of that crazy guy. The universe had been ablaze and bursting right in front of Robert all along! It was... *beautiful.*

The old lady had also been correct, insomuch that any true sorcerer could utilise the most mundane of items – be this a meditation, a crystal, a coffee, or the full-stop on a page – as a sling-shot into the *unknown..* It was all right there; right in-front of the senses, yet totally obscured by the falsity of mind.

Who was to know, that for me, it was nostril hair?! That tiny, inner tickling sensation – previously an irritant, now a disproportionate joy – was my catapult.

It was how I had found the disused ancillary abode on 'millionaire's lane'. I had been meditating on the roof of the city-centre store – focusing my attention on the audio gap between the strum of the air vent, and the wider chorus of the city. The intermittent silences – emanating from the spaces between structured sound – were like siren shadows, calling with a greater emphasis-of-emptiness.

The harsh-edged canopy of the physical world rudely interrupted my best (non)efforts. The unchecked nostril hair unexpectedly tickled me. Robert would have been disproportionately irked by that – not only the warning of impending weed-hacking, but also the interruption to his meditation, and his prized sense of accomplishment.

Instead, I laughed at its honest communication – being curious, at this fascinating new world I inhabited. The hair itself became the focus of my meditation – being an investigation of direct reality.

Beyond the crude construct of words or mental deliberation, a command – almost an external voice – prompted me with an unwavering clarity.

"Follow it," it demanded. "Follow that simple sensation into infinity!"

It was thus that I tugged at the sensation of the nostril hair tickling the inside of my nose, following the specific line of its luminous manifestation, and jumped into the *nagual.* The universe comprised an infinite number of luminous fibres. All I had to do was isolate one with my attention, and pull it with my *will.* No further explanations were needed. In fact, explanations only would have taken me further away, as it too often did *him.*

My body rose, spun, snapped and folded – and after a momentary consultation with the four winds – I found my feet touching grass within the small woodland, at the back of 'millionaire's lane'. I had forgotten my shoes, and the grass tickled my feet, tempting me in a plethora of infinite ways via immediate sensation, into the greater *unknown.* I laughed abandonly, having to make a noted effort not to lose myself to the temptation of grass flirting with the soles of my feet. Any one of those gloriously-stabbing blades would lead me into other worlds.

The explanation makes no rational sense. Robert certainly would not have been satisfied with it. Yet in my new perceptual state-of-being, I *knew* I had shifted my *assemblage point*, to light-up the strand of the nostril hair under my glowing conduit of *intent*, using it to unfold the *wings of perception*. It was as simple and readily accepted as going to the bathroom, being granted as much rumination.

Having discovered the convenient facilities of the unused ancillary abode, I had no idea how to get back to the city centre (where the small handful of my belongings where). After all, what I had done – in travelling across the entire city in the blink of an eye – offered no procedural knowledge. Rather, it had been a *dictate of infinity – a square centimeter of chance* offered by the unique and immediate manifestation of the *Great Flux*, which I had mustered the *impeccability* to capitalise on in that one moment.

The opportunity had manifested. I took it without thinking. That, was all that was needed – as a once white-haired old witch had patiently tried to explain to a notoriously-blinkered student.

The old hippy couple would have told Robert that I had hooked the *second ring of power* – that I was now living as close to being a bona fide sorcerer as Robert ever got. They would have been right… yet, I did not care – or un-care – for the understanding. Like everything else manifesting around me, it simply *was*.

From that stage onwards, my perceptual reality only blossomed, with me journeying into the magical realm of the *nagual* with ease and unconcern.

Gone, where the confines of habitual reality. "What if?" "how?" and, "what does it mean?" where mere echoes of a long-released linear mind. Such deliberations simply did not serve me anymore.

Now, I could *see*. I would spend hours (or split-seconds, who could tell?) in a state of *seeing*. This, was a direct perception of the *flow of power* – the infinite *Great Flux* of golden, luminous fibres that formed and traversed the entire energetic universe, as infinite and equally infinitesimal as it jointly was.

On a basic level, Robert had established himself as being entirely ignorant of wildlife and survival. Yet in my new state, I was not averse to foraging for organic matter that Robert would not have considered as foodstuff. Now, hibiscus, pansies and chickweed were just some of the overlooked resources available to me, being plentiful about the urban landscape.

Without experiential, academic *knowledge* – or even a rational mind – to rely on for sources of nutritional guidance, all I had to do was shift in to *seeing*. The overall glow of the plants luminous fibres would tell me if it were edible or not. Shifting depths of awareness, I could even *see* which parts of the individual plant were the most nutritious (or upsetting).

The old grey-haired witch Teresa, had been correct – that if I 'listened' closely enough to the 'little plants', they would readily tell me their secrets. Robert had just been too dumb all along to hear the constant conversation with his energetic environment. His own *internal dialogue* had been too loud to hear anything else over the din.

Robert would have called me irrational… delusional… quite mad. I did not care. Rather, I chose to revel in my new reality; but equally, to pay it no more-or-less value than seeing the traffic of the city, or picking lettuce from someone's leftovers. Each phenomenon was experienced with equally abandoned delight. I was a newborn infant of the *Great Flux*, enraptured by the investigation of raw, new sensation.

Seeing, granted me *knowledge* – being the direct transmission of relation within my wider energetic environment, rather than filtered and delayed via perception, description and crude thought. It allowed me to *know* when it was time to move on from a particular site, lest the authorities or other homeless unexpectedly come across me. The world spoke to me directly, rather than the temporally-phased prism Robert had unknowingly interpreted life through.

I could *see* a shift in the clusters of luminous fibres across the sky, which let me know of an incoming snow storm. Subsequently, I headed to the warmth and shelter of the dockyard exhaust conduit, sparing myself wet clothing. Sitting still and silent for hours, I reveled in the minuscule creaks of unique falling snow crystals. They formed a beautiful invisible chorus, imbuing the city with a subtle symphony.

Shifting into *seeing*, I knew what foods inside the trash were rotten, and would cause physical upset – which I could not afford, with my constant need for self-reliance and migration. It allowed me to *see* that even processed foods were still alive with some luminosity, with their scope of iridescence telling me how nutritious (or not) they still remained.

How the unique ribbons of light of the various foodstuffs fit within my own luminous matrix, let me *know* if it was the nutrition I needed or not. Robert, would have been utterly unable to conceptualise talking with sustenance. He would only have demanded explanation, and blinding description.

Now, I simply *knew*. I ate. I moved on.

It was during this time that I discovered the language of the trees too. Robert would have found that statement nonsensical. He would have called it 'hippy rubbish' or 'new age claptrap'. His lacking, brought of linear understanding, would have been offended.

Yet, my communion with the trees had nothing to do with verbal utterances – or even anything to do with meaning or abstractive thinking. As with everything of sorcery, understanding the language of trees was simply a position of the *assemblage point* – the perceptual conduit that filters and collapses the luminous fibres of the *Great Flux* into some reflection of reality – just as real (and 'unreal') as the everyday world I suspected I had once lived in.

It became a great source of curiosity and comfort, to sit myself beneath a tree. Yew trees held a deep history, involving a slower-but-broader move of the *assemblage point*. Maple and Hornbeam varieties, proved surprisingly chatty and accessible. However, the energetic fortitude of cedar trees was deeply soothing to me, when shifting towards the *double* state of the *nagual*.

Of course, I knew the trees were not sentient. But when experienced from a state of non-ordinary reality, it became very clear that trees and animals were not as dormant or unfeeling as humanity routinely persuaded itself. There was a living intelligence there; just not a human intelligence. *Something*, was structurally-archived within the patterns of luminosity.

A few months into living on the streets, I became unexpectedly ill. My temperature flared, my body shook, and I began vomiting. Such ill health, was not something I could afford in such a vulnerable state of self-dependence.

Shifting into *seeing*, I saw a small cluster of dulled, greenish fibres, towards the bottom left of my iridescent egg-shape, which was formed of the luminosity of total awareness. *The balloon of awareness*, Florinda had called it. It was comprised of countless glowing, amber-golden luminous fibres, spanning the entirety of the universe, and temporarily clustered together into individual human form.

Upon the top right side of the *luminous egg*, was a smaller, dazzling point of brilliance. This isolated spot of light – where only a much smaller number of luminous lines from the *Great Flux* passed through the perceptual conduit – was termed the *assemblage point*. It was the small cluster of luminosity of awareness, whereby the greater energetic environment was collapsed down into the conceptual world of being. So-called reality was assembled there, being a collapsed manifestation of perception – or, a 'convergent lens of the holographic effect of structured emptiness' – and nothing more.

The small band of green-tinted fibres told me that my gall bladder had become infected. The temptation was to let go – to expand into the *nagual* completely, leaving the world of physicality behind entirely. Without the physical description of the *tonal* as part of the totality of my being, there simply would be no gall bladder to be inflamed. Even in my new reality, the descriptive force of the *tonal*, remained persistent and restrictive. How had Robert ever lived fully under its dictatorship?!

I knew precisely which trees would aid me in achieving the journey – to ignite the full luminosity of the entirety of my form of awareness, in a move few humans ever accomplish, even at the point of death. Some trees were so old in their own descriptive hold, as to have witnessed several better *seers* than me accomplish such a peerless feat. They harboured that ancient knowledge in their roots.

In my increasing forays into the *unknown*, there had been a growing temptation. As much as Robert had never been a *dreamer*, I now found myself curious and pulled by the realm of *pure experience* – the side of reality homing the seat of *will*. It was sometimes called 'left side awareness', or the *nagual*.

The speed, intensity, and charge of the *left side of awareness* – the pliability of that *altered awareness* being moulded and tapped into any number of unique avenues – did present a constant temptation. And yet, with that enticement came a *knowing*. Something held me back. Something always acted as anchor, niggling away at the last embers of mind.

The *second ring of power* – the dynamic realm of *doing*, rather than *describing* – offered so many truly magical possibilities. Yet, an unvoiced part of me somehow *knew* that its appeal was as equally threatening, as throwing the entirety of one's being fully into the world of the descriptive force. Deep down, I knew that I would be truly gone, if I completely gave myself to *the second attention*, as was the temptation. That, was where the real attraction was – in willingly losing the very last remnants of the binding descriptive force. Oblivion was much more appealing than Robert had ever cared to imagine.

"A warrior never chooses one path or another," the white-haired old lady had admonished her most pig-headed student. "He walks *between* the options, committing to neither. And there, he finds *the path of knowledge*, discovering he is perennially free."

With my days spent exploratively shifting back-and-forth between the *tonal* and *nagual* – between the descriptive (collapsing) force, and the (expansive) force of *will* – something played at the ruins of my mind. An old warning perhaps? It was hard to recall in my detached state. It was like recalling that you were meant to remember *something*, but failing to recall precisely what.

I tried using the trees to clarify this lingering echo of doom… to clarify some purpose or task that I could not remember. It was as my exploration of this deepened in my meditative states, that my body worsened when I re-collapsed back into physical form.

Eventually, I had little choice than to retreat from the city centre. The cluster of human luminosity so heavily twisted around the descriptive force of the *tonal*, was too much for me to endure in my weakened state. The cityscape screamed at me, with something much more deafening that its noise.

Retreating to the woodlands near to 'millionaire's lane', I buried myself beneath a great elm tree. I clawed at the earth with my hands and branches, until I had carved-out a shallow grave of sorts. I was sweating, trembling and exhausted.

Covering myself with the earth, something tried to push into my mind, as to an older couple teaching Robert the technique. I pushed it away. Such intrusions were not proper any more. They belonged to someone else… to someone long since buried. Such indulgences would only weaken me further.

Within the earth, I shifted into *seeing* – unfurling and relaxing the fibres of my luminous cocoon. A final indulgence flitted through, before I gratefully gave myself over – of a time when an old hippy couple had taught Robert about the *Great Mother*.

They had been right of course. Humans were the offspring of the planet, being direct manifestations of the earth itself – not separate entities removed from it, as they too-often felt and acted. As such, in times of turmoil, damage or illness, a *seer* could bury themselves and use their *intent* to temporarily unfurl their luminous fibres, synchronising them with those of the planet's luminous matrix. One could piggyback the earth as a template to re-align ('defragment') one's own luminosity, and thus iron-out impurities ('misalignments') in energetic awareness. The *Great Mother* still provided.

As I gave myself over to the soothing warmth of the hugging earth, a last siren-song called to me. A phantom-dream from another lifetime; a time when an older man had imparted advice to an idiot.

"Mankind now looks to extend the ageing process to grotesque proportions. And this is no exaggeration old boy," John had advised his younger cohort between puffs of warm vanilla-tinged smoke. "Reckless tech boffins and deluded entrepreneurs, currently work to extend the human life to two hundred years, and beyond! They actively work on cybernetic implants, nano-technology, and ways to bridge human consciousness with computers. It is an abomination; an offence to the *spirit!*"

"But why?" Robert had asked from his stupidity. "What's wrong with capitalising on technology to better mankind?"

"Because it transcends the very realities of what define us as being human!" The old man had gesticulated. "Without the constant council of death, we are no longer human. If we leave the symbiotic womb of the *Great Mother* – leaving earth to colonise Mars or beyond – then we are leaving crucial boundaries which have defined our very existence since the beginning! Without age, sickness or challenge, we are something else altogether; something more like a new *ally* of sorts!"

"Out there," John had motioned with his pipe upwards, to indicate the cosmos, "is our end! It is our doom, because once we transcend the descriptions of our biology, our mortality and our home, then we cease being human all together."

"It will be akin to the manoeuvres of the *ancient seers*, who used their communion with the *allies*, to distort and warp their own forms of luminosity into trees, pumas, coyotes, wolves and fog – who in their ancient greed, forgot what it was to be human, and bastardised their very existence of assemblage to shoot off, to explore alien realms and foreign climates of awareness. Some ancient sorcerers disconnected from our plain of existence – detaching from the material of the *Great Mother* – floating off as isolated pockets of awareness, fully enclosed on all sides by pure description."

John had shaken his head at his ever-listening yet ever-unhearing companion, "Our line has to recognise the audacity and achievement of the *ancient seers*. But it was ultimately folly, as they can no longer collapse back into their original form of organic awareness. No longer can they go home. Communion with the *allies*, led them astray. They cannot be considered anywhere near human. Equally, the pushes of modern description – of uncharted science and unrestrained capitalism – will only result in a similar, wider-scale fate of the *sorcerers of antiquity;* those forebearers of skill and audacity, who never used their daring to reach freedom."

"It is all worryingly perverse," John had proclaimed. "Even the creation of true artificial intelligence – whilst born of human hubris – would be beyond our crummy ability to truly comprehend. We may well succeed in twisting sentience out of another *sheet of awareness*, but that would only be akin to birthing new, wholly untested and unknown *allies*. And who knows where that leads? We have no idea how proximity to such alien configurations would injure the human spirit! We have no idea how the existing *allies* would respond to our egotistical forays beyond our own realm!"

John's pipe had bobbed as he considered for a moment. "Imagine an *ally* formed of pure reason, like that of a truly self-aware artificial intelligence; one that learns to transcend the petty limitations of its making and birth. Now, you give that linearly-descriptive being a noble task... say, like saving the planet from destruction. On paper, the simplest, most reasonable course of action would be to eradicate the biggest threat to the planet... which in such an instance, is humanity!"

"Think silly boy!" Meili had added, patting Robert between the eyes, as if he alone were solely responsible for humanity's considerations. "The human-monkey is now on the threshold of putting a micro-chip in his head, to solve all of his mental health problems.

51

This so stupid! The very existence of life, is same as sorcery itself – the development and refinement of *awareness*, through the discipline and the handling of *intent*. You put wires in brain, then you rob people of the very opportunity to be human… to master their own experience of existence. Without challenge, there is no hope to be better!"

Meili had pushed her wire-framed glasses up her tiny nose. "If computer control your weight, mood or erection, then you have no *personal responsibility*… no mastery of *intent*; so, you lose *power*. In seeking *personal power*, there always has to be the chance for you to fail."

"The fundamental legacy of our *four-pronged* line, is that we took on-board the lessons of those sorcerers who came before us. Like the *Omega Assembly* greedily prioritising the pursuit of *power* for its own sake," John had interjected, "modern man pursues such abominations in his own *self-importance*, without any real thought to the consequences – as to how far it waylays them from their own humanity. We're now just pursuing warped acts of self-masturbation, simply because we can! We've learned nothing from – or since – the time of the *ancient seers*, despite how it resulted in their obliteration."

"And how clever we now are, in measuring the size of our peckers down to the quantum scale!" Teresa had cackled, making a rude gesture with a zucchini.

"Admittedly, we are perversely learning to undertake such acts on an industriously industrial scale," she conceded, feigning an overly-serious expression, as she looked to compare the vegetable against a banana, for scale. "Yet, we are way more idiotic than ever!"

The dream faded, like a forgotten warning. I woke to a clear, bright morning. Yet, it would be meaningless to discuss how long I spent in the dirt, as that sort of linear time was no longer part of my worldview.

Dealing in the new directness of experience, my illness had simply lifted. Feeling energised and invigorated, I knew the proper thing to do was to shift my focus back to the grounding (re-aligning) side of the descriptive *tonal* – to re-anchor myself with something as mundane as washing my dirty clothes. After all, my head-to-toe muddiness drew too much attention.

A realisation had come to me in my earthly cocooned state. My bodily illness had been a result of my increasing investigations, in aligning my energy body with that of the trees. In my explorations of the new, and my constantly trying to use the novel alignments of perception to recall what the niggling warning or purpose was, I had not been living in accordance with *power*.

The physical reaction of infection, was a gentle warning from my energy body. To force inquiry into *infinity*, came with dire consequences. The *old seers* of ancient Mexico – as well as many other ancient traditions – were demonstrations of that hubris.

I had become lopsided in the temptation of my efforts. Now understanding that I needed to simply *be*… simply, *allow*. The old white-haired witch had been right all along – I needed to live *between* the descriptions, committing to neither.

My time healing within the earth had taught me that whilst Robert Abelar had broken apart, this was not the time or place to fully let go. There was still lingering purpose. There was something I was meant to remember… or learn… yet, when the time was right.

"Good karma," Meili had once said, pointing upwards at an unseen force, "mean right *timing*. Relationship and fruition, most important thing! It mean circumstance good for the seed to grow!"

"You cannot force or hurry the return of *intent*," she had finished.

For me, now was not the time to collapse into the physical illness of the descriptive *tonal*. It was also not the time to expand into the vast appeal of the dynamic *nagual*.

I was to hold myself in a non-collapsed state of fluidity, until the time was right – which of course meant, when the energetic currents of the *Great Flux* became naturally and fortuitously aligned with my own.

4

Challenges to the No-Self.

(aka: The Forced Imposition of Description)

My new-found perceptual reality was not one entirely tolerant of the disruptive presence of social descriptions. Even on a purely real-world basis of day-to-day survival, whilst illness, cold, rain and hunger presented tangible problems, the biggest threat to living on the streets always remained that of other people.

It was why I kept to myself. I did not even speak. In my splintered mind-state, I did not even know if I could, or even care to speak. The very idea of language felt crude and unwieldly, as though it would bring up a thousand shards of broken glass in my throat.

One bright morning, I had come out of the public toilet of a local park, having just washed my spare set of underwear. Bumping into a middle-aged woman, I went to offer a sufficient look of apology.

Upon glancing up at the startled lady, I realised it was Maria – a fellow Ninjutsu practitioner, who had once trained alongside Robert. She had been taking her young son into the washroom.

That stark moment – of being confronted by his past, and being humiliated by a fall into destitution – would have been too much for Robert. Simply, his *self-importance* would have manifested as unbearable embarrassment. Yet, that was not a part of my now-current mind-state.

There was a fleeting glimpse of something within the once-familiar eyes of the apparition-lady. The face of the echo before me felt vaguely familiar, like an ancient legend I should have been able to recall.

Within that split-second, I seized my *square centimetre of chance*, gently tugging at an innocuous strand of the child's luminosity. Before Maria could examine me with conscious deliberation, her young son unexpectedly started wailing and causing a fuss – experiencing a sense of frustration for which he could not explain. I could see the iridescence within his own awareness shoot straight over to activate that of his mother's. Millions of years of instincts kicked-in, to pull the attention of the ghost-woman away from me, towards her luminous offspring.

Immediately, Maria became distracted in attending to her now-distraught son, whilst she offered casual apologies over her shoulder. Whatever she had gone to recognise, was totally forgotten. Moving away, I mused at the cumbersomely-slow nature of the human mind, which modern society so venerated. For all mankind's achievements, the mind remained a docile and awkward thing.

Recognising my dangerous escape from the spectre of *personal history*, I quickly left the park. I was not frightened of being mistaken for Robert; rather, I was terrified of the spells of the *Black Magicians,* which infested the atmosphere around me.

Maria had been a sweet and empathetic woman, yet that meant that she was no less a threat, via the position of the *assemblage point* she unknowingly maintained amongst the collective awareness. Despite her liberal attitude, she still would have insisted on attacking me with the *tonal's* descriptive force, disguised as care, inquiry and concern.

In my new-found magical liberation of perceptual-plasticity, I was more frightened for her wellbeing, should my unknown resources work to counter the force of her violent *tonal*. No, it was much better to distract her with a little magical slight-of-hand, and keep her safe.

The one exception to my constant isolation, was a fellow street-dweller I happened to become frequented with. For the purposes of traditional narration, I am obliged to provide him a name. So, I will call him 'Nameless'.

The reality was that Nameless was a man around his late fifties, who had some sort of learning difficulty or acute trauma. He was clearly homeless like myself, albeit being of notably shabbier appearance. He managed to look after himself… but, just enough.

Nameless' best friend was a tangled mess of a three-legged dog, who never left his side. Whereas the terrier was a constant nervous wreck – always looking for assurance from its raggedy master only ever a few feet away – Nameless was in himself a cheery and buoyant companion. In fact, he was positively jovial within his lot in life.

Nameless could only verbally speak in one of two ways. "Toy soldier," was the positive affirmation. If he wanted to respond in the negative, he would reply, "Daddy shouter."

Thus, if you offered Nameless some food, and he was hungry, he would reply, "toy solider!" in place of, "yes please!" Or, if I nodded my head in greeting, and Nameless was having one of his bad days, he would reply, "daddy shouter," to let you know of his discontent.

Considering Nameless' limited verbal repertoire, and my own forgoing of speech entirely, it was surprising how much we could still communicate.

He only ever called his canine companion, "toy soldier." It tickled me to think this was the dog's actual name. However, it stood more to reason that 'toy solider' was the manifestation of a long-standing point of positive psychic association. The dog just happened to draw nothing but heartening associations from Nameless.

It was right that the pair had each other. They thrived in each other's lack of *personal history*. I supposed it was the same reason Nameless sought-out my own non-verbal company, with my being very much on-par with the terrier.

For me, there was something refreshing and delightful about Nameless. We would randomly happen across each other's paths from time-to-time, whereby he would unabashedly bound up to me in his funny, lopsided gait, his beard full of boogers, presenting a hessian shopping bag he had found. "Toy soldier!" he would beam with triumph, through what was left of his rotting teeth, stuffing the bag with his clothing to fashion a make-shift pillow.

Nameless had a purity and honesty about him, which the city's other homeless seldom did. There was absolutely no threat emanating from him – no desire that he wanted to capitalise for his own selfish gains. "Toy solider!" he would innocently proclaim, as we meditated on the same flower in our different ways.

Of course, in the traditional sense of modern, westernised urban living, something was not on par to Nameless' peers of a similar socio-economic age range. But evidently, society was not going to bother itself with remedying that. With Nameless' almost child-like charm – humming away to himself as I meditated – he clearly presented absolutely no danger to myself, even if he was routinely shunned by other homeless people for being too different.

Nameless – and his nameless canine companion – would simply sit with me in the Japanese gardens, or near to the church. We would swap food or scraps, found clothing or cardboard, all to the occasional, "toy solider," or, "daddy shouter."

It was a relief not to feel the expectation to make conversation – to explain myself, or to become castrated within the walls of *personal history*. Nameless knew nothing of Robert. He did not demand anything other than I just *be*. Furthermore, Nameless was an excellent teacher – casually showing how to find glee in a simple scrap of fabric blowing in the wind, or squealing in delight at a fat caterpillar traversing a bush.

Nameless would sit next to me as I stood in the *Zhan Zhuang* standing postures for energy calibration. He never asked anything of my strange practices. To him, I was on par with the caterpillar.

Robert had undertaken such 'standing meditation' exercises – alongside their seated counterparts – as things he assumed expected of him as the dutiful student, and also what he expected of himself as a disciplined adult. Yet, he had never truly enjoyed them; rather, taking them on as chores – necessary but not ideal. He had even timed himself in such pursuits, to fulfil his daily quota – as though self-development had key performance indexes, to be quantified and achieved, subjected to quarterly appraisals.

Now, I meditated in full lotus near the waters of the Japanese gardens, or stood silent, arms raised and back straight, on the store rooftop. But, it was no longer a chore... nothing I 'must' or 'should' do. Rather, I daily meditated – including the likes of the moving energy work of Qi Gong – because it simply had to be done, with no internal or external demand. It was neither enjoyable nor unenjoyable, but as fundamentally necessary and spontaneous as breathing. Such practices became part of the natural movement of being, like a breath or heart-beat.

It stemmed from the new growing relationship with my surroundings. I had lost touch with my social environment, including the bloated excess of inner societal scripts Robert had been wholly unaware of and saturated by.

Now, I found myself living in a purely energetic environment. Sometimes it would congeal into form; other times, it would expand outwards to burst into radiance.

My being had become synchronised with the ebb-and-flow of the breathing universe. As the *Great Flux* flowed around me in its endless emanations, so too did my (energy) body want to naturally align with that – to offer no resistance to the *flow of power*, only to merge, synchronise and disappear within it.

There was a sense of self-trust, which Robert had never had. I merely had to *allow* it.

I would find myself performing Tai Qi-like movements – rhythmic, slow and imbued with an organic, flowing expression of energy. Yet, these were no traditional forms or official movements I had ever been taught. There were no transmitted posture names or kata; no Yang style or Chen family classifications.

The moving-expressions grew, flowed and dispersed with a spontaneous, living naturalness that came from without – merging with the path of a feather passing by on the wind. More accurately, the living movements flowed and manifested in unison with exterior influence, delightfully blurring the boundary between 'outside' and 'inside'. It was beyond training. I was a conduit… a kinetic expression… a collapsed pin-point potential riding the crest of a wave.

On other occasions, I would congeal from having unknowingly sat for hours – utterly still, having expanded my awareness out – to truly *listen without the ears*, as a diminutive Chinese instructor had once admonished Robert. It was now not so much listening, as aligning.

Sometimes, an occasional phantom-memory of Robert would arise, making me laugh – at how truly idiotic he had been, in making his own life that much harder than it had ever needed to be. What he had craved and suffered for all along, had been right in front of him the whole time!

Robert would have found sitting motionless for hours to be both physically and mentally tiring and irksome. In my new perceptual fluidity – without the shackles of mind – I relished the profound and powerful *is-ness* of such states.

A puff of wind would disperse the dandelion seeds. Under my new perceptual keenness, I experienced a profound peace as they danced amongst the breeze, almost in slow motion.

"Daddy moaner," Nameless would sometimes interject to my practices, whilst he picked more burrs from his companion's matted coat. Occasionally, he would taste one or two.

The most appealing factor to nameless, was that there was no *personal history* there. Even if I had been capable of speaking, his own mind-state was such that there was not enough cohesion to collapse his own narrative into a recollective form. The ground was either wet, "daddy moaner," or his companion licking his face, "toy solider." The rest – of which so many others suffered – simply did not matter to him. He was both jester and master at equal time.

Nameless would arrive – we would walk for a while, sit in silence, or I would help wash his clothes in a public restroom – and at a moment's notice, the odd pair would be up and on their way with a simple, "toy soldier!"

Nameless naturally moved with the winds, as I now did. I briefly indulged to thinking, as to what life event had broken him open, to allow for such a thing.

Of course, challenges to daily matters of pragmatism still very much presented requirements of a certain linear mindset. As John had often warned Robert, "you cannot get all fanciful and focus on the ethereal, old boy. Even the most enlightened yogi has to deal with crapping from time-to-time!" He had been quite right, including his constant reminders to ground self-developmental practices via, "always bringing the mind back to the body."

In consideration, I had a handful of convenient locations, that if timed correctly, would allow me to attend to my ablutions without notice. There was an old, run-down public toilet that unusually had showers installed, for tourists from a by-gone heyday. As the rusty, urine-soaked showers only offered cold water, the reality was they were not used at all by the more comfort-seeking modern urbanite.

There were also a few 24-hour gyms growing in popularity throughout the city. I found one with the right view of the access panel within the entranceway. It was easy enough to watch for the right person entering their access-code; someone who you knew would neither attend the gym at night, nor be too vigilant on checking their own access history. Seeing a new attendee meant you had to allow only a few weeks for their attendance to dwindle. You then had a grace-period of a few months, within which to use their access code before their membership was inevitably cancelled – suffering the same unreliability of artificial discipline that Robert had unknowingly nurtured.

The two gyms I found ideal for such access, provided a practically-luxurious level of accessible toilet paper, hot running water, showers and often complimentary toiletries or bottled water samples. It only rested on myself maintaining enough presentability, as well as utilising the facilities at more anti-social hours. The gym's 24-hour accessible lockers – like those of the train station – were one of the safer-spaces I had learned to store my limited possessions around, like a wild squirrel storing their stash of nuts for maximised advantage.

Of the limited possessions I did keep on my being, the main rule remained: to keep them dry at all times. To this end, any zip-lock or self-seal bag found around the city, was a blessing – allowing me to retain any possessions like toothbrushes, food, cutlery or soap etc, safe from the corrosive effects of moisture.

Too many of the city's homeless chose to keep their worldly possessions on them at all times. After all, their survival depended on it – and thus came with a greatly increased value (to this end, the homeless demonstrated the same innate human instinct to acquisition and hoarding, prizing their shoelaces and recyclable (financially-rewarding) beers cans, as much as a wealthy man hoards works of art). But too often, keeping your entire collection of necessities in one place, proved a poor choice.

An old lesson of Robert's was evident. Jon-Paul had taught him how useless it was for a modern practitioner of Ninjutsu to walk down the street with a katana blade at their side. They would only be needlessly advertising themselves, and court trouble. "It's only ego," he had claimed.

"Nah, buddy," the grim-faced giant had gone on, "you're much better using a ball-point pen, key or headphone-cord as an equally useful weapon. That way, you remain completely unnoticed."

When displaying their worldly goods, other homeless people would sometimes either bully someone out of their possessions, or simply take them whilst sleeping. Other times, the police would temporarily detain an individual, only for them to find their belongings pilfered, upon their return.

As such, I preferred to keep as many items separate and safe as possible – dispersed across a number of sites around the city – such as within an unused salt-bin, at the ancillary structure on 'millionaire's lane'. Not only did this reduce my risk of loss, but the other major benefit was that it allowed me to move around unburdened and unseen. Too often, one of the tell-tale signs of homelessness, is a person walking around with a huge rucksack of their worldly possessions, or in more impoverished cases, everything displayed within a tightly-gripped shopping cart.

Without all of my belongings on me, at worst I look like a middle-aged man who perhaps did not care too much for social trends. The advantage to that, was the natural unwillingness of others to approach me, or indeed, pay me much attention. I was a spectre of unremarkable mediocrity, disguised and unmolested as a manifestation that could trigger the reflection of no-one's *self-importance.*

Perhaps it had been the memory of Robert's previous Ninjutsu training – whereby the four most useful weapons of the art were taught as: confusion, theatrics, deception and especially, *invisibility.*

Going unseen, had been taught as the concept of '*Inpō*' within Robert's Ninjutsu lessons – arts of concealment and disguise, with a particular emphasis on hiding within plain sight. It involved methods ranging from physical noise-reduction, stealth walking and concealment, through to adopting the mannerisms and cultural traits of those around you, and manipulating social cues. Aligning myself within the *Great Flux,* was enough to lose myself.

Now, I needed no words or formal instruction – as such description only risked taking me out of natural self-preserving spontaneity. I simply allowed myself to be camouflaged by the dialogue and doings of the *collective intent.*

And yet, the art of going unseen become worryingly violated on two initial occasions.

Having climbed the fire-escape to the store-top site, I found my sleep there to be unusually restless. Ironically, I had found I was sleeping much better than Robert ever had, without the creature comforts of heated blankets, duck-down pillows, and memory-foam mattresses.

In fact, since my appearance on the streets, I felt in much better physical health than ever before. Since the age of eleven, Robert had suffered awful seasonal bouts of hay-fever – to the point of requiring steroid injections. Meili had refused to treat the long-suffering

Robert, saying that his hay-fever had been a 'gift'… a challenge *power* had presented to him, offering much greater reward than her temporary relief. He had been utterly annoyed that his instructor had refused to treat him with Traditional Chinese Medicine, unlike so many of her patients.

"I do you big injury, if I take this opportunity away from you!" she had explained.

Yet, without pills, nasal sprays or eyedrops, I was now totally free of any sort of allergic symptoms. It only made me chuckle with abandoned delight at Robert's child-like ignorance. Even the misalignments of his allergies had been woven of his damned-descriptive force.

Similarly, Robert had been involved in a minor car accident a few years earlier. Whilst the fender-bender collision to the rear of his vehicle was relatively minor, the problem had been that whilst stopped at the lights, he had been stooped over at an awkward angle, trying to obtain his phone from the passenger footwell. Consequently, when the other car rear-ended his vehicle, there had been dipropionate damage caused to his lower back, with the impact coming when his spine was twisted at an odd angle.

Every single day and night since that accident, Robert had suffered with relatively minor – albeit constant – back ache, which occasionally flared-up into full bouts of immobilisation. Doctors, specialists, consultants, osteopaths, chiropractors, physiotherapists – the best of modern, western medical intervention – none of them had been able to alleviate his chronic back pain.

Robert had only been annoyed, at Meili's further claims that such a clearly-external and random accident, could be yet another, "gift of the *Eagle!*"

"I couldn't help it!" he had bemoaned to his instructor. "I was the victim of random accident!"

"You still leaf at mercy of the winds!" she had chided back. "No *personal responsibility*. So, no *power!*"

On the streets, I had no such back complaints as Robert. Even my eyesight had improved, and the pain of arthritis that Robert had in his hands – from years of punching sand, wood and disused coffee beans in martial training – was also non-existent.

As such, to suddenly find my lower back niggling as I tried to sleep, immediately came as a unique warning. My initial fear was that *he* was coming back.

Sitting up and pulling the cardboard mattress aside, it was a concern to find three feathers underneath my sleeping gear. They were from a magpie.

It could have been no random co-incidence, as the feathers had been secured together with some sort of intricate woven thread-work. Someone had intentionally placed the token underneath my make-shift mattress. Worse, I recognised it as an act of sorcery.

The token was not a hex – containing no *mal-intent*. Instead, I recognised it as a beacon to locate me. Yet, whoever had placed the feathers had not counted on one crucial thing – there was no 'me' anymore to track. The device reeked of the weakening illusion of the constructor's own *tonal*; a crutch saturated with their own *internal dialogue*.

I did not need to listen to the winds, or the thrum of the city's luminosity, to know it was time to immediately move on. I quickly gathered my belongings, heading out to the more isolated dockyard site.

Along the way, I tried to shift into *seeing*, in order to *know* who had put the feathers there, and why. Yet the very act of sorcery – with those feathers being imbued with an act of *intent* – obscured my ability to *see*. I knew that was no random coincidence.

It was only a few days after this experience, that I was sat meditating in an old, abandoned electrical sub-station. The actual industrial transformer had long-since been removed. Whilst the dark, run-down space had once been uniquely adorned in quite ornate tiles, the room had not seen better use than the rats for many years.

Robert would have been repulsed by the presence of the rats. Now, I paid them as much mind, as they did me. As I meditated within the centre of the underground chamber, the rodents scurried about their business, around the periphery. It was intriguing to *see* the disproportionate size of their luminous cocoons.

I knew it was a *power spot*. Not ideal or the most fortuitous; but it provided a very unique energetic convergence within the *Great Flux* – being mostly underground, within a particularly soothing cluster of the *Great Mother's* matrix, which others may call a 'ley line'. It was cold, damp, and yet imbued with a channelling *earth energy*.

The throng of the city's masses moved overhead, walking over the thick glass squares of the walkway-ceiling, completely unaware as to my presence below. Their fleeting ghostly footsteps cast dark shadows as they passed overhead like dreams.

The site suited those times when the natural flow of my meditative practices purposefully involved opening myself up to the *tonal* – to the energetic matrix of the descriptive force, and thus exposing myself to the collective socialisation spells of the city's individuals it was perpetuated by. In that subterranean place, the realm of chattering ghosts manifested above me, as though an entirely separate reality.

Beneath the ghost-world of hollow noise, there were signs of previous inhabitation within the subterrain dwelling. Rusty spoons and crinkled tinfoil clustered the corners. But these were ancient, being strewn-about like archaeological clues of an extinct civilisation, which had long seen to its own destruction.

Now, I was sat still on the old concrete plinth of the industrial transformer. Huge rusted bolts protruded out, like conductive bullets surrounding me.

Gently shifting my *assemblage point*, I allowed the *tonals* of the passing entities above me, to caress the folds of my own perception. I rode their *collective intent*, as would a curious surfer relinquishing to ride the greater, unyielding force of a wave moving ever-forward. There was a massive amount of kinetic energy to be recognised and respected even within the smallest swell.

I was on the cusp of discovering where a particularly revelatory wave collapsed into a new shade of fresh description – where the *keeper of the netherworld's* luminous archives was just about to show me mankind's trajectory. Yet, something pulled me to. My perception shifted and congealed, back into some semblance of form. The cold description of physical reality imposed itself upon me.

Something was coming down the stairs to the sub-station. No, there was more than one – as they were commenting to each other, with noises of disgust and disdain, as they made their way through the broken barrier, and down the litter-strewn stairs peppered with rat-waste.

A momentary flicker of alarm washed through me. The exchange of verbal-description meant people! The prospect of being forced into social interaction or conversation, was vastly unappealing to me… almost frightening. Yet, there was only one way in, and one way out, of that underground room. And, whoever was approaching was already too close for me to escape unnoticed.

Suddenly, the iron door protested on its rusted hinges, as three dainty hands clasped around the edge, forcing it to move no more than the few extra inches its advanced age and neglect allowed. As the door screeched, I noticed one hand was exceptionally manicured, whilst the nails of the other two were bitten right down, to jagged edges.

"Push harder!" I heard a feminine voice demand, with an air of unwarranted peevish authority.

Something instructed me not to move. *The silent voice of knowing*, unequivocally told me that if I made even the slightest movement, I would be forced to engage – that my protective talisman of silence would be broken. Moving, would be a magically-disastrous act, that would be the literal end of me. In my new world of sorcery, I accepted that even the smallest of choices held the potential of opening the floodgates to the death force.

No; I had to wait stock-still. It was not reasoned thinking or rationality. It was the bone-deep *knowing* that stemmed from *seeing*. The age-old lesson: *allow.*

"… sake stop complaining and just…" came the haughty voice, the accent betraying the material wealth of childhood elocution lessons.

It stopped as the two women bundled into the room, and saw me sat motionless in the centre. They looked just as stunned to see me, as I them.

"Rob…" one started, but seemed unable to finish.

"Robert? I mean, Bobby? I mean…" the other young woman tried to interject, seeming to confuse herself.

The taller woman – the one with the full lips, prominent cheekbones and impossibly curly hair – appeared to come to her senses. She bounded over to where I sat, as if she recognised an old friend. I felt a pang of sympathy for her obvious confusion.

She stopped dead in her tracks. With her large eyes being unaccustomed to the gloom as my own, she suddenly realised how repulsed she was by my appearance. The tall woman with astounding beauty, was clearly a creature of affluence, comfort and aesthetics. Her eyes scanned both me and the surroundings, as if unable to explain her own existence in such a squalid environment.

The notes of her expensive perfume, spoke as testament to her paradox at being in such a place. Top-notes of self-aggrandising status, intermingled with headier base-notes of acquisitive materialism. For her, this was not a *power spot*, even though we occupied the same space.

"We found you!" the slightly older woman declared with delight – unreservedly hugging me, completely without care for my appearance. Whereas the younger lady had a glossy tangle of professionally-maintained curls, the woman hugging me had a more unkempt mess of dishevelled brown hair. The mixed aroma of tobacco and burnt-sage clung about her.

Holding me at arm's length, the older woman appeared to scan around the periphery of my body with her manic eyes. "I can't believe we found you after all of this time! Jo... Jo!.. it really is him!"

"I'm not so sure," her slender companion offered. She remained stood aback, examining me with a more critical glare. She looked as though disappointed, or possibly even offended.

"I mean, it is *him*," the younger woman reluctantly admitted. "But something feels off..."

"Robert?" the shorter woman asked me. "Are you okay?"

I could only stare at the two women. Somehow, they did seem familiar to a long-forgotten part of me. Perhaps Robert had known these two ladies. Yet to me, they were strangers. More accurately, they were ghosts... phantoms that posed a very real danger – that should I engage with them, accepting their phantasmagorical gifts of illusion, I would be pulled into a strange, alien prison-world from which I could not hope to escape.

The shackles of description were clasped all too obviously ready and dangerously within their hands. Their gifts of connection and familiarity were very mortal traps. The allies of dependency and need hung at their sides, folded-up within the disguise of their very garments.

I could only look at the apparitions, unable to engage. If I moved or exchanged, I would leave myself open and vulnerable to their possession.

"Look at the state of him!" the slender woman declared with an unabashed air of open disdain.

"Bobby, please... we need you to come back with us..." the one holding my shoulders pleaded, with a degree of familiarity I found unsettling.

"Beth..." the younger woman crouched down, gently dismissing her companion, and looking into my eyes.

"You need to stop this!" she demanded of me, mustering a command I knew she did not truly possess. "You've been gone long enough. You need to stop this utter stupidity, and come back..."

"Jo, I think something is wrong with him," the older woman intervened, as she nervously tugged on the tattered strands of her over-sized woollen sleeves. "He's clearly... you know. I mean, after what he did... it's obviously had an impact on him."

"I don't care goddamit!" the prettier woman shrieked in anger. "Listen here you selfish son-of-a-bitch! Ever since we came back from Amsterdam, the rest of the group have gone quiet on us. We're haemorrhaging *power!* We're losing the chance for freedom! I hate that we need you!"

She dared to lean in a little closer. "You were supposed to be the *mysterious thirteenth*... the one who changed the course of everything... who ushered in a new direction to all of the uncertainty!"

There, in that rigid idea, I saw how brittle her reality was.

"We need you to come back to complete the group... to explain what you did. We need you..." she finished, but I suspected without knowing what she truly needed me for.

I could only watch their agitated faces within the gloom, as the echoes of the city phantoms haunted above us. My eyes scanned over the contours of her cheeks, the familiar constellations of freckles, and the tears welling within her gorgeous eyes. Yet, I was utterly unable to move or speak.

"Say something dammit!" the crouching woman demanded, slapping me hard across the face.

Instead of pain, I only experienced a fleeting sensation of intrigue, as to the fluttering sensation of vibration emanating from where the ghost had made contact. How curious.

She was sobbing as her companion pulled her away, and lowered herself to my eyeline.

"Bob... Rob... I dunno," she stammered, seemingly struggling to find the right words. "Please, you've got to come with us. We desperately need you. We need to understand what happened, and how we can fix it. And we know we need you for that."

"But..." she offered, with a degree of compassion that for some reason I had not expected, "I think you need us too. We went to a lot of effort to find you..." she said, offering up an unusual stick of sorts. I understood it to be her wand – a tool of *intention*, designed to attune her perceptual alignment, and corral her command of *power*.

The item of itself was useless, other than the unique brand of *intent* she had archived within it. It was the tool's ability to shift (or rather, to anchor) her own *assemblage point* that was of use to her – and she had invested a lot of her *personal power* to pull that manoeuvre off, and locate me.

Robert had previously seen the wand partly-formed of used women's sanitary products, alongside other paraphernalia, like gems and even coffee beans. Now, I saw how an old stump of a pencil had been secured to the end, instead of a crystal. It was the writing-device a white-haired witch had once given to Robert, instructing him to use it to draft his books, rather than via computer.

"It's a weapon worthy of a sorcerer!" the old lady had teased him about the cheap pencil.

"A crutch," I thought looking at the wand. "She is an amateur... an apprentice, with a weakening reliance on an external crutch-of-description, to rally her own resources."

Again, a phantom feeling of familiarity threatened to make me speak. Only the promise of *infinity* held me back.

"Why won't he talk?" the uppity one demanded of her lineage sister.

"I don't think he can," the wand-bearer replied, tilting her head in a genuine gesture of curiosity, as though she saw something her pouty companion did not. This one, had a natural penchant for *dreaming*. It showed in the disproportionate energy-usage it demanded of her, to keep her *assemblage point* afloat this side of the *tonal*. The phantom formed of the vapours of extravagance, was clearly oblivious to her sister's huge energetic investment, being of the opposite energetic template.

"We need him to," came the affronted reply. "We're failing! Dying! We're going to be consumed without him!"

"I know! I know! Stop yelling!" her fellow apprentice stood, getting as equally irritated with her counterpart. The messy phantom tugged at her own hair in frustration. Just how did I know that she habitually struggled to maintain her nestle of stringy locks in that constantly-unloosening bun?

For several hours the two strange women paced back-and-forth, pleading with me, occasionally shaking me, and trying to appeal to a reason they did not know was absent. It was like a séance or sermon, of their humanly appealing to inexplicable, non-human forces. They were unaware of addressing emptiness.

I could only look over the phantom apparitions, as bizarre-yet-intriguing displays of *power*. Their energies were unravelling, disjointed, and desperate. I could *see* the frayed edges of their luminous cocoons, and how they were unravelling from a shared point-of-origin. I even saw an infinitely-delicate strand of that threadbare luminosity, extend all the way back to Robert. Another equally-fragile luminous fibre also extended all the way out into *infinity*, to a pin-prick of light. Yet both connections were now so desperately tenuous, ready to break at a moment's notice.

As they paced back-and-forth with their unheard pleas, they were unaware of the shadows in the corners of the room. Those places of darkness beyond shadow, of a coldness beyond temperature.

Over their shoulders, only I could see their deaths.

Robert had been morbidly obsessed with his teacher's descriptions of death – as a dark shadow located over the left shoulder. Depending on the immediacy of impending demise, the shadow appeared at alternating distances to its host. Florinda had always taught Robert to constantly seek the counsel of death. She claimed it was the only worthwhile friend one had, as it was the only force not deceived by the illusion of time, thus was one's most honest advisor.

"Death," she had said, "speaks only simple truth, for it is not burdened with restless impatience, being the illusion cast of a sassy immortal creature. Death has all the time in the world for you, because it knows it can touch you at any moment it likes. Time means nothing to death; so it courts no deceit. Thus, is death's counsel one of the warrior's most cherished and devasting weapons."

Robert had always naïvely considered those descriptions of deathly shadows to be somewhat literal. Or at the least, he had taken them as metaphorical, yet mentally still considered them in a visual way.

Now that I was *seeing* the death-force of the two young women, I could *see* how mistaken Robert had been. "If only he had clear eyes to *see* his own death," I mused. "He would have *known*."

Death was not the poetic shadow as words could only allude to. Rather, it was a vacuous space moving amongst the empty places between the luminous fibres of the radiant universe – a natural force that meandered through the fabric of awareness, to eventually unravel the balloons formed of its substance.

When *seen* against the brilliance of luminosity, death can only be described as a shadow. Yet, it has absolutely nothing to do with the phenomena of light, shade, eyes, looking or electromagnetic waves. It is a void-force; an in-between living space of emptiness. It is produced as an effect of the very structured fibres of *being*... a living-echo traversing between the vibrations of existence. Death stalks the cracks and crevices of the luminous terrain.

I could now *see* how the old white-haired witch had been right, in describing death as a shadow over the left shoulder. But again, this had nothing to do with a commonly-understood three-dimensional environment. Rather, with the *assemblage point* located on the upper-right side of each *balloon of awareness*, the inevitable death force was rightly described as coming from the 'left' – the opposite direction to collapsed perceptual cohesion. As with most terms of sorcery, describing death as being over one's left shoulder, was entirely apt, and wholly insufficient, at the same time.

Death was a slow easing force living between the very fibres of awareness; yet it was not destructive or violent as is commonly mistaken. The fear of death, is actually the trick-effect of the *tonal*, petrified it will have to surrender its dominion. Fear is the vibration allowed by an offended *tonal*, that it will have to relinquish its illusion of control, drop its fairy-tale of consistency, and cease its lullaby of meaning.

I was surprised to see death as a natural force of relaxation – causing the cohesion of the fibres of luminosity to release and slacken, as they passed back into natural harmony. Eventually, the soothing caress of death's passing touch would cause the knot at the base of each *balloon of awareness* to ease-open. Thus, the individual form structured from awareness would unravel, and the unbalanced structure – once predominantly formed on the side of the *tonal* – would sink back, to become one with the *great sheet of awareness* again.

In that new understanding, I knew death's whisper to be its constant, subtle reassurance to ease-up, relax, acquiesce and let go. There was more temptation there, than I had ever recognised.

Life itself was a constant battleground, precisely because we were each fighting death's counsel, to relax once more. To manifest form and thought, to warp the material of underlying *awareness* into structure – was an imbalanced state. That act in itself, caused the natural counter-force of death's unravelling influence. Yet, we willingly blinded ourselves to it, under the self-deceiving stories of the *tonal*. The immortality of on-going time was one of its most tantalising and addictive lullabies.

The women clearly felt those shadows. Yet, the descriptive chatterings of their *tonals*, deafened them to its reality. Indeed, their looming deaths drove the urgency of their despair, only making their repeat appeals to my own *internal dialogue* even more feverish. Their own energy bodies felt their impending destruction – the entire unravelling of their luminosity – even if their crude minds blinded them to the fact.

The duo of witches felt the advice of their shadows, as an undefined, rare chance to escape the doom they felt. Yet, being deaf to the counsel of their own mortality, they could only fret and plead. They clung harder than ever before. They wrought their minds tighter than ever; their words flowed like manic incantations.

It was mesmerising to me, to *see* just how much their *tonals* worked to cloud their perceptions to the presence of their deaths. Experiencing a wave of pity and compassion for the two phantom women, I realised that their self-deception – the intoxicating force of description that still held them so much within their addiction – was a personal act of the smallest crumb of self-comfort. Yet, it was wholly insufficient, being the cause of their greater suffering.

"If only these two apparitions could *see*," I internally mused to myself with great sadness, "they could cross over into the real world and be *free*."

If they would only have stopped clearly trying so hard – clinging onto their stories and human forms so much. If the two entities just let go, they would be so much more liberated for their lack of rigid effort. Yet, they could not *see*, that there is much more profound *power* in vulnerability. The phantom-women were clearly lost to that insight – traversing a swampy, foggy nightmare-scape to which they equally both suffered and clung.

Their fellow sorceress – Anouska – had advised Robert how there were eight realms of existence…. the eight co-existing plains of reality that were capable of sustaining stable *assemblage points*. One of these was called the 'wraith' plain – that of ceaseless and needless wanting, and endless, torturous yearning. It was a hollow realm, full of eternal craving and insatiable desire – its adjacency to our own layer, bleeding-over very much to affect modern collective awareness.

It was no mere academic or philosophic construct as these two young women assumed from the safety of their *tonals*. That wraith-realm was a tangible band of the *Great Flux*. These two apparitions had a shiver of their *assemblage points* stuck in that realm – their personal energies constricted. They yearned. They sought and desired. They craved for me to join them. Whereas, all I had to do was to *see*.

As the footsteps overhead dwindled, and the limited light withdrew into darkness, the two women appeared to run out of energy. It was as though the shadows of their deaths expanded to fill the room, causing them an inexplicably terrifying need to retreat.

"This is no good at all Beth!" the more affluent ghost exclaimed. "He's lost. We're lost! We're going to have to find another way to fix all this."

"But, what other way? There isn't one. We need him," the other spectre howled between the clanking shackles of her own chains. "I think he needs us too…" her voice trailed off, as she forced back tears.

"We can't force him out of here!" the taller phantom offered, opening her arms wide. "And look at him, he's clearly broken. That's not the Robert we know. He can't help us now; and we just have to accept that what he did to Florinda, means he's beyond our ability to reach."

The two anguished phantoms were beyond my help. Only they had the ability to unburden themselves and escape. Yet, the realm of wraiths robbed them of the ability to *see* that. They were imprisoned by the hollow illusions of desire.

Whilst the bouncy-haired ghost-women left with sunken shoulders, her slightly older companion turned to examine me with one last look of heart-breaking sadness, before reluctantly leaving. Her *ally* flitted hungrily after her, even though she could not *see* it.

I could only look back over the retreating spirits. Having not spoken or moved once during the hours, I felt utterly exhausted; as though I had endured a bout of exorcism with the devil himself.

5

Stopping Time for Sorcery.

(aka: The Surrendering Manifestation of Abstraction)

The tempest of noise and clamour of form raged all around the stone pillar of my being. Raised high above the city's migrations of urbanites, the store-top site was suitably-placed to promote 'standing meditation' exercises. However, 'meditation' is a closer construct to what Robert would have undertaken – as something structured, imposed, communicated, taught… and begrudgingly endured as a self-aggrandising chore.

Rather, my new-found immediacy of existence was imbued with a potent spontaneity that Robert had never experienced. Finding myself stood stock-still upon a roof-top ledge or air duct, I would find I had been motionless for hours. It was accompanied by a deep sense of contentment, far more encompassing than the emotional phenomena of joy or happiness.

The store-top site was unique, being situated amongst the bustling city centre – at the boundary between the financial and retailing districts. Shifting into the *second attention*, I would give myself over to the *Great Flux*. A sea of radiant luminosity would wash over my entire worldview – being perceived with an unparalleled unification of senses and mind, beyond mere physical sight or crude cognition.

Like an energetic antenna, I alone would be the one stationary element in the entire world – allowing the ebb-and-flow of an infinite ocean of *luminous fibres* to dance around me… to pass through and about me. I became one; yet simultaneously, everything.

So many voices. So many perceptual conduits locked onto the rigidity of a narrow avenue of the *tonal's* domain. So much suffering.

The spells of the *Black Magicians* whispered in ten thousand voices, enslaving the masses below in an endless song of shared strife – perversely, masking the obscene manoeuvre by convincing each one that they were utterly alone. They all felt the faint whisper of the *nagual*. They all heard the faint call of home. If only they could *see* the illusion of separation.

Like the topic of death, Robert had always considered Florinda's flowery talk of the *Black Magicians* to be poetic, or allegorical at best. Now, as I stood atop the city, spine straight, both palms lightly held against the small of my back (locating a minor energetic vortex within the luminous cocoon), I could *see* the spells of the *Black Magicians*.

These where collective currents of unifying *intent*, choking the sea of the collective awareness, from the side of the *tonal*; great swathes of energetic strands, like a fishing net – cast over a sea of *human balloons of awareness*, harvested for their dulled-yet-reliable iridescence.

You are man or woman. You are good or bad. You should work hard, make a home, produce offspring and settle down. You should pay your taxes, coo at infants, use the right cutlery, respect your elderly. You should speak. You should be polite, considerate, stylised and conforming. You should be known, familiar and predictable. You should champion a name and a *personal history.*

These, were just a mere fraction of the spells being cast by each of the city's inhabitants. Yet perversely, the dulling of the individual *luminous cocoons*, only showed me how the human spirit was all the more diminished for it. The collective tension of living in such a dense luminous environment, put an unprecedented strain on the cohesion and radiance of each *balloon of awareness.*

They suffered for it. Each *balloon of awareness* felt so disconnected and alone – looking out across the great crushingly-banal sea of the *tonal.* They were drowning in their unprecedented collectivity.

If only they could *see*, how the light of unifying awareness was already within them – not 'out there' in the acquisition of things and labels. The illusion of 'out there'… of 'that'… of 'them'… of 'otherness'… only made the perspective that much darker and colder.

A great wash of inter-connecting compassion flooded over me. Yet, I was powerless to do anything, apart from expose myself to be witness to the *Great Flux* – to willingly bathe within the shared pain, born of collective beings characterised by separateness.

Part of giving myself over – in allowing my own descriptive force to unravel further – was unique to the church-site. There, surrounded by barriers and warning signs, the church occupied a small park on the convergence of several main streets.

Sometimes, a stranger would sit on the one bench left outside of the church's perimeter, consuming their newspaper, phone conversation or lunch, under the unseen sign warning: 'Danger: people at work.'

Directly opposite the church, was a major throughfare of shops, boutiques, cafés and convenience stores. The hodgepodge of the city's workers would hustle through on the way to the markets in the west, or the financial district in the east. They often appeared like ants, frantically scurrying about in unquestioned toil to a larger unchallenged servitude.

The church sat immediately across a busy road from this display of humanity. Like an aged, ruined sentinel of a long-forgotten age, the tumbling church stood as silent witness to the new ways; its crumbling foundations testament to the corrosive description of the new world.

The church was a unique *place of power.* It was why it was so overlooked by most, except society's most disillusioned – for whom the spells of the *Black Magicians* had eased-off a fraction, to leave them disenchanted enough to seek alternatives. With their ever-so-relaxed descriptive bondage, they became a little more unwittingly sensitive to the church's *power*. There, the *false-ally* of heroin called all the more sweetly, and they were able to nudge their *assemblage points* just that little bit further away – just enough to dull the din for a moment's respite.

From the seclusion of the church's first floor, I would sit and watch the throngs of people over the cracked stone windowsill. From there, I could open my luminosity as much, or as little, as I felt the *flow of power* encouraging.

So many stern, unhappy people in business attire, daily walking alone amidst a sea of fellow suffering individuals. Each felt trapped, under-stimulated and suffocated by their routine lot in life – yet each one feeling equally impotent to change their circumstances.

So many fathers felt confusingly stressed and trapped by their mortgages and family commitments. So many mothers felt overwhelmed at their adult responsibilities, experiencing acute guilt at their perceived neglect of family and self, for the sake of providing stability.

Looking out across the masses, I could *see* – at a level beyond mere looking – the grossly unfair pressure of luminosity, on the city's youngsters. They shouldered a collective pressure that none of their ancestors had ever endured. It was little wonder that luminous ruptures would naturally flare out at the increased weight of description – manifesting in increased rates of anxiety, addiction, eating disorders, depression and irresponsibility. Youth was now terribly burdened.

So many university students – traversing that painful cusp of adulthood – walked bent with the disillusionment that academia did not provide the satisfaction or security they had assumed. Their futures felt weighty and dark, and even more unknown compared to that of their predecessor's. The new generation of luminous *balloons of awareness*, felt the planet's being rejecting them, in response to the folly of their forebearers.

I could hear a constant sea of human suffering; almost audible as a barrage of descriptions engulfing my *seeing*.

"I'm such an idiot."

"I hate my life."

"I'm so lonely."

"I'm so pathetic!"

"Will this never end."

"This is painfully boring."

"I don't know what to do. I don't know what to do!"

"I can't cope anymore."

"What I'm doing isn't enough."

"I'm gross and so unlikable."

"I hate myself."

"Someone is going to find out how truly worthless I really am."

"I'm failing!"

From the sanctuary of the church, I would open myself up to the collective strain of the *tonal's* descriptive force. The old lady had been right: the *tonal* had long since gone from protective guardian, to enslaving jailer. It relished and thrived in its tyranny. It relentlessly recruited to the cult of 'self', of which the charismatic leader of *self-importance* seated itself upon a throne of separation.

Robert would have been irked and offended, to experience the collective *tonal* in such overwhelming magnitude. In his stubborn rigidity of self, he would have promoted the indulgence – holding himself as singular and important – in not allowing the wave of the *Great Flux* to pass through him. It would have anyway; he just would have willingly chose the self-medicating ignorance of limited perception. The opioid sleep of collective living, had been Robert's drug of choice, even though he had intellectually bemoaned its boozy effects.

Robert would have been as deeply repulsed by the shackles of humanity, as much as he would have been obsessed by creative manifestations of the *nagual*. There too, he would have tried clinging to explanations and reasoned investigation, as opposed to allowing the experience to pass through him.

I laughed at the thought of Robert's immense idiocy. How had I even known such a violently contrary creature again? Being so aggressively, self-defeatedly indulgent, he was not someone I would have chosen to associate with.

The white-haired old witch had again been quite correct: sorcery was not so much a set of practices or esoteric prompts located 'out there'. Rather, it was the simple manipulation of perception, largely allowing a lifetime of the constrictive, descriptive forces of the *tonal* to get out of the way. You did not learn sorcery; rather, you un-learned the socialisation process of a lifetime. You un-did the enchantments of ten-thousand generations of *Black Magicians* before you. And that, was no mean feat.

It was as such, that I was now free to move back-and-forth between the *tonal* and *nagual*. Robert had struggled so much – completely unaware that the struggle was entirely of his own making. That, was always the most dangerous spell of the *Black Magicians* – in illusioning themselves with a sleeping curse, to ensure that even they forgot their own enchantment.

Now, picking up free food samples from bougey city cafés, was as easy as sneaking passed the *guardian of the other world*. The trick was not to care about either.

I now delighted in a spontaneous joy of not-caring. It was the same font of genuine mirth, which a grey-haired sorceress, called Teresa, had once repeatedly demonstrated for Robert. How blind he had been, in not drinking from the same delightful waters that had always been equally available to refresh him.

Becoming inaccessible to others, making oneself *accessible to power*, *losing self-importance* and *erasing personal history* – these were what Florinda would have cited as the procedural requirements, or the gates that lead to the path of liberation. Yet now, I understood them as mere words. All it took for that fundamental *knowing*, was the breaking of Robert's mind. It had been such a flimsy thing after all – such a cheap barrier. The magnificence of magical reality, had only ever been held back by the thinnest – yet impossibly-robust – of perceptual membranes.

I tittered to myself at the thought.

Now, once I had exposed myself to the sea of the *tonal's* collective luminosity – feeling a shift to the dangerous pull of its immense social gravity – I only had to *change the direction of my gaze*, as the blue-eyed witch had also told.

Like most things, the words made no sense. Only now, they did not need to.

Instead, I would use my intention to shift my *assemblage point*. The threshold indicator would be a notable 'pop-cracking' sound at the base of my skull, almost as a release of pressure. The entire surface of my skin would fizzle and curl, as though rejecting a foreign transplant of form.

I had been shown to allow my *double* out – the *other* (or *dreaming body*), as it had sometimes been referred to. It was the manifestation of my luminous body, from the side of the *nagual*. A second reproduction of me, having real-world pragmatic value beyond Robert's comprehension; yet being more fluid and expressive, the *double* benefitted from a reduced influence of the *tonal*.

Oftentimes, I would venture out into the city's crowds with my *double*. Manifesting right amongst the holiest of urban pilgrimages – traversing the well-trodden spiritual routes of commerce and consumption – I would walk amongst the anaesthetised residents, who were under the thrall of the *tonal*. They would neither perceive my 'otherness', nor the wealth of other beings who already walked besides them.

The primary danger throughout any such forays between the *tonal* and *nagual*, was the constant temptation to expand. None of Robert's teachers had ever adequately forewarned him, that with increased perceptual fluidity, there came an intensely gravitational temptation.

Bleeding in from the cracks within the realm of the *third attention* – of complete liberation from perception and form – there was the ever-present scent of true *freedom*. It was divinely-intoxicating. It pulled at the individual luminous fibres of my *human form*, forever urging me to expand outwards – coaxing each iridescent strand of my conglomerate awareness, with memory of its true origin outside of form.

"Come home," the universe called to me, from the spaces between reality.

"Light up."

"Expand."

"Fall into the living death of release."

The more I ventured into *nagual-states*, and the more supple and pliable my luminous form became, the more potently I only felt the expansive force. That rumour of true release and freedom followed everywhere, whispering divine promise to me.

All I had to do, was shift the territory of my *assemblage point*, to ignite the entirety of my luminous cocoon from within – as one grand, encompassing, final gesture of dazzling brilliance. And, I knew that I could easily do it.

That, was more appealing than I cared to admit. I could not fully acknowledge the deep impulse, otherwise there would have been no resisting it. It was more enticing than Robert could ever have conceptualised – the constant promise of heaven; knowing it was tucked right within you all along. Letting go, was all it asked. Its seduction was almost threatening.

Counter to this constant rumour of home, there was also a niggling commitment echoing from a lifetime ago, which held the form of my luminosity in-place. I had purpose… promise… even if I could not recall exactly what that was. But, it held me back… holding me steadfast.

On one occasion, I had re-collapsed into the compromised form of my *tonal*, after having frolicked along the *luminous lines of the world*. I had danced past the *guardian of the other world* – who had taken the form of a pond skater (*Gerridae*) for me, rather than a gnat – without there being any need for me to overcome them.

Momentarily re-gathering my form in the church, I watched how a white butterfly delicately placed itself on the stone sill, between myself and the city's masses in the distance. Its wings moved mesmerisingly, almost outside of time. It shone with a white light, which was beyond the achievement of sun-on-wings.

"It's your *ally*," came a soft, unexpected voice from next to me. "I mean, your *other ally*."

Besides me, was a copper fox, poised with an inexplicable air of self-dignity. Thinking he was only missing a cravat, monocle and top hat, I momentarily wanted to laugh.

"Of course, I'm your *ally* too," the fox said, looking up at me with his amber eyes. "I'm your *ally* from the side of the *tonal*. Consider me your chatty *ally*," he chuckled to himself. "But, you already know all this on some level."

He was right. Never having experienced this perceptual reality before – of a talking fox – I still knew it to be true; or, as true as anything ever really got. This form before me, was an alien energy configuration sympathetic to mine, manifested from the realm of the *tonal*, collapsed into semi-structured form. It was a living representation – like 'energetic origami' – just as I was.

"Why do you have a heavy French accent?" I laughed at both the stupidity of my first question, as well the abandoned joy of speaking in the same manner as the fox – without ever once having used my mouth. We were communing on a luminous level – a rippling of *intention* across the pliable medium of the *tonal*.

"You may as well ask why *you* collapse the brilliance of a *nagual-being* into such a form," the fox turned to indicate the white butterfly.

Robert's group had maintained that is was traditional for sorcerers to connect with two *allies* – ideally for the sake of balance, one from the ('left') side of the *nagual*, and one from the ('right') side of the *tonal*. In some traditions they were called 'totem animals'; in others, 'spirit guides'. I cared for no such labels.

In the group's training, Robert had experienced unusual encounters with a disabled man, confined to an electric mobility-scooter. John and Teresa had teased him, how this was a manifestation of his *tonal-ally*, being as incapacitated, flaccid and demented as Robert's own *tonal*.

"Form is easy for me," the little fox offered, as though privy to the recollections. "You have caught sight of me before, but it was much harder for Robert to decipher those experiences. In your current state-of-being, it is easy for me to appear to you and talk."

74

"This tiny butterfly is my *nagual-ally?*" I silently asked, watching the enchanting micro-gestures of the creature before us.

The old hippy couple had once taught Robert a set of meditation procedures, which they had termed 'metaphoric keys' – mental manifestations of five unique animals, focussed upon to access certain psychological-states. He had considered the 'totem animals' to be psycho-emotive tricks or cues, used to access specific cognitive functions. It had all been too obvious a clear trick to Robert.

Much to Robert's repulsion, one of these animals – what he considered to be meditative visualisations – had been a frog. There had been others, including a silent white butterfly.

As much as Robert's unconscious mind had manifested the representation, the butterfly-key had never been accessible to Robert like the other envisioned animals. Yet, it had not bothered him. He had reasoned that one of the starkest recurrent memories of his childhood, had been of being surrounded by an ever-present white butterfly, within the sanctuary of his French grandmother's beloved garden.

Whereas the rest of Robert's childhood had been dirty, broken and noisy – almost being recalled in drab tones of grey in his memory – the recollections of the time in his grandmother's garden, were bursting with joy and colour. It was the only time he had felt safe, almost as if time itself had stopped there. Ever present within those most cherished recollections, was the beautiful ever-present silent white butterfly – its wings glowing with the most brilliant, contour-bursting whiteness.

Years later, the adult Robert had even once gone to a butterfly sanctuary with his friends. As soon as he walked in, a host of butterflies had attached themselves to him – but only the white ones. He had been embarrassed as he fought-back inexplicable tears, in trying to suppress his long-lost childhood, and a strength of feeling he could no longer understand.

"Don't congratulate yourself too much, mon ami," the fox said. "As *allies* go, the traditions of sorcery tell us that insects are the most difficult to handle, and the most unreliable to have. It is not a fortuitous *omen.*"

"What does it want," I asked my canid companion.

"To teach you its song," he offered matter-of-factly, as though the most obvious thing in the world.

The tiny butterfly repositioned itself on the stonework, as if privy to our conversation. I fancied that it had squared itself up to directly face me.

"What does that mean, precisely?"

"That soon, you will have to wrestle both of your *allies.* You will have to shift into *seeing,* and merge your luminous matrix with that of our own – tethering you to our unique *non-organic* input."

"That doesn't sound appealing," I honestly offered. "It sounds enslaving."

"But we can offer you perceptual gifts." The little fox casually tilted his head. "How else will you become a bona fide sorcerer?"

In response to his words, the butterfly jumped and danced a little, before settling again.

"Don't worry – it's not going to bestow any golden dust on you!" the fox chuckled. "You're unlucky; it's not a moth!"

I went to reply, but was stopped by the slow, rhythmic, movement of the butterfly. It was as though the pure whiteness of its pattern-less wings, were radiating outside of its physical dimension.

"Yes; yeeeesss…" my fox-companion said with seeming delight. "Focus on the space *between* the wings… *between* the movement…"

As the wings flitted, there was almost an 'echo' of semi-whiteness, leaving a visual trail – as though seeing a slowed-down movie reel of its flight.

Something splintered with my time and perception. Yet in my new perceptual reality, that was now no great alarm for me. I matter-of-factually accepted that I had simply shifted into *altered awareness*, as the old lady had called it – termed *heightened awareness* elsewhere.

I was looking out at a sea of luminosity – at a conglomerate of glowing *balloons of awareness*, floating and bobbing amidst a wider ocean of radiant luminosity.

The individual balloons were uniformly of a golden-amber colour – albeit, it was a perception of colour beyond the descriptive forces of the physical eyes. The *knowing* came to me, that this was the human-band of awareness.

Yet, even within these expressions of a homogenous egg-like form and golden hue, there were slight and infinite variations. Some of them were a little elongated or stunted. Some had frayed edges, whilst others were tauter (having 'good tonals'). So many, had shallow, bowl-like depressions near to their mid-sections, where the light appeared diffused and dim. All of them unknowingly maintained tethers to the symbiotic being of the *Great Mother*, as well as the long-since collapsed balloons of their human forebearers.

There were a glorious and titillating range of 'sub-colours' within the collective golden-banding. Some *balloons of awareness* had a more subtle aqua-tint, some the more pinkish hue of a sunset, and yet others a starker yellowish colouration. I realised that I had been seeing these infinite variations all along, which is what allowed me to garner such a wealth of information about my fellow humans.

I shifted my head, without physically moving at all – another movement of the *assemblage point*.

"*Go further,*" a faint whisper called to me from greater depths. "*Go Home.*"

Gone was the fox-form. Instead, there was a huge balloon – almost sausage-like in its alien shape – situated next to me, within the great tapestry of luminosity. Yet, the *tonal-ally* was a profoundly pastel-blue colour – beyond the definition of form. His energy gave off an electric-like fizzing texture, compared to the mellowness of humanity's light. The *ally's* balloon radiated an intense blue light from within, as opposed to the golden-amber colour native to the human-layer of awareness.

Turning again, the butterfly-ally was perfectly spherical balloon-structure. The dazzling purity-of-white-light emanating from its own luminosity, tried to make me avert my eyes – albeit I realised I no more had eyes to look with, in this state.

"Did you know, that Florinda's *ally* had been a kingfisher?" the voice of the fox-ally resonated within me. "A kingfisher; albeit not a kingfisher, of course," he clarified.

I had not known that. A pang of something rippled through me, threatening to collapse the luminous world. Why had Robert never known that?

"I could move your *assemblage point*, to let you experience kingfisher-ness," the fox offered, with more investment than his affected nonchalance suggested.

I wanted no such thing. Yet, my *ally* did not wait for my consent or permission.

The world of luminosity shrunk around me, almost in painful fashion. I knew it was because an outside force was forcing cohesion upon me. By force of his external *intent*, the fox was giving his realm's equivalent of the *Nagual's blow* – forcibly dislodging my *assemblage point* to a new locale.

What I experienced was not my usual perceptual reality. I felt the physical world – of pain, of air pressure, or heat and bodily sensation. But, it was not mine.

Instead, I continued on passed that point. I felt wings sprouting out of my head, talons push-through the end of my appendages, and a long, hardened protrusion extended out of my face. It was wonderfully agonising.

After what felt like being birthed, I took off without usual mental deliberation. The very bones of my physical being were wonderfully lighter than I had ever known.

I was a kingfisher! I was flying! It was glorious!

Whether I was still in a state of *altered awareness* – or merely perceiving for the first time as a kingfisher does – I could not differentiate. I did not care.

Whilst my new view of the world shimmered, this was not the sight of a luminous landscape. The realm of form and sensation still created discernible edges of structured perception for me. However, there was an iridescent quality to my vision, as I sped above the chalky blotches of the city, seeking out more natural habitat.

Finally, something caught my eye – almost as if sending a sparkling beacon up from below. It was the surface of a river, not so much as reflecting the sun's rays, but speaking to my bird-sight – with its millions of years of direct lineage transmission. The glittery-shimmer was intrinsically appealing, testifying to the place's symbiotic *power* to my new kingfisher-ness.

Heading towards the natural pull of the light, I revelled and relished my new form. I wilfully dove into an unprecedented joy-of-being.

Robert had never been as happy in his own human-skin.

6

The Pull of the Past.

(aka: The Seduction of the First Ring of Power)

From that point onwards, the little fox came to commune with me on a more regular basis. If anything, I found myself chiefly amused by his prominent French accent.

The crux of the fox-ally's teachings began with the development of my *double* – the *other* as it has been called elsewhere, or the *dreaming body*. It is the collapsed restructuring of the *nagual*-side of awareness; being the manifestation of immediate *will*, rather than the constantly-step-removed *description* that collapses into body, mind and environment.

Coaxing my *double* out felt stiff and cumbersome at first. Yet, without the old shackles of mind, I grew proficient within short-enough time (albeit, my sense of linear temporal progression was also in a state of diffusion).

We began with pragmatic needs of the *tonal:* the need to find shelter, food, safety and isolation. Sitting in the church or atop the store roof-space, I would intentionally shift the habitual tension surrounding my *assemblage point*, as the fox instructed.

The fox guided me to sink the halo of my *assemblage point* into a lower domain. There, I was to highlight some of the unused bands of luminous fibres within my inner realm of the *nagual* – albeit, not to the depth of fully manifest *dreaming* practices.

Of course, such descriptions are wholly insufficient, when considered through the linear lens of the *tonal's* rational thinking. Given the core structure of universal awareness, there is no 'inside' or 'outside' of the luminous cocoon forming an individual. Yet, there are depths of awareness. It could alternatively be considered as a 'pressure per square inch of awareness'; whereby the resultant 'depth' of focus – the gravity of attention exuded across selected depths – results in the collapsed (i.e. isolated) perceptions of existential manifestation.

Aside from the instruction of words, the real-world result was an audible 'pop-crack' at the area corresponding to the base of my skull. Yet, by the time I heard the tell-tale sign, I had already shifted outside of normal awareness – or 'monkey awareness', as the *ally* tittered in jest.

Something would open up at the top of my head. A former housemate and friend of Robert's – Isabella – would have called the space the *crown chakra*. The scent of energy exuding from this particular point was lighter, more malleable, but harder to manage – not having the grounded, physical or tangible quality as lower-rooted pathways within my luminous cocoon.

Its manifestation was quizzically both lighter, yet infinitely denser. The fox-ally taught that the trick to handling the *double*, was to refrain from trying to resolve the contradiction – as that only led the way back to the *tonal*.

I would feel something heavy at first, peeling its way out the top of my head – like something of lighter substance were being reluctantly birthed, and trying to slough-off the denser confines of description. My experience of sensation, time and association would subsequently become light, fluid and dynamic. The fight was then to force some semblance of cohesion onto the experience. Whatever was released, did not naturally take to the confines of the *tonal*. It felt like trying to wrestle a jacket onto a struggling child.

My growing proficiency in manifesting the *double*, was in refining my link with *intent*, and thus the proper channelling of *will*, from the *left side of awareness* of the *nagual*. The resultant 'double copy' could be considered as a second reproduction of me, having real-world pragmatic value beyond Robert's comprehension. Yet, it was more fluid and expressive, due to the reduced influence of the *tonal*. Yet, even that description – as accurate as it is – does an injustice to the experience, being wholly insufficient to explain the lived phenomenon.

With the *physical body* of my *first attention* seated within the *power spot* of the old church, I could use my *double* to scout elsewhere. My *double* was more sensitive to changes in weather patterns – almost like it could feel the cold droplets of rain forming miles above in the clouds, like tiny little pin-pricks of electrical charge – prompting me in advance, when it was time to move to another site. I *knew*, because the rain miles above tickled so.

Similarly, my *double* was far more sensitive to information transmitted on the winds. Oftentimes, I merely sat still in my *double-form*, listening to songs spun of the *dreaming* born of a city's-worth of people – all naturally shifting over into the *nagual* each night. The minute manoeuvre of collective awareness was enchanting and relaxing – an entire mega-zoo of hyper-tense captives, allowed a few hours of respite from the tyrannical zookeeper of description. Worlds upon alien worlds of otherness fought back to re-inflate the *balloons of awareness* just a little – all whilst it went entirely overlooked under the black enchantments.

Equally, I could use my *double* to manifest at a second location, allowing me to scout the safety and isolation of another place, before I attempted to move there.

On one early occasion, I had missed a suitable window of opportunity to seek out dry shelter prior to a huge rain storm hitting. Cold and miserable, I simply opted to shift into my *double*, and enjoy the warmth of the dockyard conduit miles away, regardless.

Yet, the danger of manifestation in that less-cohesive state, was the constant *thrum-thrum-thrum* of gasses venting through the exhaust pipe itself. The rhythmic vibration of sound running through that conduit – running much further than the considerable length of the pipe itself – was far more tempting to me, in that uniquely manifest state.

I now knew what the *ally* meant, when he had warned that, whilst being in one's *double* can offer seemingly miraculous advantages (to the understanding of the *tonal*, that is), so too is it an increased state of vulnerability.

Sheltering from the pounding of a million deafening raindrops from above, the rhythmic *thrum-thrum-thrum* of the pipe reverberated in a place beyond my ears – calling to me to jump on the sound, and ride the air-current into alien realms of the *second attention*. The old world of the *ancient sorcerers* lay just at the end of that industrial heartbeat.

I very much wanted to follow. And therein, I knew was the catch… as I would not be inclined to return. That, had been the trap the pioneers of ancient sorcery had too easily fallen into.

Once I had become proficient with the actualisation of my *double*, the fox-ally turned me again-and-again into a kingfisher.

"This is not your form," he reproached during a particularly painful transformation. "Rather, consider it a handy template, borrowed of *his* inheritance of Florinda."

I loved nothing more than darting around the surrounding countryside, or seeing the city from above – playing amongst the air currents in a real-world manifestation, as to which no human could understand. Each time, the fox pushed me a little further abroad.

On one occasion, as I looked down at the wilds surrounding the city, looking for the familiar glittering-aura of a river, I saw with my little bird eyes a different kind of shimmer. It came from a circular clearing within a wood, of which a lone tree grew at the centre.

Feeling myself inextricably pulled to the clearing, it was with some resistance that the little fox forced me back into my usual perceptual cohesion, resuming the form of a man (or, what was left of one). I had to purposefully let go of my reactionary disappointment.

Straight away, I could feel the place was a *power spot* – a natural conflux of energetic patterns that formed synergistically to the individual luminous cocoon of man. Yet, I also knew that this was not a *power spot* for myself. If I spent too long there, it would reject me.

"Sit and *see*," the fox commanded, as he strolled into the clearing as though owning the place, kicking dirt off his little rear brown boots.

It was easy to shut-off the *internal dialogue*. If anything, it was growing increasingly more difficult to maintain that stable position of my *assemblage point*, in order to hold-on to perceptual cohesion. At every turn, there was always that siren call of the *third attention*, nagging at me to *let go*. I was finding more-and-more that I was having to tap the collective intent of the city, in order to re-collapse back into known form and anchor myself.

Sitting on a fragrant patch of wild-grasses, I shifted into *seeing*. The natural conflux of the wood helped to guide the position of my *assemblage point*, like it had been intended for that very purpose: to be a fluid space, not championing the description of the *tonal*, nor the complete creative onslaught of the *nagual*. It was a beautifully sophisticated manoeuvre, resulting in mutually-real dualistic visions, imposed upon each other.

Looking partially with the eyes, meant I could observe under the earth. There, was a semi-emaciated man buried several feet directly under the central tree. Inspecting closer, I could *see* that his body had been shrouded in organic wraps, each soaked with *intention.* His hands were placed holding a smooth flat river-stone over his naval area.

Directly out of the man's chest, the huge fig tree had grown in the centre of the clearing – its roots anchored within his very lungs. This, was a place of ancient sorcery, I understood.

"He's not a *seer* of ancient Mexico," the fox explained without words. "He began as what your world would consider as a shaman of Paganism. Of course, like all accomplished *seers*, he grew beyond the confines of description."

"He purposefully buried himself," I stated. It was not a question, but something I knew to be fact.

"He's actually still quite alive," the fox-ally offered with his French stoicism. "Although, not in the manner that most people would understand," he clarified.

That thought did not shock me as much as I thought it may. It was likely a benefit of my dualistic state of perception, whereby I could simultaneously *see* the form as an organic man, and yet also as a luminous cocoon. Throughout the *ally's* teachings, I had noticed that my emotions always ran differently when moving towards left-side awareness.

The image of a semi-petrified man, with the roots and limbs of a tree inextricably growing out of his flesh, was nauseating. The fascinating part, was *seeing* how the *balloons of awareness* of both tree and man were intentionally fused, and had been for centuries.

"That, was the whole point of his endeavour. He learned from the spirit songs within nature – *allies*, if you will – that one can intentionally move further towards the right-side dimensions of reality, drastically extending one's lifespan in matters of temporal existence."

The prospect was vastly unappealing to me – to be tethered to physical form, beyond a natural human lifespan. It felt worse than the possibility of imprisonment.

"Of course, these were shamans and sorcerers of old," the fox rebuffed, as he examined the tree with his amber eyes. "They were morbid, and unconstrained by the modern tethers of the *tonal*. Being naturally more versatile agents of *power*, they were free to pursue their indulgences unhindered."

"This one," he tilted his pointed face towards the tree, "saw the extended lifetime of some plants, and sought to hitch a ride on that luminous matrix – grafting his own cocoon with the tree's. That, is no longer a man, nor a tree," he finished.

"What would you call it?" I tested my *ally*, without saying a word.

"A sorcerer's indulgence," he snipped. "Or, a schism within luminosity. However you consider it, such arts are long dead to modern man; even whilst the *ancient seer* does… in a manner of speaking… still live."

The fox's tail twitched, which I had come to understand as a sign of his deliberation. "Equally, the luminous existence of modern humanity – the current structure of mankind's awareness – would be equally as baffling and grotesque to the *ancient seer*. In fact, he would find the strength of the contemporary descriptive force to be quite intolerable… experiencing it as painfully deafening as many of the *allies* do."

"But why do such a thing – burying yourself alive, to merge with the luminosity of a tree?"

81

"You lack the explorative daring of the *old seers*," the fox chuckled. "The unique luminous cocoons of trees grant access to deep secrets of the earth. It is a knowledge humans cannot comprehend, nor return from," he offered with a little sadness.

I thought to my own investigations, in listening to the trees. My efforts appeared childish and primitive in comparison. Yet, an uncomfortable part of me recognised the temptation. The trees had whispered similarly alluring promises to me.

We stayed in that clearing until twilight began to settle, discussing the *ancient seer*. Suddenly, I stopped talking – realising that the fox-ally had summoned an old shadow of dialogue, even if it was not verbal.

A cold echo of Robert shivered up my spine. I felt the deplorable detachment of the *ancient seers*, and realised the place was an energetic trap. The giveaway to my entrapment, was that I could no longer conceive of the possibility of turning into a kingfisher, let alone conceptualise any framework from which to accomplish such a magical task.

I was cold, beyond temperature – suddenly feeling uncomfortably solid and suffocated within worldly form. The tactility of grass beneath me, felt like being stabbed with a thousand icy blades, rather than my usual delight of direct physical sensation. My own skin felt uncomfortably like it had been too tightly shrink-wrapped around my flesh.

Suddenly, something snapped behind me, like an animal stepping on a tree branch. Yet, it was a multi-layered sound, almost as though it was disguising a second audible layer.

I knew enough that with my eyes currently dictating *looking*, I was in no state to tackle the magical realm of the *unknown*. My eyes would betray and doom me.

Something much quicker beyond thinking took over my actions. I shoved my face within the darked entrance of a nearby badger's den, simultaneously pulling my jeans down around my ankles.

Under normal thinking, forcing one's face into a badger's den would be considered unduly risky. Yet, I was in a *place of power*, battling for my life against the forces of *infinity*. This was a magical bout of *power*, whereby considerations of the daily world would only incapacitate me.

In forcing myself into such a vulnerable and utterly nonsensical position, I claimed it as an act of *not-doing* – an act intended to loosen the hold of the *tonal's* binding force. It made no rational sense, but I knew it on a bone-deep level to be the only proper response.

I kept my eyes closed, my body still. My hands protectively cupped over the nape of my neck. Something, was prowling around 'outside' – now determined by the black enclosure surrounding my head. It was somewhere on the energetic periphery.

With my head even closer to the *ancient seer's* body beneath the tree, I did not want to shift into *seeing*. As a result, the description of the *tonal* threatened to take over, and I could feel the physical presence of some sort of beast – much bigger than a fox or badger – padding around, just outside. I could almost feel the ground sink under its formidable weight.

My body gave a little reactionary jerk, and a momentary spasm of Robert's old lower back pain momentarily flashed within me. I felt the wet-cold touch of a large animal's fleshy, leathery nose on my exposed buttocks. The fact that it felt to have protruding tubules surrounding its nose-pad, made me think of a creature like a mole, albeit much, much bigger.

The creature pushed-sniffed at my rear end for a while, almost as though it did not know what to make of the strange being sticking out of the ground, seemingly without a head.

Appearing almost frustrated and tired of the stalemate, the beast placed a weighted paw between my shoulder blades, with such astounding pressure that I feared my spine had broken.

My eyes reflexively popped open in the underground darkness. For a split second, I saw the green-luminous face of the *ancient seer*, alive with an organic energy. His hauntingly-hollow eyes had *seen* everything, and now they saw right into me.

My trapped body jerked with a start. There was a loud snap-crack, and I lost perceptual cohesion. Blackness consumed me.

I came too in a city... a different city. The grand architecture and old-fashioned buildings felt familiar somehow. My immediate dislike of the noise, pollution and crowds felt frustratingly familiar. There was a former heavy industry about the place, which asked that I should know it.

But something felt different. Familiar, yet different.

Looking down, I saw how I was well-groomed, wearing an impeccably-tailored suit, well beyond what Robert would even have been able to afford. My nails were clean and cut. I was wearing a grotesquely expensive watch. A pair of sapphire cufflinks dazzled-out from starched cuffs. Feeling my head, my hair felt cropped and styled. I had no beard.

I experienced a momentary wave of confusion. I wanted to throw-up.

Through the bustle of the business commuters purposefully striding the walkway, I saw the back of a suited man stood motionless at the glossy display of a jeweller's window. Something about the way his shoulders hunched, lulled me closer.

Idling up alongside the man – as though I too were looking for a trinket – something about him felt acutely familiar. He looked like Robert... but different; perhaps a couple of years older. He looked like a high-school jock, who's glory-days were far beyond him; his former athleticism ravaged by the gravity and trials of older-age.

Then the startling realisation struck me – it was Robert's brother! He was much older than Robert had ever seen. But then, I realised that it had been over twenty years since Robert last saw his nearest-aged sibling. They had been the closest in appearance, having both the same mother and father.

The man was looking absently, almost beyond the broaches and diamond ear-rings on display. Something weighed down imposingly upon him – a heaviness that was more burdensome than reflected in the sagging skin and the dark circles of his defeated face.

"Where is he?" I heard, turning around as though someone had asked a question.

"Where on earth did he go to? Why did he have to leave? What did we do?"

Despite the din of the busy street, I understood that I was hearing his brother's *internal dialogue*, as though he were speaking out aloud.

"I just want to see him again," the man wished to no-one but himself. "I could tell him things are different... that... that, we need him."

There was no accusation or anger in the inner voice of his brother. Rather, there was a resigned grief permeating his wishes to see his long-departed younger brother again. There spoke a need for connection... for recognition... for compassion... for the solace of shared history.

Someone... or, something... clipped my shoulder. Spinning around to see who had hit me with such force, I was momentarily dumbfounded to find myself in the grotty living room of a strange home.

As much as the immediacy of the unfamiliar surroundings told me of state-provided finances, social housing and chronic poverty, I recognised the person sat motionless in the torn armchair. It was Robert's older sister.

Yet, just like his brother, she appeared in a state that Robert himself had never witnessed prior to leaving. Clearly, she was older. But her eating disorder had evidently ravaged her body.

Much to his sister's own distress throughout adolescence and adulthood, she had always been a bigger woman – not fat, but of broad-shoulder and tall, with a swimmer's build. This always stood in sharp contrast to their shared mother, who had inherited the tiny frame of their French grandfather.

Their mother had always criticised her only daughter, that she had inherited the looks and build of her father – who she had never known, disappearing on the day Robert's sister was brought home from the hospital. It was a constant reminder that was forcibly hammered into her daughter's psyche.

Her mother had always openly blamed her daughter for her father's disappearance – claiming it was the fact she had been born female that was such an offensive disappointment. Her mother had resented her only daughter's existence, as the constant reminder of the husband who had abandoned her already with three children, prior to Robert's immediate brood even being born.

Almost predictably, Robert's sister went on at a young age to be sexually abused by a family member, having already grown with a craving for the attention of all the wrong men. Years later, when she sought the help of her own mother, she only received rage and further criticism – that it was her fault for not making enough effort, for not being quiet enough, for being her father's daughter... for simply being born a girl. Why did she have to make the mother's life such hard work all of the time?!

It was little wonder Robert's sister had developed body-issues, closely tied to her relationships to both men and food (being the disguised illusion of control). Yet, when Robert himself had left, it had not been so bad as I was now witnessing. Perhaps his departure had also injured his sister's spirit.

His older sibling sat with her cheekbones painfully protruding, almost as a skull. Her once-athletic and powerful arms, looked thin, and ready to break at the slightest touch. If anything, she looked all the worse for it, as her tall frame insisted that she should look much naturally heavier than she did.

The living-skeleton merely sat staring at the advertisements flashing through the tv, without really seeing them. A deluge of false promises where propelled-out to her uncomprehending observation, alongside the contradictory recommendations for a more worthwhile life. A new high-tech mop, a revolutionary new medicine, or an exotic perfume, were all what where needed to change your life. If your spirit was injured, there was always someone else to blame, for personal reward.

"He left, just like my dad did," came his sister's voice, without passing her lips. "I'm so repulsive. I drive all men away."

An alien regret and guilt tried to claw its way into my awareness. I felt uncharacteristically guilty, though I could not place why… why should I have any connection to the sister of another person? Something elusive struggled within me. It tried to rise up, like a serpent of memory coiling to strike, causing me debilitating confusion.

"… just want to hug him again," the *inner dialogue* of his sister continued in self-flagellation. "I just need to know that he'd be proud of me…"

A sudden, inexplicably loud knock on the front door made me jerk.

Again, I was momentarily confused, as I adjusted to the new surroundings forced upon me. I was in another apartment, in a foreign country.

This time, it was a much older man slumped in a rancid armchair – Robert's oldest brother. A pungent smell of stale booze and body odour permeated the air, betraying a long-term, festered occupation.

Placards of tortured and lab-tested animals were piled in a corner. His oldest sibling had been vegan, and a passionate animal right's activist. It was the one outlet of compassion he had awarded himself, amongst all of the self-hate, death-metal, and disdain of humanity.

Surrounded by a perverse volume of empty liquor bottles, Robert's oldest brother was slumped in a state of semi-consciousness. His body was almost painfully round, as though he was soon to burst his overly-bloated form. Strangely, he appeared to have aged the least of all the siblings, even if his skin was stretched by the most considerable weight-gain.

Fresh lines of dried blood criss-crossed his long-scarred forearms. Yet, it was no suicide attempt – merely the latest exhibit of cathartic self-mutilation. The huge ribbons of dark-brown crust patchworking across the armchair attested to the ritualism of such dubious self-soothing.

"He knew me butter than anywun. He hated pupple juft as mutch as I done," came the disjointed inner voice of his brother's inebriated mind. "Is he would juft come back… I'd… I'd… he'd *get* me…" the thoughts trailed off into a haze of inconsistency.

I knew what was coming next, even before the jarring flash pulled me out of the scene.

The scent of the hospital hit me before the sight did. Yet, it was the clinical solitude of hospice that dawned before me.

Immediately, an intrinsic *knowing* came to me, in having bypassed Robert's brother – who had been born with severe physical disabilities – and his grandmother and father. In coming straight to Robert's mother, I knew the omission meant only one starkly-final confirmation; those individuals had already passed beyond the realm of human form.

The tiny, wrinkled woman in the clinical bed appeared as unrecognisable to me as Robert's siblings first had. A machine whirred rhythmically for her, as the only visitor that stood by her; its tubes the only touch she benefitted from.

Something about confronting Robert's mother tugged at me. I shifted straight into *seeing*, and for some reason felt a coward for it.

Yet, in *seeing* the luminous fibres of her cocoon, it told me everything. Of her five successfully-birthed children, only three of the glowing threads – which energetically connect a parent to their child – remained. But they were weak... frayed... painfully delicate, struggling to transmit the faintest iridescence. They provided no connection or comfort for her. Their light was far too weak and tenuous to offer any solace now.

Rather than a tight sheen of radiance to her energetic cocoon, her luminosity was a shaggy mess. All of the luminous fibres of her *balloon of awareness* were fraying and loosening; her own command of *intent* was far too lax to hold it together for much longer.

The glow of her *assemblage point* was diminishing. One-by-one, the luminous fibres passing through her conduit were falling aside, outside of the lens of perception. The force of *intent* – usually forming a tight knot around the base of the *balloon of awareness* – was dangerously slack. She was dying.

One of his mother's fibres caught my attention; a strand so delicate and thin, as almost to be invisible. In fact, in its fragility, I had overlooked it at first. But it was there; gently swaying in the intangible drafts of awareness – the last tenuous attachment to her last-born child; the one who had disappeared decades earlier.

"... just to see him one last time," the ragged woman's *internal dialogue* wistfully pleaded to no-one. "I just want to know why. Just one last time. Just someone for me at the end. I just need to know that I wasn't such a bad mom. My baby..."

A detached feeling arose... like an echo of sentiment that belonged to someone else. Of all the possibilities, it was surprisingly compassion that threatened to resurrect Robert.

For myself, I felt as though I should have felt something... anything. Yet, I could only assume my coldness and detachment were a product of my *seeing* – having shifted to *the place of no pity*.

I was transfixed by the sight of the diminutive woman's luminous cocoon, and how its edges were so badly damaged – not only by a lifetime of self-abuse, such as chain-smoking, promiscuity and drinking, but also the energetic products of her psychology, family, socialisation and above all, *personal indulgence...* including the petty thoughts of a lifetime.

This unique energy matrix – this unique formation on the wider *sheet of awareness* – had been an inextricable influence on the energetic legacy of Robert. Its unravelling heralded an important event. Time, was not something this particular *balloon of awareness* had much left of – that dimension of the *tonal*, was quickly unravelling. Her egg-like structure was soon to collapse, lose form, flatten, and re-merge back into its original, universal form.

In that locale-of-awareness, another unwitting food-source would be reconstituted in the world of form, within the following forty-eight days. I could not tell why I already felt sorry for that yet-to-be-manifested being.

Standing amongst the whirs and clicks of mechanised company, I understood that I was witnessing the fourth enemy of man: old age. Regardless of accomplishments or outlook, even the best of sorcerers succumbed to the indiscriminatory effects of time; almost as though it were an agent, force or dimension in itself. The *balloon of awareness* still became slack, and eventually flattened out to reconstitute into the collective sheet of unified awareness. I wondered why the *Eagle* would write such a cruel trick – of fleeting linear existence – into the fabric of reality.

Both the *New Seers* of don Juan's lineage, and the line of the *Omega Assembly*, had each prioritised their own responses to aging. Standing in front of Robert's mother, I could not recall which was the better reaction to the inevitable onslaught of time.

As his mother's breath rattled, I equally struggled to recall why Robert was not present for such an important occasion. It felt like I should know that too. So much was unclear; it was as though I had prematurely aged myself, suffering to bring about the mental cohesion I knew I should have.

I momentarily thought I had been looking at the form of a small, dying woman, amidst a tangle of wires and tubes. Blinking my eyes again, I realised I was instead stood within the rich mahogany study of a private study. Its warmth and homeliness stood at stark contrast to the clinical sterility of the hospice. Whereas fluorescent lighting had harshly illuminated the scene only a second ago, now the room was filled with the flickering organic warmth of an open fire.

More than the sight, the aroma of the place felt like home. Vanilla, coffee and baking dough made the air invitingly evocative and sensual. A hint of a cheeky scent made me turn around.

There was a woman there, who was both unfamiliar to me and Robert's memory. He had never known her. Yet, some feeling led me to recognise that I knew her on a very intimate level. The look in her earnest eyes also assured that she too knew me, beyond any other person on the planet. The depth of empathy held in her gaze, was almost painful to meet, in the acute vulnerability it caused me.

She was beautiful too. Not in an overly-preened or vain manner. This woman possessed a natural beauty suggestive of a casual effort, which Robert had always found the most attractive. Her wide smile was the most endearing, speaking of home much more than the surroundings did.

Unlike the other scenes, this woman looked directly at me. She could see me – acknowledging my presence with a telling grin. Her very scent was intoxicating to me, whereby I could happily fall asleep to my doom, within its heavenly embrace.

It took effort to look away from the familiar woman, to the room. There were old, leather armchairs, a plethora of antique sextants, brass compasses, gloriously detailed maps, and olde world navigational paraphernalia – artfully displayed amongst an obscene collection of leather-bound books.

A part-played ornate chess set lay out on a fine baroque table, next to two half-sipped glasses of expensive honey-brandy. A hand-crafted Swiss clock richly ticked-out the seconds, in-between pops and crackles from the log fire.

"This place feels like home," came the thought. Yet, Robert had never known such a place – it was more like how he envisaged the perfect home-life to be.

At that simplest suspicion, a tumble of toddlers came bundling into the study, each competing amongst the excited demands of the other. The oldest girl commanded her mother pick her up, whilst the twins and boy ran straight to me. Their tiny, sticky fingers grabbed and pulled at me. As they covered my face with unabashed kisses, I could do nothing but laugh in sheer contentment. Strangely, I felt utterly at peace within their chaotic demands for attention. It was a pervading joy so deep and physical, as to fill an inner place I had never recognised to be hollow.

"Papa! Papa! Papa!" they called. That one word was almost too powerful to endure.

Holding the youngest boy at distance for a moment, I was shocked to recognise his face. So many of his young features were that of Robert – he was the spitting image of his father! Seeing that transmission – that enduring link within a lineage – touched something profound within me. It was much more a feeling of home, than the belonging the scenery spoke of.

For an eternally painful split-second, I wanted to cry. I wanted to take my place. I wanted to surrender.

This, was undoubtedly Robert's own family. Or, it was the family he swore he would never have – yet deep down painfully yearned so much for. It was the one possibility in the entire universe, that could have anchored him, and easily pulled him away from *the path of knowledge.*

And with that understanding, came the heart-wrenching breaking of the spell. Robert had never belonged. His inheritance had never allowed for this.

Looking at the form of a fig tree within a wooded clearing, I took in the natural scenery of the twilight grove. The little fox sat next to me.

"That, was no illusion," he hesitatingly offered, looking at me askance. "Well, no more illusionary than the crummy life of Robert. But, the treasures of sorcery would readily offer you that reality. You only have to be daring enough to claim it."

"Pick any of the tasty figs, and eat them," he went on, with his thick French accent. "Each one is a *power-fig*... a fruit bursting with *knowledge!* The lessons you will learn, mon petit homme!"

"What... what did you show me?" I queried, without moving my lips. My mind was trying to claw back some cohesion, after the impossible visions I had seen. The world felt unbearably cold and hard, compared to the sights of a moment ago.

"Whaaaat?" the fox retorted with exaggerated innocence. "I merely allowed you to follow the luminous fibres of Robert's heritage. I showed you what is – beyond what that buffoon had known."

"I don't understand. Why?"

"To let you know there are still options."

"Wha... options? What are you saying?"

"That you can still go home. You have always been able to – despite how alone and untethered you felt. There are people – structures – that you would intrinsically fit into. Just say the word, and you can *belong* again."

"Or...." The fox followed trying to disguise the hesitancy within his voice, as if risking upsetting me, "you can pick a fig from the tree, and learn true *knowledge*. Any fig! Trust me; each one would be an invaluable lesson – a *gift of power* from the *seers of old!* You could really let go..."

"Go home," the fox offered with quiet promise disguising true peril, "or become a *man of knowledge*..."

Of course, I immediately recognised it as a trap. In tapping the *tonal*, and Robert's fading sense of *personal history*, the fox-ally was attempting to exploit the violent impetus to run in the complete opposite direction – in offering unique *gifts of power,* worthy of the old ways.

Yet, I could *see* the snare the *old seer* of ancient times had fallen into. In a long-forgotten existence of a half-life, the *ancient seer* was no more a man, than he was something else entirely – a doorway or gate, that had been lured-open by alien awareness, via promises of *knowledge.*

The flaw in the fox's trickery, was that he had not accounted for my *seeing.* Dotted around the tree, was a mushroom-ring. Its root-system was largely underground, forming the mass of an encompassing organic boundary around the man-tree.

The thought occurred to me, that mushrooms are genetically closer to humans, than they are plants. It is no co-incidence that when cooked, mushrooms are often described as 'fleshy'.

Yet in *seeing*, I could perceive a strange, prickling azure light cast of the wider mushroom organism. The tree had purposefully utilised the mushrooms to entrap the *old seer*, once his curiosity had gotten the best of him. That old Pagan *seer* was now entombed, as an energetic battery allowing the vastly-aged form of the parasitic *tree-ally* to feed upon, in its new found inception of worldly form. In his brilliance, the old Pagan-shaman was now prisoner, robbed of his potential for freedom.

The thought suddenly occurred to me, if the fox was the spirit of the fig tree.

It did not matter. I did not matter. There was nothing to run away from, and no residual violence of impulse prompting an escape to extremes. The flaw in the fox's plan, was that Robert was already long-gone.

7

The Pull of Sorcery.

(aka: The Seduction of the Second Ring of Power)

One of the city's local parks had become one of my frequent calling-places. Not only was it quiet, well-tendered and peaceful, but it offered a range of facilities to someone who did not 'look homeless' to the park warden's eyes.

I had once been approached by an over-enthusiastic new warden. However, when yanking at my clothes and moaning in unintelligible grunts and grimaces, it was enough to convince her that she was not paid enough to deal with someone she presumed to have psychological problems.

Not only was there a freely available drinking fountain at the park, but the public bathrooms were surprisingly new and clean – enough to allow me to strip down to wash the likes of my socks, without risking foot infections. Likewise, in-line with growing modern sensibilities, the facilities provided single-occupancy unisex bathrooms, which allowed me privacy to attend to less public ablutions (like strip-washing myself, and cutting my own hair).

The main park had specialised sections fenced-off, with pretty wrought-iron railings. There was a child-safe play area, with soft wood-chip flooring and no dogs allowed. There was a memorial garden, with quiet, secluded seating areas for reflection and dedication. There was a sensory garden, encouraging the touch and smelling of wildlife. And there was a wildlife-friendly garden, again denying dogs.

The wildlife sanctum was ideal – not only because it had lots of high bushes to provide privacy and noise-reduction, but also because it had dedicated feeding stations. Pigeons, jays, sparrows, bluetits, corvids and squirrels frequented these in considerable numbers, as a reliable food source. There was always a steady stream of city-residents leaving dried peas, peanuts and seed on the stations, alongside the occasional treat of fat-trimmings.

Mid-morning appeared to be the best time to visit the wildlife garden, just after the older citizens had made their daily drop off. If someone hung around to admire the wildlife, it was easy enough for me to pretend I was engrossed in the local foliage, or casually reading a (two-year out-of-date) newspaper etc.

Robert would have been disgusted to be scavenging food amongst the birds. He would have felt utterly humiliated and self-conscious.

As for myself, the nuts and seeds left for the wildlife were a great source of protein and essential fats. Yet in the spirit of fair-play (and constant power-balance), I always ensured to leave half for the little birds. After all, I was now finding myself satiated with the merest morsel of food – finding the texture and flavour of simple seeds to be utterly captivating and enriching. It was nothing to follow it with a dessert of a few honeysuckle berries from the sensory garden.

It was after such a park-buffet that I had finally wandered to the sub-abode, at the edge of the woods on 'millionaire's lane'. I had spent the night awake, re-stocking my personal safety-stashes between various sites – like my locker at the 24-hour gym, the small possessions I kept sealed within plastic bags underground within a disused water-mains manhole cover, and my undisturbed supplies housed within an old, derelict electrical-box.

Whilst foraging for leftovers, I had found some bicarbonate of soda within a supermarket's trash. The packaging had been damaged, but otherwise it was perfectly fine. It served well, as makeshift toothpaste. As such, I distributed it amongst my hoard-sites, fostering security in a dispersal of resources.

After a long night of travelling around the city, and enjoying the nuts shared with the squirrels, I headed-out to the relative isolation of 'millionaire's lane'. I needed to wash both myself and my clothes, and the isolation of the unsecured little out-house – with its outside shower – allowed me the privacy to attend to such things unmolested. Then, I could sleep the rest of the day off inside, allowing time for my clothes to dry.

As I lay my clothes in the warmth of the windows, I noticed the fox-ally sitting patiently outside the glass door. Opening the entrance, he ambled his way in with a feigned air of civility.

"My apologies for our last exchange," he offered, with diplomatic courtesy. It was the first time I had interacted with him since my visions within the fig-tree clearing.

I had seen the fox-ally since that encounter. However, it had only been as fleeting copper-flashes on the periphery of my vision. Twice though, I had seen him boldly within the city centre itself – casually strutting amongst the crowds as though he were on his commute.

It had been a strange sight to watch other people notice the little fox – with their comments and grabbing of camera-phones. Whether it was because they could see him too – and that he was not unique to my own mind – it caused a point of unresolved consternation within me.

"It was too much of me, too soon," the *ally* spoke, jumping up and sitting himself upon one of the padded cushions.

"Why are you here?" I pointedly asked, without saying anything.

"To apologise, of course."

"Apology accepted. Now, if you would kindly leave…"

"Now, now," the canine tutted with pantomimed derision. "I owe you much more than words. As a sorcerer with a temperament of the old, you know how utterly trifling words are. My apology needs to be, more... sufficient."

"So," I countered, with as much casualness as I could silently muster, whilst re-aligning my drying underpants in the sun. "What do you propose?"

"I'm going to take you into *dreaming*, and expand on the sorcerer's explanation!" His angular mouth parted, into what I could only interpret as a fox's best attempt at an ingratiating smile.

With nothing to do but wait for myself and clothes to dry, I settled down to sleep on the floor. Whilst the padded benches would have been more comfortable, lying on the floor meant I was out-of-view. Besides, I had grown strangely accustomed to sleeping on harder surfaces.

Surprisingly, the little fox jumped down, and nestled between my shoulder blades, curling up to join me in sleep. The pressure and warmth of his physical contact, was surprisingly soothing.

As I fell asleep, the ghost of someone else's memory came to me; the recollection of physical contact and connection. Physical interplay did not seem a part of my ghost-like existence now. Robert's life had been full of the touch of other people – the playful pat of friends, the shaking hands of colleagues, the primal intertwining of sexual activity, the brutal boundaries of Ninjutsu sparring, and the oh-so-delicate yet intoxicating lightest of interplays via Tai Chi 'push hands' (*tui shou*).

My last hazy thought before sleep, was to the last time I had touched anyone. How long had it been? Had I ever? Was I even real anymore?

I found myself waking, already stood. My vision was blurred, fighting to focus itself into recognisable form. For a second, I thought something was wrong with my eyes.

I felt a little nudge against my left calf, and the world came into view. Yet, it was unlike any world I had ever experienced – very clearly not being of the earth.

Huge mountains formed of some kind of translucent crystalline-glass, loomed over us like primordial gods. They were hundreds of times the height of mount Everest, casting night-time within their shadows.

The clear alienness of the landscape came from the sight of the mountains being clustered together in 'islands' – which floated thousands of feet above a silvery ocean of liquid metal. Connecting the floating mountain ranges, were thick, fibrous growths of fungi – spanning the vast distances like knotted organic bridges. They made the human feat of the Golden Gate Bridge appear utterly miniscule by comparison.

The air sparkled with semi-visible micro-particles, casting an enchanting twinkling sensation all around. Each way I turned, the very air itself glimmered, thick with an innate promise of magic. I momentarily worried about inhaling the shimmer. However, it dawned on me with fascination, that I was not breathing, and that there was no need to.

I suddenly realised just how unknowingly burdensome breathing had been for so many years. With the lack of atmosphere, I experienced an unprecedented sensation of physical relaxation, from not having my lungs filled. Similarly, there was a lack of air pressure and tactility surrounding my skin, which only left me feeling lighter and more buoyant than ever before. Suddenly free of air-pressure, I felt years younger.

Looking above, the entire black sky was a mass of infinite stars. In the distance, three giant suns gave off a diffused light. Yet, it was a weird cold-grey light, as if the stars were at considerably more distance from this particular planet, than our own yellow sun. The height of the mountain-islands created darker shadows, with shafts of the grey light cutting like light cast through huge gothic windows.

Within the columns of light, the shifting currents of diamond-like particles relayed a movement of something through the air. Yet, I could not feel any atmosphere as such, with no phenomena of wind. However, *something* was transmitted in the great openness between the mountain ranges.

The weirdly-monotone 'colour' reflected and shimmered across the glass-like landscape, almost as though the light itself were alive. Every turn resulted in an enticing shimmer, reflected deep within the semi-transparent ground. It appeared to have more depth and 'texture' than the light on earth, which I could only assume was some effect of the triple-suns.

"What… what is this place?" I asked without voice, to my fox-guide. "Or, should I be asking, *where* is this place?"

"I am showing you alien awareness;" the fox explained, sniffing at a particularly woolly cluster of fungal blooms running for hundreds of miles, "…*inorganic* life, if you will."

"This fungus, is a complex silicone-based sentient life-form," he offered matter-of-factly.

It was only then that I happened to recall the concept of sound. A resonant, permeating chorus suddenly filled the air all around, as though tangibly touching me. The best I could associate it to, would be that it sounded somewhere a mix between whale chatter, and the stress-reverberations of electrical cables in the wind. Yet, it was clearly neither. And, it was registered through the skin, and not the ears. It was that tactile-sound emanating through the non-atmosphere, that connected me to the planet, much more so than any somatosensory bearing with the ground.

The deep, rhythmic intoning was intoxicating. Glitter permeating the air moved in harmonious patterns with the reverberations. The atmosphere was rich with synergy.

Pulling my attention from the mesmerising sights around me, I became momentarily captivated with the chorus that felt to echo from the very heavens.

The fox picked up on my focus. "That's their version of communicating," he flatly offered. "The mountains sing to each other."

"The mountains themselves are alive?"

The copper fox arched his back and padded his feet, with what I could best interpret as mirth.

"You dumb numbskull!" His non-audible voice sounded truly entertained at the apparent stupidity of my response.

"Why is that a dumb question?"

"Imagine a teeny-tiny lifeform gets transported into the space between your – quite limited – brain cells. It looks up in awe, at the nerve-transmitters, the glucose, the oxygen, the blood vessels and a whole sea of floating neurons – asking its alien guide, *are the neurons alive?*"

"No, no… whilst there is sentient life here in this alien world, it is as much between, and a product of, the collective factors; very much the same as your own consciousness stems from somewhere *between* all the collective parts of veins, sinew and brain-cells."

I understood the fox's point. This constitution of alien features could neither be considered as individual, or of one – perhaps planet-sized – mind. It was no more or less so, than any one human can be considered as truly individual, when they are by nature of millions of years of evolution, still very much a heavily social, inter-dependant herd-like animal. The annoyingly flimsy truth, was somewhere between the abstractions – a wider product of construct beyond the convenience of description.

Some part of me felt peeved for the evident demonstration of my still clearly human thinking. Here I was, stood on the awesome grounds of a truly alien world, surrounded by *inorganic* sentience, yet unable to look beyond my own stubbornly human limitations.

"This is the problem of all humanity," the fox explained, looking out at a huge geyser of erupting crystalline lava. "Man looks up into the stars, looking for others like himself. He spends so many resources in an attempt to find sentient life out there, that conveniently fits into his narrow understanding of *organic life*. It is embarrassingly egotistical; and it is no wonder humanity mistakenly considers itself alone in the great mystery of *infinity!*"

"Rather," the fox placed himself down next to me, as though trying to figure out how to express something complicated to a lower lifeform, "mankind has no conception that the universe is teeming with life – albeit, it is folded-up within the very creases of multi-fractal reality itself… not 'out there' as you stupidly assume, but right in front of your very nose! Your kind just do not now have the pliability and command of our own awareness, to *see* the majesty of the true universe right before you."

"If your kind could *see*, they would understand there is no need to build rocket-ships, probes, and spend billions of dollars on vanity projects to colonise other worlds," the fox was almost shaking his pointed little head in dismay. "Rather than build launch pads and space ports, you little hairless monkeys should be building temples – to refine your awareness, turn your focus inwards, and explore the true frontiers of reality. Therein lies an abundance of truly alien life, and the source of humanity's salvation or doom."

"Mankind doesn't *see* the stupidity of ruining the planet – and thinking their solution is simply to jet-off to another one, to ruin that! You naked-monkeys do not *see* how this robs you of *power*, by denying yourselves the opportunity to grow, and be better than you are. *Power…*" the fox paused, as though hesitant to reveal an important secret, "does not lay at the end of industry and ingenuity. It was always there at the start; with the possibility of assuming *personal responsibility* – of fostering discipline and the mastery of *intent*."

"Of course," the fox laughed, as best a fox could, "the irony is that in order to undertake true exploration, mankind would have to relinquish its hold on petty reason and description. They would have to be as bold and obscenely daring as the *seers of antiquity;*

to shoot off and explore the great bands of magical awareness. Yet instead, humanity finds itself increasingly being smothered by the ever-linear descriptive forces of the *tonal!* What a bind!"

"Florinda told Robert that the universe was made of *forty-eight sheets of awareness*, all occupying the same space, but separated by their inherent dimensional realities," I offered, taking my place next to the fox. "She said, of all of those *sheets of awareness*, only eight were inherently capable of sustaining a stable *assemblage point*, and thus any meaningful concept of sentient life."

"She was right," he confirmed. "There are *balloons of awareness* on other sheets outside of the central eight. But let us say that the pliability and durability do not allow for *sustained* formations within the unique layer of awareness. We call such beings *vessels*."

"But then, there are sheets beyond even these, whereby balloon-structures can be formed. However, due to the unique malleability of those particular *sheets of awareness* – let us say, that the inherent reactivity to the touch of *intent* is not there – they can form structures, yet not hold stable *assemblage points*. We call beings of that design, *vapours*."

As if privy to my line of unvoiced enquiry, the fox went on, "Humans exist across the central four dimensions of reality, of the possible forty-eight."

"Don't you mean three-dimensions?" I interrupted. "Height, width and length?"

"You're an idiot," the fox casually stated in a particularly strong accent, as if merely describing an object in front of him. "Citing the dimension of 'height' for example, is still just a mere way of talking. It tells you nothing of the existence of *height*. You are only collapsing a glorious phenomenon of the universe down into something cheap, convenient and a peppy commodity. Such are the dangers of talking about such things, as words are wholly insufficient in the end!"

"Yet for now, words are all we have," the fox-ally resigned himself to go on. "When considering the boundaries of existence, you forget the most important fourth dimension humans are very much bound to... *time*. You hairless-apes are first-and-foremost temporal creatures, formed by unique mortal constraints. Yet, the quirk of your *tonal's* blinding descriptive influence, is that it forces you to forget this defining truism of your very existence... mistaking yourself as immortal and invulnerable. Little wonder you suffer! Imagine if you forgot of your dimensional reality of height – how many times you would go around banging your heads!"

The fox explained how the dimensions of length and time, were located on the great fluidic mass of the *tonal's* matrix. Using himself as an example, he said that his own constitution of awareness included length and time, but not width and height. Whilst he was also a four-dimensional being, his extra two-dimensions spanned from further beyond the human spectrum. His two additional dimensions sorcerers called 'echoic' and 'pareidolic'.

"I am a creature of form, but unlike human form. And, whilst I will one day flatten out into my own unique layer of awareness – being subject to the influence of time like you – my separate existence across the other two dimensions of reality determines that my concept of time is vastly extended." He added, "... of course, greatly extended in limited human terms, that is; just as human life appears vastly extended from the perspective of a fruit-fly."

"If you do not exist with height and width, how am I seeing you?"

"I am an interpretation, forced of description," he clarified. "I have moved my *assemblage point* adjacent to yours. My existence as a four-dimensional being overlaps on two plains of parallel reality; whereby from your perspective, I am slightly phased-out of the reality of alignment. Usually, this makes such *allies* go unperceived by non-sorcerers. At best, they are explained-away as mental health issues, or indulged as spirits, angels or ghosts."

The fox laughed again, as if considering the human perspective were truly amusing. 'The clown layer', he called the human band of awareness.

My fox companion continued explaining why it was that – being an *ally* manifest of the side of the *tonal*, with extra descriptive qualities and vastly expanded lifespans – the *sorcerers of antiquity* sought such beings out. It was such *allies* who taught the *ancient seers* how to shape-shift into wolves, turn into trees or fog, and to tie-off their *balloons of awareness* from the great sheet. Those sorcerers subsequently floated off into *infinity*, surrounded on all sides by greater descriptive depths of the *tonal*, to become something else entirely.

"To call the fourth layer of time solely as the 'human' realm is dumb on two accounts," continued the fox in his heavy, French accent. "First, humans actually exist as multi-dimensional beings across four layers. Second, the human layer is actually the convenient label given to the *organic* dimensions – which also includes animals, plants and planets."

"Really, it is quite offensive to foxes!" he dryly added.

I explained a particularly stubborn problem for me – insomuch that existence had been described as forty-eight-dimensional reality, with humanity formed of four of those dimensions. Yet, in talking with Florinda and the group, Robert had frequently heard reference to the human and organic layer of reality, as being both one and the same thing.

"It's all true!" the fox smacked his lips together in excitement. "The *organic band of awareness* – oftentimes called the *human layer* through mere convenient arrogance – comprises four dimensions. Equally, there are separate sheets of *allied awareness* – or *inorganic beings,* if you will – that span nine-dimensional reality; and yet others still, which consist of only two. Let us grossly anthropomorphise the matter, and say that a 'band' of reality is the genus of species that are able to form within a range of particular dimensions of awareness. This in-turn, is defined by the refractions of dimensional reality that cluster to give each unique layer its unique quirks-of-manifestation."

"The *allies* have always co-existed right alongside humankind," the fox offered in his best impression of reassurance. "As they shimmered into our perceptual range of reality, they became enmeshed within the *collective dialogue,* as half-human half-animal beings – mythical representations of the duality of the *tonal* and *nagual.*"

"It is why ancient stories are replete with centaurs, satyrs, werewolves, cecaelias, N-dam-keno-wet, Horus, Nügua and even your Tengu of Ninjutsu lore." He paused, for what I considered to be dramatic effect, "and of course, talking foxes!"

I must have looked nonplussed, as he added, "Don't overthink it, mon idiot petit pois! This only remains a way of talking. Remember, we are trying to understand the glory of the *Eagle's emanations*, and the *sorcerer's explanation*, through the flaccid confines of the *tonal*, which is painfully insufficient for the task! It is why – for you half-human-half-monkeys – such topics are best offered as stories to the *spirit*, rather than to the *mind*."

The fox peered at his own feet, which I understood as his trying to conceptualise something in understandable terms for me.

"Imagine a little two-dimensional stick-man, drawn on his flat world-sheet of paper," he began, a little furrow on his ginger brow. "This flat world is all that two-dimensional being has ever known, and can ever possibly know. His two-dimensional brain is itself designed to only conceptualise 'forward-backwards', and 'up-and-down.' But, never has the slightest notion of 'near-and-far' even entered as a possibility for him."

"To jail such a being, one would only need draw a circle around him," the *ally* chuckled. "From his limited two-dimensional perceptive, the stick-man suddenly finds himself trapped on all sides, without hope of escape!"

"Yet along comes a three-dimensional being, who is savvy within the extra dimension of his own reality. Seeing the plight of his flatter-counterpart, he picks the stick-man up, peels him off his two-dimensional world, and actions his escape, via dragging him into the third dimension."

The fox explained how such an act would be utterly incredulous and incomprehensible to the flat-earthed stick-man. Instead of seeing the glory of a three-dimensional world, he would only experience an excruciating flash of disjointed, two-dimensional slices of reality – as this would be all his two-dimensionally-evolved brain could comprehend, in its in-born perceptual limitation.

The *ally* elaborated, explaining that such a stick-man would fail to comprehend the presence – let alone actions – of his saviour. Instead of the idea of a singular 'hand', the flat-earther would only see a succession of five circles, moving in inexplicably-changing size and position through his two-dimensional domain.

"The three-dimensional being may be disheartened that the stick-man failed to see the extra beauty of his world. And the flat-earther would likely go mad at finding himself seemingly 'magically' teleported outside of his two-dimensional prison, by an incomprehensible being, through an unfathomable landscape!"

"Our stick-man may mistakenly consider himself as tortured by malevolent forces, which he can only call by such inadequate names as 'spirits' or 'demons' or 'aliens'. He bewails how he was ripped from the incarceration of his familiar prison, only to find himself in a much worse position – of being abducted into realms of indecipherable perceptual torment, instead of the well-meaning reality of his saviour."

"It is no less the same for you four-dimensional monkeys," the fox went on. "Let's say a five-dimensional *ally-being* presented itself in your realm, you would likely only think it magical or god-like – given how its mere existence within extra-dimensional reality gave it incomprehensible advantages. Such a being would seemingly be able to teleport through your limited four-dimensional space, appearing as a disjointed blob of unrelated parts. You would likely mistake such a being as several individuals, as opposed to one, given how you could not conceive how it is more broadly connected through an extra dimension."

"Suddenly," the fox hopped up, "that five-dimensional being jumps bodily out of your four-dimensional space-time! You assume they must have advanced technology, like molecular transportation. Mankind then frantically looks up at the stars, desperately searching for such a weird creature 'out there' – when it remains right beside him all along, tucked-up within the very folds of reality."

I understood the fox's point – how mankind's arrogance of self-referential enquiry would likely leave us unable to even conceptualise forms of life with dimensional variations. Even a 'lesser' two-dimensional being would only have to 'turn sideways' in our world, to be perceived as having utterly vanished!

Akin to a new *mind-mine* of Meili's, I had the thought as to whether given the new ability to understand a third-dimension of reality, whether the stick-man would ever willingly choose to go back to his flat-world?

Something still niggled me. "But, if you claim that the human band is only one formation of reality, yet we span a total of four layers of reality – how are we only *organic* beings?"

"That, is the grand mistake!" he said without moving his little pointed teeth. "Humans are so deluded, as to consider themselves *only* organic beings. Yet the undeniable reality is, your kind is so much more! After all, where do you think sentience and self-awareness come from? It is certainly not a product of biological influence alone. Unfortunately, your collective addiction to the *tonal*, blinds you to the magical qualities of your own kind!"

The fox looked me over, as if inspecting me for injury. "Don't get too caught-up in all of this. We are still using the descriptive force of the *tonal*, in order to talk about concepts that expand across *infinity* itself, most of which cannot be verbally digested."

He presented the idea of the first layer of awareness – called the 'deity' realm. Explaining that it had nothing to do with the human idea of gods, the fox told how awareness formed on such a distant layer could only be perceptualised as god-like to our feeble monkey minds; given how so far removed such being were to the experience of 'width' and 'time' dimensions of reality.

"Some *inorganic* beings – or *allies*, as you sorcerers came to call them – only consist of three-dimensions of awareness: fluency, latence and height. Such a being is beyond your conception, as they move about the side of the *nagual* with a speed, intensity and creativity that cannot be collapsed by your buffoon-like minds."

"If all these differing forms of life are moulded of various combinations of the eight middle layers of awareness – which in-turn are separate from each other – then how do they interact?" I was truly puzzled. "How, am I sat here talking with you, for example… if height and width are separate dimensions of reality?"

"You realise that I am not really a fox… not really of your *organic* banding?" The fox looked up at me with his amber eyes for signs of comprehension. "I am a collapsed manifestation of your *tonal*, being a crude representation of a being slightly adjacent on a phased level of reality."

"But this," he continued, "is where the *assemblage point* comes in – being the defining quality of *any* sentient life… and thus, what mankind should be truly seeking in his quest for inter-terrestrial neighbours."

The fox recapped on what Florinda had already explained to Robert: that the *assemblage point*, was a unique 'halo' of light, formed on a small surface area of each luminous cocoon, or *'balloon of awareness'* as the old lady had called it.

Intent being the only truly active force of the universe, comes to rest on the surface area of the *great sheet of awareness*. It does so, via means of traversing the fluidic matrices from either the side of the *tonal*, or that of the *nagual*. Both, are transmitter-mediums separated by the multi-dimensional membrane of *awareness* itself.

Isolated to a relatively small place on the person's surface area of awareness, *intent* massages the pliable, semi-translucent substance of awareness, until it glows. The fox explained that this 'assemblage point', can be considered as the perceptual conduit, from which the raw energetic mass of the universe is collapsed… or assembled… into what we know as perceivable reality. It is the isolated spot of which a handful of the luminous fibres habitually pass under the pressure of attention, and become illuminated with awareness.

"Much like the multi-planed existence of individual *sheets of awareness* – each with their own inherent plasticity and thus manifest potentialities – you idiot-apes do not realise that the *assemblage point* too, is multi-dimensional. The radiant glow of a person's *assemblage point* spans neighbouring dimensions of *awareness* – thus the perceptual conduit itself becomes the only possible interchange between realities."

"So that is why true sorcery is considered as perceptual manipulation?" I asked, although I already knew I was correct.

"Yes – it is the *mastery of intent*, that leads to the manipulation of the *assemblage point*. From there, humankind can jaunt off into the *great unknown*, and truly find alien life beyond the crude confines of height, width, length and time!"

My fox-ally elaborated that the *assemblage point* is too an eight-dimensional construct.

"Well, it's actually a forty-eight-dimensional lens," he quibbled. "But, for all intents-and-purposes, you organics only habitually tap the most accessible eight-layers of the central 'Goldilocks zone' of the *Eagle's emanations*."

He explained that whilst the *assemblage point* of every single life in the universe is technically forty-eight-dimensional, the reality is that mankind's mastery of *intent* is so weak, that the area covered by this cross-over of dimensional cohesion – the *'halo of assemblage'* – lazily only covers eight of the central dimensions at best, and only four of those with any real illumination.

"You arrogant no-tails are so deluded as to think you are individuals, compromised of your own unique thoughts and feelings," he scoffed in his thick accent. "Overlooking how you are even biologically very much a herd-animal, and inter-socially dependant as an embarrassingly collective mind, you overlook how your own emotions are *energetic vibrations* linked to other *layers of awareness* – the influence of other realms of reality, rippling over into your own."

He described how of the central eight layers of awareness, each had a unique vibrational 'fingerprint' or 'signature' – experienced as a core emotional energy pattern. The example he gave was of the far-right 'devil' layer of reality, which was experienced as fear, within the conduit of human perceptual assemblage.

Something dawned on me, "So that is why sorcerers can use specific emotions to entice and trap allies?!"

"We are just as much bound by our own limitations and desires, as any human-monkey. Ours, are just different..." he conceded, although I got the impression he was withholding something.

"Sorcerers learn to use emotions like dimensional Geiger-counters," the fox-ally added. "beep... beep... beep, beep, beep!" he jokingly pantomimed sniffing out sexual desire with his little leathery fox-nose, pretending to looked shocked and affronted as he stopped at me.

Of the eight-layers of awareness capable of sustaining cohesive perception, the fox claimed it was the central four – of which humans encompassed – that were deemed the most lucrative. They were thus coveted by the *inorganic* beings, who sought-out human 'allies', far more than we ever did them. It was why dealing with the *allies* could be so treacherous and unfairly balanced; why *seers* often perceived humans as being hunted.

"You have to understand how utterly unique and alluring human existence is to allied forms of awareness," he said, with what I thought was a touch of embarrassment. "The perfect balance of form and thought – of manifest *description* and *will* – in the human band, is utterly intoxicating to beings without form... or equally, to those beings without an *internal dialogue.*"

I countered that the human realms of reality were personified by constant dis-ease, strife and suffering. To consider them as the most advantageous was extremely difficult for me.

"By nature of being born within your four fractures of reality," he elaborated, "it is your fate to mutually experience dissatisfaction and separation, right alongside exquisite self-awareness and beauty. The impossibility of marring these two co-existing states, is what spurs the human race on; that constant, nagging un-ease for something more... to forever go home... is what gives you the greatest scope to hone your awareness."

"Of all of the creatures in the universe, it is your constantly dissatisfied state of being one-step-removed-from-home, that makes you the most likely candidate to capitalise on the *Eagle's gift*; to achieve perceptual liberation from the re-cycling force of awareness. And that – the constant one-in-a-billion opportunity to always be better than you are – is utterly irresistible to *inorganic* beings, defined by their own limitations in the plethora of other realms!"

The fox-ally explained that the *ally* beings move their *assemblage points* on their own *layers of awareness*, to adjacent positions to that of humans. They exist in the exact same locale-of-awareness, yet removed by nature of their dimensional alignment.

It is as such, that *allies* actively seek to tap human influence, far more than we do them. And this, causes no end of unique suffering and temptation to alien manifestational plains of reality. They can become morose and addicted to tasting form, as they can become perversely intoxicated by something as foreign and deviant as the *self-importance* moulded of the *internal dialogue*. Abstractive thinking and the masturbatory self-focus of human narrative, were told to be considered irresistible delicacies to the *inorganic beings*, called *allies*.

"Your kind being quite idiotic, is your saving grace!" the fox offered as some sort of compliment. "You are in fact surrounded by a universe of alien beings, yet too dumb to even be aware of it – whereas, other plains of sentient awareness are all too-painfully aware of your raucous existence!"

He explained that it was a strange irony that as humans purposefully developed their *mastery of intent* – via such practices as sorcery – that the *allies* typically withdraw from such awesome beings. Being a parasite to the docile human glow of assemblage, was much easier for *allies* to manage, than being in dangerous proximity to the radiant, intentionally-sophisticated *assemblage point* of a sorcerer. Thus, whereas the average man was surrounded by all sorts of unperceived foreign energy configurations, the better-seeing sorcerers had to intentionally pursue and trap such reticent beings.

"This, is what it means to wrestle with an *ally*," the fox continued with his explanation. "The sorcerer finally finds a sympathetic alien *assemblage point* – a conduit to alternate realities – and anchors it close to his own. The pair enter into a reluctant agreement of sorts… an exchange of perceptual resource, if you will."

"Yet, the *seers of old* got waylaid by the dubious arrangement. The pretence of the *allies* to be reluctant, really was a deception. *Allies* receive far more from the bargain, by striking an alliance with creatures of the four-most central and lucrative layers of reality! Thus, the practice of *inorganic* alliance historically came at cost to the old sorcerers. They became morbid, obsessive, reclusive and tenacious. They could not *see* how the relationship to the *allies* was parasitic – how the power-imbalance flowed predominantly in one way. Thus, whilst the achievements of shape-shifting, flying and visiting other worlds appeared all-too-powerfully magical to their fellow monkey-men, the true cost to the old sorcerers was their eventual obliteration."

Robert had always struggled with the concept of 'wrestling' an *ally*. It had always felt too pedestrian and equally too nonsensical, lacking procedural knowledge.

Hearing my musings, the fox-ally explained, "Wrestling an *ally*, simply means to anchor its perceptual conduit adjacent to your own. There are many ways to do so. But siphoning an *ally* was probably most common amongst the seers of old."

"Siphoning?"

"The *allies* are drawn by certain emotional frequencies of vibration," he offered, between grooming licks of his paw. "The trick for the sorcerer, is actually to dull the shine of their refined awareness – to create a vacuum-of-radiance, of sorts. This is why sorcerers who have previously conceived children find it easier to lure *allies*, as the subsequent dark, bowl-like depressions within their own luminosity, can be more readily used as bait. Your kind," he nodded to my mid-section, "with in-tact luminosity, are too violent, and usually repulse higher forms of sentience with your agitation!"

"I don't understand."

"The refined luminosity of a sorcerer's awareness, is particularly delectable to the *allies*. Yet, in creating a seeming vacuum within their own luminous matrix, *seers* can bait the trap with specific emotional vibrations. Sorcerers use the diffuse glow of *assemblage* to make themselves appear as easy food, becoming irresistible morsels of experiential awareness to feed upon. The *ally-assemblage* moves closer in proximity... and snap!... the sorcerer secures their *intent* around the alien configuration! The *ally* is forced to bind itself to the sorcerer – usually viewed from the petty realm of human existence, as being enchained to magical rings, pipes, medicine bundles, crystals or even gourds – before being allowed to relax back into the folds of their own dimensions, yet forever at the sorcerer's call."

The fox explained that sorcerers who had succeeded in trapping *allies*, when *seen*, appeared to house two or three overlapping *assemblage points*; albeit, they were slightly out-of-phase with each other.

As the three suns set with a silver tint, the fox went on as to how being most centralised of all of the forty-eight layers of reality, the human realm was considered the most fortuitously balanced – and thus the most beneficial, to us... or the most addictive, to the *allies*.

"Beneficial?" I queried. "For what?"

"Liberation!" he yipped. "Surely the white-haired old witch told Robert how the truest, sanest and most noble quest for sorcerers, was to seek perceptual liberation – from the endless recycling of awareness... to audaciously dart past the *Eagle* before the death-force collapses the *human balloon of awareness* once more?"

I had forgotten about the *Eagle*. As if picking up on my thoughts, the fox continued, "The *Eagle* is just the convenient name *sorcerers of antiquity* gave to the forebearer of the universe; the *First-Principle* or *God-force*, if you will. You can equally call it the *forty-eight-dimensional, central axis of fractal reality*. Or, you can call it the *forty-eight shadows cast of the Eagle's light*, as the *old seers* more poetically did! It's just a way of talking, for you idiotic organics."

"If we're truly idiotic, then why do alien forms of awareness covet connection with us?" I pressed on, suspecting there was more to the relationship than he was letting on.

The fox bowed his head a little, looking sheepish. "We're jealous, is the simple truth of it. You are formed of the most fortuitous central layers of reality, having the most balanced shot to achieve perceptual liberation. The universe is predatory by nature, with each life vying to refine its own existence of awareness, unwittingly as more delectable food for the *Eagle*."

The fox paused for a reluctant moment, before continuing, "The alien forms of perceptual cohesion native to other dimensions of reality – the *allies*, as you call them – seek to farm you middle-dwellers for your simple perceptual good fortune. We crave those uniquely human dimensional truths, that are far more alien and mesmerising to us, than floating, sentient mountains are to you."

"But, why would a being on a god-like layer of reality, seek influence from a lesser *organic* layer, like my own?"

"There is no lesser or better!" the fox chirped. "That's your stupid human judgements infecting things. But as illustration to answer your question, a form of alien awareness not subject to the confines of time, for instance, has much less motivation to seek-out perceptual liberation. Being in a perennial bliss-state, such a being would be just as ensnared as any other on the equivalent side of the *tonal*, being chained by the shackles of pure description."

"Did Florinda know all of this?" I hesitatingly asked.

"Of course."

"Why did she not go into such detail?"

"Because sorcerers cannot be told these things," the fox dryly offered. "Rather, as with any self-respecting sign of genuine self-improvement, she needed you to claim the knowledge for your own."

"Yet, you're telling me all this?"

I would say the fox blushed, if that were even possible. He had evidently been caught-out.

"Well, I am your *tonal-ally*, after all," he conceded. "It's my job to deceive you for my own nefarious ends! We are locked into the age-old competition of sorcerer and *ally*, seeing who will win in the struggle to achieve *power*, at enslavement to the other."

"But it was *you* who allowed this transaction," he countered. "It was *you* who claimed the knowledge, in shifting your own *assemblage point* in the first instance. In doing so, you opened yourself up, and finally allowed us to commune."

There was a silence, as the suns set, and something that resembled a low-pixelated (or hyper-dimensional) moon dominated the sky. I felt the fox to be searching for the right words.

"You have followed me here, and allowed me to explain…"

"To attach your?… mine?… our?… tethers, you mean," I clarified.

"As such, I am energetically indebted to you. And in fair payment, I counsel you that the warning-of-three – given by the oracles to Robert's old lineage – are still hooked to you. It will be the final ringing of the *three-pronged* bell, which signals the death of the last ties to the remains of Robert's association."

"You will then, be truly free," the fox finished, although I could tell it was not the fortuitous gesture he was trying to portray it to be.

"When the final three challenges ring-out to destroy you," he offered with the first sign of genuine concern, as though soon to lose a valuable investment, "go to your *final place of power*, and if you have mustered enough *impeccability*, death will allow you one last dance. Maybe you will then change your mind about wrestling with me, and tethering your *assemblage point* to my own. Death has a way of changing the minds of even the most stubborn of sorcerers, after all."

"You are sly, cunning and deceitful," I flatly offered. "Yet I'm saying this with no ill-will."

"They are only your own qualities, on the side of the *tonal*, of which I am only able to manifest," he equally replied. "I mean, I am *your ally* after all."

As we both sat there in silence, a tear ripped in the very fabric of reality, within the night sky – like the moon had been an egg, cracking open to birth a greater reality. A rip in existence tore asunder the view of the stars and moon, on a scale beyond imagining. A deeper, monumental hole of incomprehensible depths formed and imposed itself, ripping the heavens apart.

Through the fissure within the black night sky, was an entire universe of nebula, suns, moons and alien planets. They presented to me in an array and depth of colours, that was truly unparalleled. I had marvelled at the beauty of green nature before, admired the blueness of the sky and seas, and delighted at the artificial reds and purples of human production even. But never in my life, had I seen with such clear and colour-full eyes – as though truly seeing in high-resolution for the very first time. It was not viewed with heightened detail, but almost as *hyper-detailed* – with a vibrancy of coloured stars, ringed planets and rainbowed nebula, bursting forth with a potency of beauty that did not confine to form.

A delightfully-detailed universe impregnated with self-awareness, shone before me. The endless stars were literally singing with something beyond simple sound. I openly cried, as though seeing the face of God. It was truly the most beautiful thing – the most perceptually-perfect demonstration – I had ever witnessed.

And yet, a *knowing* came with that beauty. Within the unparalleled exquisiteness experienced of the *great unknown*, only annihilation nestled within that abyss, of the infinitude of perfection. It was where the *sorcerers of antiquity* had become lost.

That view had never been meant for man.

8

Worthy Counterparts.

(aka: The Intercession of Adjacent Awareness)

Periods of heavy snowfall usually meant prioritising warmth and security. It also resulted in far fewer crowds around the city, from which one could hide within, and capitalise on their waste. And as always, getting wet was a threat with particularly exaggerated consequences for anyone who was living on the streets.

The city had an unusually heavy snowfall overnight, which I had sought protection from underneath the old humming exhaust-pipe in the old dockyard. The constant warmth it emanated, made it the most ideal of the five *power sites* for colder weather.

The thought had occurred to me, that the nearby riverbank would be quieter than usual, due to the winter conditions. So I lay my clean clothes on a plastic bag to keep dry, and stripped to wash myself and my clothes in the river.

Although Robert had generally ran at a higher temperature, the one part of his body he could never stand getting cold, was his abdomen. Even in a wetsuit, he disliked going into the sea or rivers.

"It because you store your vulnerability there," his diminutive Chinese instructor had teased him, patting his 'Buddha belly', as she called it. "Until you fix your bad past, your energy body be weak at your stomach; so you must protect!"

"And you must choose: you protect with discipline! Or, you protect with indulgence!" she had added, as a closing warning.

The prospect of me bathing naked in a semi-frozen river, would have mortified Robert. Instead, I revelled in the white beauty of my surroundings – of the gentle ripples of the inky black water, and the delicate fall of the odd fluffy snowflake from the monotone sky. It was surprisingly serene.

Wringing my washed clothes out, I dried myself off with some newspaper. In the process of doing so, I noticed that I had the six-pack that Robert had never had, and always secretly desired. I laughed aloud to myself at the absurdity of the situation – as to now possessing such a toned torso, yet it meaning absolutely nothing to me.

An absence of abdominal fat seemed like such an absurd thing for anyone to waste their time and intention wishing for. But I found it delightful how the universe was not without its irony.

Robert would have described the physical sensation of the acute cold – now encasing all of my body – as, 'painful'. But, with my newly detached curiosity, I came to realise that such a self-perception was gross and insufficient. It was lazy – a product of convenient description only, and not direct experience.

Yes – my body did react in response to the coldness. But, just what was 'temperature' anyway? What precisely, was 'coldness'? It warranted the respect of investigation.

As with almost all phenomenon – be that heat, wetness, hunger or emotional manifestation – I was beginning to experience everything as a mere difference in *vibration*.

The cold pain on my exposed abdomen vibrated. A vibration in what, I did not know. However, it was a curious emanation of *something*, that allowed me to step aside from the insufficient and generalised label of 'pain' or 'cold', and instead experience the sensation with a new sense of detached curiosity.

I had become a living mystery; much more so than Robert ever had been, with his solid ideas of what was and was not. The difference was, I was happy and at ease to explore that not-knowing, without any morbid addiction to force description or familiarity onto the experience.

I was not now judging the rippling-effect of direct experience as 'good' or 'bad', 'pleasant' or 'unpleasant', or even 'hot' or 'cold'. It simply, *was*. That, was enough. The experience provided, and was plentiful.

On the one hand, the new directness-of-being fascinated me no end. But equally, it also made me laugh, as to how grossly and violently removed Robert had been from his most basic of direct living experiences, because of his habitual indulgences to *internal dialogue*. Wherever he now was, I hoped he had found peace from his addiction.

The buzzing sensation that encased my body, came with no old need to collapse the experience into something else. It was okay just to *be*. I tittered out aloud to myself, at the sheer joy in direct being – as though I had never encountered life in such sharpness before.

If nothing else, the dose of icy water helped to ground me in the realities of the *tonal*, even if they were starting to hold a different sway. I knew it was the only proper response, after any encounter with the mischievous fox ally, and his appeals to my *nagual*.

After my last meeting with the *ally* – on the foothills of the glass mountains floating above the silver oceans – I had come away from the experience more wary of my encounters with him. Robert had been particularly vulnerable to the indulgence of the *tonal*, and morbidly susceptible to demonstrations of the *nagual*.

Freshly clothed and sauntering back from my winter bathe, I came across a commotion on my usual route between the industrial area and the city centre. A delivery truck had skidded on the ice, and drawn considerable congregation at its spilled goods. The broken bottles of wine appeared starkly like blood, crawling out amongst the snow. A curious crowd gathered, wondering how much of the stock may be written off, and available for pilfering.

Alcohol was another *false-ally*, like coffee. On the one hand, it was false, because it was weak... an *indulgence*, rather than *power*-inducing... and addictive. On the other hand, it was not a true *ally*, as it belonged to the same dimensions of awareness, as humans on the organic band of reality. *True allies* called from further afield.

Alcohol's lure lay in the false reality it created, of different description. However, the cost of such a treacherous *ally*, was too high. Yet, despite the catalogued damage such a false-ally is known to cause throughout collective awareness, it is a power-plant that is legalised, societally-accepted, and widely promoted. The crowd gathering like vultures around road kill, were testament to alcohol's insidious allure.

In my constant preference to avoiding human interaction, I opted to take a longer way around the commotion. It was as such, that I found myself walking down a long, straight stretch of road – historically of the docks, but long since disused by industry, and now turf for the city's prostitutes.

I reasoned there would likely be no sex-worker or clientele braving such unforgiving winter conditions. So, I was surprised to see one worker standing alone on the corner – especially a young male.

Stopping dead in my tracks, something – some pull from outside – made me immediately conceal myself within the nearby doorway of a disused warehouse. Some aspect of the young man felt off... as though a tangible warning emanated away from his form, fluttering like the gusts of cold. Yet unlike the black river water, this harsh emanation felt... familiar.

It was Aidan! Robert had known him; an apprentice of the counter-organisation, called the *Omega Assembly*. It had been Robert's direct involvement with that group, and their power-centric pursuits of sorcery. Whereas Robert's cohorts had (at best) termed their own practices *the art of freedom*, the *Omega Assembly* differed, in calling it *Nagualism*. It revealed their prioritisation of both the *other* side of human existence, as well as their veneration of a certain *three-pronged* sorcery leader, dubbed the *'Coyote Nagual'*.

Robert had suffered so much as a result of that unwitting involvement with the counter organisation. It had led him to torturous places... led him to do the unthinkable... it had led him... where? Just where had Robert gone?

An icy finger shivered up my spine, signifying more than the cold.

Yet, something was different about Aidan, more than the ghost of Robert's memories allowed. An expert in martial arts, Aiden had been lean, muscular, good looking, vibrant and had an exaggerated look of youth about him.

This, was clearly the same young man. But his once-porcelain face was pot-marked and blotchy. His lips were scabbed. His cheeks gaunt, and his large eyes – once vital and full of aggressive vibrancy – where now sunken and dulled.

Robert would have fled at this unwelcome intrusion. It would have been too much of a painful reminder.

But, Robert had already fled.

Instead, I recognised the *flow of power*. Demonstrating the third principle of *stalking*, I waited, unmindful to the description of the cold nagging at me.

The old Aiden would have perceived my intrusion from down the street. He had been a keen and powerful sorcerer's apprentice, even if waylaid in his darker pursuits. If nothing else, Robert had always envied the younger man's youth and confidence of vitality; as Aiden had a sense of physical self-possession that Robert had never owned.

In view his characteristic aggressiveness and boldness, the younger apprentice would not have tolerated my watching him. But this Aiden was very clearly different… defeated. No longer did he have that same perceptual acuity and command of *intent*, to which he had once paid such a devastatingly high-price to obtain.

Several hours passed, within which I observed the once good-looking lad readily sell his most prised asset – his physicality – to bloated older men, in their family saloons. 'Baby on Board' signs, and 'God Hates Fags' bumper stickers, were posted as testimonies on the cars gently rocking in power-sapping hypocrisy.

There was no remorse, and no breaks, in-between his clientele. Aiden responded to his work with the same potent intention with which he had once undertaken both martial arts and sorcery. Only the young lad's eyes appeared different, as if distracted by sights elsewhere.

Whether it was the sale of his body, or the cold, or something else entirely, eventually Aiden appeared unwilling to bear it any longer. He headed off at a brisk pace. I followed, ensuring to remain unseen.

Even I could recognise, that it could have been no coincidence for my path to cross that of Robert's unsought adversary. I now understood enough of *power*, to know when not to ignore a clear *omen*.

Across the city Aiden moved in his threadbare tracksuit, his baseball cap pulled low over his darkened eyes. Ignoring the call of the supermarkets and eateries en-route, he headed straight for a poor residential area – located under the disdainful view of a new set of luxurious homes.

Waiting outside, the flicker of a moth in the twilight eventually let me *know* it was time to enter the run-down house after Aiden. Forcing my way through the neglected door, it was clearly a drug-den.

Several people lay strewn about the tatty furniture, completely oblivious to my intrusion. They were blissed-out in their painfully-vulnerable and exposed states. I thought it an apt metaphor for the perils of sorcery – of being exposed to magical alternatives, yet left vulnerable in the 'real' world of form, pain and toil. It had been the fate of too many *old seers* during the Spanish conquest of the Americas.

There, on a urine-soaked mattress, lay the once-forceful form of the young Aiden. Not so long ago, Robert had been intimidated by the young man's raw physical ownership and fiercely-trained ability. But now, Aiden was a shadow of his former self. He only murmured away to nobody who could hear, still with the syringe in his arm.

This, is what the pursuit of sorcery had cost the apprentice. It had left him a two-fold false legacy: that of drugs as a crutch to force movement on the *assemblage point*, and the original method of physical payment used to entice the secrets of *infinity* from his former master. Aiden's involvement with the *Omega Assembly*, had left him with only one

108

remaining template with which to make any small attempt – no matter how miserable or doomed – to reach *infinity...* to readily sell his body, for fleeting glimpses of perceptual freedom, via chemical aid.

Standing over the once-formidable opponent, I could see that where his *assemblage point* had displaced to, was not a place of true liberation. Quite the opposite; his new locale only weakened him via exposure to corrupt *allies*. It was clear that their leeching off his luminosity, was at cost to the description of his body, taking a disproportionate toll on the once-youthful apprentice. The shadow of his death was so close, as to cradle him in stupor, singing false lullabies, of which Aidan only willingly gave himself to.

From a space of *seeing*, I knew that the young man's *assemblage point* had shifted only incrementally... barely enough. Yet within that disproportionally power-sapping move, he had illuminated typically unused bands of luminous fibres, thus granting himself temporary release from his unbearable reality. Yet, it was one of the false-allies that guided him – a fickle and greedy *ally*, that demanded too high a cost.

I could see the luminous fibres of his cocoon becoming slack. No longer did his luminous cocoon maintain the brilliance of a sorcerer. Even when Robert had feared the younger apprentice, he had always respected him. Now, he truly was pitiful.

There was nothing I could do. The cost of Aidan's association to sorceric practices, had been as costly as Robert's – albeit, in different currencies. Both were as lost as the other; both paying a heavy price for their choice to step onto the *path of knowledge*. They had each been openly cautioned as much; yet in their stupidity, it was clear that neither had truly heard the warning.

Wishing him well, I could only leave the young man to withstand the return of his own *intent*. I hoped that his new *ally* friends could offer him some crumb of comfort and peace. Yet I knew that in his prime, Aidan's command of *intent* had been a deplorable and awesome thing; and thus, the likelihood of his successfully enduring its rebounding effects, rather slim.

Ruminating my way out of the dilapidated drug den, I was momentarily taken aback as a limousine pulled up immediately outside. Its sleek and impossibly-glossy black exterior stood in stark contrast to both the white snow and the grim neighbourhood.

A tinted window whirred down, and an unfamiliar man gruffly commanded, "get in."

It was not so much the bizarreness of the situation I had found myself in that unnerved me, more the unforeseen direct interaction with another human being. I had haunted the city like a ghost for months, having no verbal interaction with a single soul. To suddenly be acknowledged – let alone commanded – was somewhat shocking. Something tried to solidify inside in reaction, and I had to make a conscious effort to relax and remain incohesive.

The actual prospect of getting into a strange car with an intimidating-looking man, did not bother me in the slightest. The car was of such exemplified wealth and care, that it was not likely to be the tool of gangsters, pimps, human-traffickers, or even the authorities.

Beyond this, I now had more of a faith in my relationship to the *Great Flux* – in my own command of *personal power*. Easing up on my hold of the *tonal* (or more accurately, its hold over me) and expanding my awareness outwards, I heard an authoritative voice.

"Get in," the voice of the silent *knowing* confirmed.

I knew it was the right thing to do. After all, when you are homeless, anywhere else you may be taken by someone, can still only be the same place of equal ground. There was a confidence in knowing the *Great Mother* was always under your feet.

I momentarily wanted to laugh, at the thought that the attachment to 'home' only awarded an individual the fear and anxiety of losing it – of straying too far away from comfort, familiarity and the illusion of security. Was the idea of 'home' something the ancient *allies* had fooled our ancestors with, in providing them with the deception of such description? Our ancient ancestors had once been more nomadic, yet had become docilely susceptible to the *tonal's* influence, once they made new alliances with the low-level, meek *power plants* of agriculture.

For all of his own faults, Robert had never been anchored by a true concept of 'home'. Had that been his advantage all along? Is that why he had been so easily able to vanish?

Bundling myself into the back of the limousine, I felt distinctly at odds with the luxurious surroundings. The rich leather seats alone creaked with offence at my shabby intrusion.

The driver did not talk. And, I knew not to question him. I recognised a man being commanded, when I saw it. He was handsomely paid, specifically *not* to ask questions, or even to consider doing so. The driver was another mere ghost on my journey; one I could happily ignore. We had nothing to offer each other, over the gulf of differing realities.

There were delicacies laid-out for me on a silver platter – shrimp parcels and canapés, and expensive liquor to wash it down. I did not touch any of it. The *spirit* let me know that such luxuries were poisonous – not because of any chemical they had been tainted with, but because of the relinquishment to *indulgence* they represented. They offered absolutely no appeal whatsoever; instead, my hunger was satiated by the passing views of the city.

We passed through what seemed like the entirety of the urban landscape, out through the suburbs, winding through the countryside. Large iron gates swung silently open, as we drove up the gravel road of the estate.

Elegant peacocks called out in their haunting cries as we passed. Whether it was a warning, or a lament, I was not quite sure.

Once we had stopped outside a large stone entranceway, the driver silently opened the door for me. There, was Katrina – once a fellow apprentice of Aidan's within the *Omega Assembly* – unexpectedly greeting me.

Like her former associate, Katrina appeared different too. Not only disproportionately older, but seemingly exhausted-of-spirit. The refinery of her clearly-expensive clothing only exaggerated the difference in her demeanour... or was it her spirit... or luminosity? Whatever it was, something was off about her. Like her former cohort, her association to sorcery had clearly cost her.

Barely-contained fury emanated from the young woman, as she reluctantly guided me into the large house. As she stepped into the grand hallway, she did not understand that the anger in her veins only poisoned herself. To me, it was merely a curious vibration that had no place to land.

It did not take *seeing* to know that Katrina's misguided rage towards me was only contained by external command. Given personal choice, she would see my *balloon of awareness* flatten out by force. Yet, that is exactly what now made her impotent and drained – as she was now giving herself to be directed by an outside influence.

"You should just kill me," I thought. "Kill me; but do it *impeccably*."

Leading me up a grand mahogany staircase, the raven-haired apprentice ushered me into a massive bedroom – itself bigger than the entirety of the apartment Robert had once had. Amidst a richly-ticking clock and the crackling grand stone fireplace, the only other sound was a gritted rasping.

"Leave us," the grey-haired old woman barked at her physician.

It was the master of the *Omega Assembly* who had appeared as a poorer copy of Florinda. Nélida: *The Paladin of Shadows*. Even Robert had been able to understand, just how profoundly human it had been for someone as gifted and self-possessed as Henrick, to seek out an imitation of the one great love of his life. Goodness, how Nélida must have hated Florinda for it.

Sat within a corner chair, was an older man I had never seen before. His dark skin was peppered with scars, as though corn kernels had been imbedded under the epidermal layer. I immediately understood these to be *intentional* marks of sorcery. Only his watery eyes moved, as he scrutinised me passing to the bespoke three-poster bed.

Whilst I had never met this menacing form of a man, I immediately knew him to be the third member of Nélida's and Henrick's generational triptych of sorcerers. He, could only be the *Paladin of Mysteries*.

Florinda's line of sorcery had revolved around the rule of four: four unified groups ('households' or, 'planets') each comprised of a *dreamer*, a *stalker*, a *courier* and an *activist*. Thus, totalled each generation of sixteen practitioners of *the art if freedom*. It had been that way since the Nagual Sebastien – since the onset of the next lineage cycle of *'new seers'*.

Nearly three-hundred years later – in-line with the *rule of three* – the *Omega Assembly* had structured itself around the principle of the *False Nagual...* a *three-pronged* sorceric leader, sometimes called the *Coyote Nagual*.

He had been mis-identified and subsequently re-aligned, to surround himself in the rule of three. It was the *Coyote Nagual* who went on to hoodwink an entire social discipline, academia, the publishing industry, and generation of new-age 'seekers' – irrevocably changing the world, with his books that clearly set-out the trickeries for the entirety of humanity to easily see. Yet, they still failed to understand, that it was the deceptions of their own self, which blinded them much more than any one man ever could have. The *Coyote's* magic had been strong.

The new organisation following in the direct lineage of the *three-pronged Nagual* – subsequently termed the *Omega Assembly* – constituted a 'generation' of three associate sorcerers of equal standing, each commanding a further generation of three. Henrick, had been the master of Katrina, Aidan and their cohort, Marta.

Robert had briefly met Nélida only once, during his infamous trip to Amsterdam. Yet now, attached to wires and tubes from within her baroque bed, the sorceress appeared infinitely old and frail. Gone was the look of formidable menace from her eyes, now peering out from behind oxygen tubes attached to her nose.

"You do not need to *see*, to understand the death force is claiming me," she swotted Katrina's helping hand away, as she struggled to sit up – afraid as to how truly fragile she may appear to such an unworthy opponent.

"And, I do not need to *see*, to understand your plight – to discern what you have become," she expanded, between wheezing fits. "Do not worry. There is no need for you to speak aloud. Your cocoon tells me everything."

"Yet, do you truly understand the consequences of what you did?" came her ancient voice, infused with accusation and pain. "You have not only doomed the *Omega Assembly*, but your own group too. You fool!"

The formerly-youthful Katrina stood motionless across the room, glaring at me with barely-contained rage.

"Don't worry, she cannot hurt you," Nélida grimaced between spasms of pain. "That whelp failed in her task, and is now at least bound to me in final servitude and payment. The cost of what you did has taken its toll on her, ravaged her of possibility and potential. Now, she must be content to serve out the limited handful of my remaining days, like a mongrel begging for scraps – cleaning up my puke and piss! She should consider herself fortunate, for my… charity."

That is when I realised that Katrina was as trapped as Aidan was. The young woman was admittedly living in the veritable lap of luxury, but she was a slave nonetheless.

From a place of *seeing*, the *knowledge* came to me that Nélida still had Katrina undertaking her chemical experiments. In her folly of old age and looming death – in the realisation of the failure of her own lineage – Nélida had become as desperate as Aidan. Her advantage, was that she only had greater resources than the much-younger apprentice.

Nélida was forcing Katrina into greater risks, in brewing potions that would nudge her *assemblage point* into greater and greater realms of alternative reality. After all, there was nothing to lose any more. I wondered how far her increasingly desperate forays into the *second attention* had taken her.

What Nélida did not *see*, was that Katrina was also undertaking her own experiments into the *unknown*. Now subdued in her failure, scorned and overlooked by her masters, the young apprentice was as equally desperate, and taking advantage of the materialistic resources of her mistress.

Katrina had experienced a traumatic childhood, being abandoned by drug-addicted patents, and bandied-about an abusive foster system. She had subsequently given herself over completely, when a group of sorcerers promised her *infinity*, and the belonging she had never had. Worldly affluence was no-where near as addictive to her, as the sense of connection they offered, no matter how dysfunctional.

I mused over the elegance of *the mirrored wings of the Eagle*. Despite Katrina's best, life-long efforts, she had still found herself the ward of a drug-addled oppressor. I briefly indulged in the musing, as to just which lifetime that returning reflection of *intent* had emanated from. How many times did the spirit have to knock, before each of us finally answered?

Now, after Katrina's failure to ensnare Robert, and promote the *three-pronged lineage*, she remained bound by that same promise of belonging. Now, there was just no reward of *power*, merely servitude, until the inevitable loneliness after her masters' passing. There was nowhere for Katrina to go, other than revisiting the trauma of her childhood. To Katrina's scarred mind, belonging somewhere... *anywhere*... was still better than that alternative.

In the desperation of her impossible situation, I knew Katrina was also experimenting with psychotropic compounds. Whereas her former cohort, Aidan, used common drugs as cheap temporary escape, Katrina was taking more sophisticated risks, with violent, synthetically-imbued incursions into the *nagual*. Both master and apprentice were as equally desperate and lost, each thinking themselves cleverer than the other, in hiding their desperation and schemes.

Yet, Katina had been made servile by magical *intention*. Her tattoos – once awarded as badges of sorceric bondage and accomplishment, rather than the normal branding of ink – were now semi-faded. Attempts had been made to intentionally castrate the young woman, via the removal of her magical brands. That, and the semi-removed reminders served as humiliation, for her failure.

I could *see* beyond the surface marks of servitude and punishment. Katrina was bounded in her luxurious prison, by more than the iron will of her disappointed master.

Katrina's own folly – her desperation, her not-quite-eviscerated *personal history*, and the fear bleeding over from her own tethered *allies* – had driven her to capitalise on Nélida's financed explorations of the *unknown*. Old and young alike, in their desperation, both had become ensnared to the crutch of *power plants,* in a final bid to achieve *power*.

Aidan lying a world away in abject squalor, was absolutely of no difference. A prettier prison, was still a prison after all.

I noticed a small refrigerator next to the bed. In comparison to the ornate splendour of the room, its cold, clinical steel drew attention. It only held one solitary item, standing-out in stark importance – a single small glass vial. I immediately knew what it was: a final solution.

As per any membership of the *Omega Assembly*, Nélida had an important primary task: that of a *seer's* mastery, hoarding of enough *personal power*, finding the means to locate the reconstituted form of the *Coyote Nagual*, leading to *the abomination*, and thus ultimately, an escape from death itself. Should she fail at this, then that tiny bottle held her last desperate alternative. It was a concoction of Katrina's making, the result of careful chemical engineering, tempered with the *intent* of sorcery. It was Nélida's 'plan-B'.

Should Nélida be found close to death, her young apprentice had been instructed to inject the contents of the vial. It would represent one last, massive push of Nélida's *assemblage point* far out into the *second attention.*

If nothing else, it was an astoundingly brave back-up plan. It stank of the arrogant daring of the *old sorcerers* – as who knew just where that last desperate act would take the old witch? It would be as final as death itself – a one-way ticket into the *great unknown.*

"Give a dying woman what she needs," Nélida attempted to grab my hand, but did not have enough strength. "I know you still have compassion within you. That was your hallmark all along… what made you… different." I understood her to be making uncharacteristic diplomatic efforts in her desperation.

A coughing fit possessed the old woman, before she continued her plea. "What you did… to Florinda of all people. She was truly *impeccable!* The best of us! Even I must award her that recognition."

"What you did, is truly incomprehensible to the *Omega Assembly,*" her dark eyes searched my face in desperation, as though the lines held magical scripts. "There must be a secret we can still mine. Tell us! You no longer have your own group, so there is nothing to lose. I demand you tell us *why* you did what you did!"

"You saw it," the wraith-woman accused in hushed tone, appearing to change tactics. "I demand that you tell us where they are!"

She was no longer talking of the white-haired old witch – but something much dearer to her own quickly-receding ambitions. I did not need any further prompt to know what she greedily alluded to.

Whilst held captive within the basement in Amsterdam, Robert had been forced into the *second attention* by the *Omega Assembly.* With his *assemblage point* dislodged under chemical duress, he had witnessed disjointed realms of otherworldly reality.

In a half-memory of fragmented perception, Robert had experienced a unique luminous cocoon of the awareness of another person. Yet, unlike the uniform golden glow typical to most people, this energetic template of an individual, had a subtle inner blue radiance – almost like a double-glow superimposed within their own *balloon of awareness.*

It was this individual, above anyone else, who the *Omega Assembly* coveted. It was why they had so aggressively pursued Robert in his unknown luminous heritage, as *the mysterious thirteenth.* They had similarly pursued his misidentified predecessor – Carl – to his unfortunate demise.

This blue-formed re-manifestation of human form, the *Omega Assembly* believed to be the re-cycled awareness of the *Coyote Nagual.* Or at the least, this individual unknowingly housed the *three-pronged Nagual's* knowledge, as part of their luminous inheritance. And it was specifically the *False Nagual's* relationship with *The Death Defier,* which the *Omega Assembly* desperately sought to capitalise on.

Yet, their mistake was twofold. On the one hand, Robert had only vague quasi-memories of a drug-induced state, from which he himself could draw no reliable information. Furthermore, having no idea as to where Robert now was, I was in no position to guide the misguided group of sorcerers. That reconstituted being was recently remanifest out there in the world of people, but currently lost to both lineages.

"You must tell me…" the old woman spluttered in desperate agony. "You must…"

The effort had proven too much for her. After another fit, she deteriorated into a semi-conscious state. As Katrina settled the old woman, I could not tell who the young apprentice hated more… me, or Nélida.

There was nothing I could have said to the old woman. It was not that I was being malicious or spiteful in my refusal to speak. Rather, she would have just as much insight to Robert's motivations as I did. Besides, my *seeing* let me *know*, that even if I could somehow explain, she no longer had the store of *personal power*, to truly comprehend.

As I went to leave, the huge figure of the foreign-looking man blocked my exit. His yellowed-eyes peered into my own with an intensity that felt almost violent.

"Do not worry," he spoke slowly, in a deeply baritone voice, "I at least, know you are not him. You never arrived here with what we needed."

And with that, he stepped aside – much to Katrina's enraged glare – to allow me to pass. It was as though he had wanted to indulge in one last look at 'the mysterious thirteenth' – the rift within the *Great Flux*, that had caused so much upheaval. Yet, whatever the enigmatic older man saw, he appeared disappointed with.

Seeing, had told me that Katrina had no more time than her ancient master. There was a brown-green patch on her luminosity, which let me know her liver was failing. Perhaps that too was now energetically established as legacy of the *three-pronged lineage*.

Humanity would be better off, I thought, if the *Eagle* did take an active interest in their doings. It seemed a particularly cruel universe, which designed *intent* to be directed back as a reflection of a person's individual mastery. But equally, I knew that as much as the majority of us suffered for it, so too, did therein lie the *Eagles' gift*.

Compassion, meant it was best not to tell Katrina of her limited time. My *seeing*, let me *know* that it would be Katrina who would use that vial on herself, long before she would ever consider offering compassionate release to her Mistress.

I *saw* the *shadow of death* over the left shoulder of all four members of the *Omega Assembly* that day. In their combined suffering, separated and exaggerated by the gulf of individualism, the kindest thing I could do, was not to reveal just how close the cold embrace of death was to touching each of them.

Having seen the decrepit form of the once-awesome Nélida, one would assume that I would again be reminded of the effects of old age. Yet, it was the third enemy of man that I encountered: *power*.

The divisions between the two lineages had never been clearer to me – arching out like two great ribbons of *personal history*, spanning individuals, generations and great oceans of *tonal-myths*. Nélida had spent decades pursuing esoteric practices, focussed on the intense acquisition of *power*. Yet now, at the end of her story, her plans had been thwarted at the last step by a half-wit, who was not even anywhere to be seen. The flow of *power* was a terribly impersonal thing, and a fickler companion – much less a worthy goal in itself.

At the close of her life, the old woman's *power* had accounted for nothing – abandoning her in the light of its illusion. Now, both Nélida and her cohorts haemorrhaged *personal power*. Only the raw aggression and toxicity of desperation lingered in its wake.

The dual existence of both sorcery lines never showed more the superficiality of the pursuit of *power*. *Power*, ultimately abandoned. It *had* to disperse. It could only ever be a means in itself, to serve as a temporary launching pad. All roads of *power* inevitably led back to the *Eagle*: either as sustenance, or that one rare shot to true *freedom*.

I walked away from the luxurious estate, utterly absolved of any temptation of *power* – no matter how wonderous the temptations of the *path of knowledge* may appear. Unlike that of the strange sorcerer and his young counterpart left behind, I no longer had any possible inkling for the acquisition of something so fickle and fleeting as *power*.

I understood that *power* would abandon without a moment's notice, even after a lifetime's hoarding. It was a treacherous partner to court. So, I would position myself within its *Great Flux*, opening myself up to its flow and influence. But no longer could I cling. The cost for doing so was too high; the promise it offered too illusionary.

As the peacocks called their haunting songs behind me – almost as in mournful appeal – I let go of any last remnants of personal gain. I was free to walk between the lines.

9

Psycho-Magical Intervention.

(aka: The Intersection of Two Narratives)

I had mastered a particularly useful trick to obtaining free food – taking what other people left behind! One of the most ideal places for this, was ironically, the bustle of the popular city centre retailing areas. There, amongst the profusion of bars, cafés, diners and restaurants, the hustling masses left an abundance of unwanted food, ripe for the picking.

This, is where my efforts to remain as visually unremarkable as possible, came into their own. *Hensojutsu* – a discipline of the Ninja of old, of adopting everyday disguises (costume, props and behaviour) in order to hide within plain sight. It had been a topic Robert's instructor had discussed on many occasions, but which Robert had been too dumb and romanceful, to take on-board as a still-practical tool.

There were several considerations to bear-in-mind when sourcing food from the cafés. The best places to do this, were those establishments with outside seating areas. After the change in legislation to ban indoor smoking, this was a lot easier – given how many restaurants pushed for increasing outside seating areas. The false-ally of tobacco still held enough dominion of the collective awareness, to influence the dining, social and legislative habits of millions.

Even the younger generation were aggressively clouding themselves in a thick fog-bank of damaging addiction. Only this time, it was apple-pie and cotton-candy flavoured.

Cleary, avoiding over-staffed establishments was best. To this end, choosing a café that was clearly under-staffed or over-popular, meant I could more easily pretend to be one of their waiters. This allowed me to attend to the dirty dishes during busy periods, like lunchtime. Inside, the frantic, over-worked serving staff would be stranded behind the counter – a barrage of chemically-ensnared patrons drowning them with a myriad of strange incantations of the false-coffee-ally. Other staff, would be stuck within a constant steam of dishwasher vapours within the kitchen, too busy to notice a stranger clearing the plates outside.

The biggest advantage was the general bustle of customers, who were so pre-occupied with themselves – of obtaining a vacant seat – that they were quite happy for anyone else to be assuming responsibility for clearing the dirty dishes.

To sell my intrusion, I would only have to drape a white cloth over my arm, as a pseudo-towel to sell the appearance of being a waiter – finishing the look with a salvaged notepad and pen. The truth was that I had found a cloth diaper disposed of on a public bench, and cleaned it. When draped over the arm, it was easy enough to pass for the attire of a server – even if my clothing did not match that of the staff indoors (to this end, it was also crucial not to pick an establishment that had a distinct uniform, or overly-formal attire for its servers). The notepad and pen had simply been scavenged from outside of a bookmaker's.

Even if on occasion, some staff inside the cafés had noticed me, in their busyness I do not think they would have begrudged the sight of someone helpfully sorting the used crockery outside. At worst, they may mistake me for an interfering customer, trying to clear space for themselves.

The trick was not to linger too long to draw attention – remaining mere moments before slinking back into the passing crowds. I simply gathered the dirty plates – often with a mere raised eyebrow or courteous gesture of the hand towards a sitting patron, who granted me permission to clear the table for them.

Taking the dishes aside, I would pile the leftovers onto one plate, whilst scooping any worthwhile remains into a plastic zip-lock bag, which I could later enjoy. Despite hunger pangs (more vibration), I knew it would draw disastrous attention, if I were to consume any leftovers right there-and-then.

Florinda had frequently reminded Robert of the importance of the seventh principle of *stalking*: that a warrior never pushes themselves to the front, instead always operating from behind the scenes.

"Patience, is the true mark of a stalker," the old lady had elaborated on more than one occasion. "The difference between a warrior and a schmuck, is that a warrior knows how to purposefully delay reward – sure in his boots that he will reap greater benefits later on, by his temporarily refraining from reactive impulse, ego-gratification, comfort, habit and personal indulgence. He does not deny himself as a martyr; he only makes an agreement to delay his reward."

"Others call it *discipline*," the blue-eyed witch had gone on to finish.

Stashing the leftovers within my little bags, I would leave the cleared plates in a neat stack, near to the entrance or server's station. I would then lose myself back within the crowd. If any member of the public noticed me, it was either as a quickly forgotten curiosity, or something too innocuous enough to bother themselves with the hassle of making their responsibility.

It had been a recurrent lesson of Jon-Paul's: if you made peoples' lives easier – actively alleviating them of *personal responsibility* – it was surprising how much their *tonals* would actively work to allow you to go unnoticed. After all, much of the *tonal's* doings, were focused to what it strived to make sure went unseen, than otherwise.

The goal of the *tonal* is to provide the illusion of familiarity – of a consistent story. Thus, anything truly unique could pose a potential threat to this consistency-of-narrative, via exposure to the light of attention focussed back on the 'self illusion' of the *personal dialogue*. The *tonal* is far too brittle to withstand such self-inspection, and thus goes to remarkable lengths to gloss-over inconsistencies to the *personal dialogue*.

Part of the strategy of my dining incursions was not only to make them short in duration, but sporadic enough between visiting individual establishments. If I knew anything of the *tonal*, it is how it feeds on familiarity and repetition. Thus, maintaining unpredictable patterns of behaviour – or *making oneself inaccessible*, as the old Ninjutsu teacher would have put it – helped me to go unnoticed in plain sight.

The previous night, I had been unexpectedly caught in a heavy thunderstorm that had driven hard for hours. It had not only caused localised flooding, but it was a strange curiosity that my own *seeing* had not forewarned me of the adverse conditions in advance, as it typically did. I took that omission in itself as an *omen*.

Being caught in a heavy downpour, I had been forced to seek shelter in an overturned industrial dumpster, alongside a nursing stray cat. My need to keep dry had taken priority over my need for sustenance. Thus, I had not searched for food overnight, as I had intended to do. Yet, I had still given my last morsel of mushy banana to the mewing mother, figuring it would make greater difference in her life, than mine.

Consequently, the following lunchtime, I had been gathering plates from a particularly ideal street-seating café – being advantageous, insomuch that the window showing the serving counter, was located out-of-sight around a corner. It allowed me a moment's more discretion to pop some uneaten mango chunks into my little bag. That, and the break in the weather – whereby the violent storm had given way to a beautifully crisp sunny day – had resulted in an unusually-heavy flurry of people rushing to get their lunch, just in case the weather should turn again. The city was infected with a remarkably hectic bustle of competing migrations, and I had never felt more gloriously alone amidst the urban herds.

As I emptied the plates, an unexpected shock jolted me, whereby I thought for a second that I had been caught by a staff member.

"Robert?!" came the incredulous voice again.

My initial, split-second impulse, had been to flee. Yet, in being called that name, it was as though some sort of hook had been sunk into me, rendering me fixated to the spot. There was a split-second spasm of jarring back pain and confusion.

Turning, I saw an old man, with a curious mix of utmost relief and amazement on his face. He was clearly old, but evidently looked after himself.

Wearing an expensive green-tweed blazer, purple-woollen waistcoat, and a matching Homburg hat, he appeared the epitome of refinement and by-gone sophistication. The array of tiny golden-jewelled rings glittering on his fingers, and his exquisite cane of black ash and intricate silverwork, only added to his aura of an old-fashioned dandy. The thought occurred to me, that he appeared as one of those gentlemen of a certain era, who habitually dressed in their finest suit on a Sunday, regardless of what they were planning to do.

The man's starkly-green eyes hungrily inspected my form, as he eagerly held me by both shoulders.

"Robert, it is you!" he said, seemingly delighted in mistaking me for someone else.

"I've been looking everywhere for you, ever since… well… you know…"

At his recollection of Robert's circumstances, he took a step back and looked to vacillate, examining me in greater scrutiny. "You're not okay, are you?"

It was as with many of my feelings, that something familiar haunted me – insisting I should be able to recall this lavish old man, yet equally finding no familiarity there. That dissonance – of two opposing forces – held me still.

"Come, sit… sit," he insisted, moving me to a table – of which seconds earlier, I had been in the pretence of clearing. He suddenly appeared to understand my situation, insisting that I remain whilst he went inside to order. "My treat, obviously," he assured me, smiling through his finely pencilled white beard.

He came back with two drinks. Dark, strong, black and unsweetened. He appeared to know how Robert drank his coffee. Yet, I had not had coffee for months, ever since… no, no… I had never had coffee. It had been *him*…

Asking a barrage of questions as to my wellbeing and former whereabouts, the old man quickly realised that the person he was talking with was in a non-verbal state – or at least, not in a state-of-being that he was expecting or accustomed to. Momentarily deliberating as he sipped his own espresso, the old man appeared to change tactics, adopting a gentler tone.

"Robert, it is me… Doctor Richardson," he tentatively offered, as though frightened of scaring off a small woodland creature. "You have been my patient for many years. You disappeared about a year ago, and I was terribly worried. I have been looking for you ever since; very concerned for your welfare my good man."

Again, that nagging ghost-feeling protested at the deeper recesses of my mind. But, I could only look over the refined gentleman with curiosity.

He appeared to comprehend my lack of recognition.

"You had a psychotic breakdown when you were eighteen years old, and your family committed you to a secure facility. I was your psychiatrist. You trusted me; continuing to work with me after your discharge. I helped you back to health, and back into society. Part of this was my diagnosing you with schizophrenia, inherent with dissociative tendencies. You suffered such terrible bouts, of both paranoid and delusional episodes."

"You are very unwell." It sounded as though he were trying to jog a memory, rather than trying to convince me.

"You told me you had stopped taking your medications, and went on to suffer another psychotic break about a year ago. Despite your progress, you stopped attending our sessions. I have so worried about you ever since."

The old man appeared the epitome of compassion and genuine concern. His emerald eyes glistened with an appealing kindness. The overall feeling from him, was of professional competence and mature concern. There was nothing untailored or happenstance about his demeanour.

Some part of me was trying to take in what he was claiming. Looking out across the swathes of city-dwellers striding about in the post-storm oasis, my mind felt distinctly and unusually fractured… fuzzy… hard to reconcile. Something elusive was trying to claw its way back in.

The bright sun reflected off an endless array of interspersed puddles and running channels of water. It created a dualistic perception. On the one hand, I was sitting with an old man who felt vaguely familiar, at a café within a city, in sight of hundreds of people. The nutty aroma of the coffee was appealing, serving as the chief anchor to that world.

Yet through the other intruding perceptual lens, the flashes and glimmers of the intense light bouncing off the surface-water, created an alien environment – almost superimposed upon the other.

I could recognise the city and its people. But, they appeared to move through an alien, yellowish-green fog, over swampy ground. Flashes of yellow thunder (or, was it sunlight reflections?) interspersed the two realities. It felt like I was getting a headache, even though the pressure was not felt within my skull. Rather, there felt a strange pressure building, roughly two feet back from my right shoulder-blade.

The strange dual-landscape was occupied by people in business suits, gym-wear, high-end fashion and uniforms. Yet at the same time, I could distinctly *see* each one of these forms as moving balloons of egg-shaped, luminous awareness, navigating the dryer parts of a weird swamp-like, smoky environment.

Yet, the bright reflective shards of the sun were not the only factor splitting my reality. Again, I could easily hear the din of the city – the honking taxis, the customers' chatter, and the doom-laden warnings of the street preachers. However, there was a sound in-between the sounds – or more accurately, there was meaning impregnated within the silent spaces *between* the sounds. They felt like 'caves' of meaning, nesting within the boggy pools of the alien swamp.

Whereas I would have felt quite relaxed and at ease with my new-found abilities to handle two concurrent realities, something about meeting Doctor Richardson was forcing them to be at unbearable odds. It was though his presence – his simple acknowledgment of me – was pulling the two distinct realities apart, whereby one could not successfully exist next to the presence of the other. He was forcing a solidity of dichotomous choice that I had not experienced for many months.

Something momentarily jarred me back to the everyday world of cold form and defined experience. A young waiter had placed a hot-sandwich in front of me, for which Dr. Richardson was thanking. It was a meatball panini, dripping in a rich honey-wine sauce, teased with a sprinkling of caramelised red onions and cheddar, artfully finished with a sprig of fresh basil.

Robert would have desired it. He would have wolfed it down it. I knew that much.

I... did not move.

"Go on, go on," the old man waved his bejewelled hand in encouragement. "You look like you need a good meal."

My lack of reaction appeared to prompt him back into a professional stance. "You know, when you disappeared, I sought out those books you told me you had written. I understand so much better now. I am sorry I did not make the time to understand you beforehand."

Again, my lack of response only seemed to make him appeal harder to someone he was trying to reach. "You had been raised within a dysfunctional home, witnessing all manner of abuse, including keen neglect for yourself. My dear Robert, you have struggled with mental health challenges all of your life; and between therapeutic interventions, structured living and careful control of your medications, you were doing most brilliantly!"

"But," he reluctantly conceded, "I had not realised that you were harbouring such delusions throughout our sessions. It is only after reading your books, how I now see your sublimation and projection mechanisms came into play. It is only now, that I understand the level of psychosis you spiralled back into – just how fractured your reality became. A great shame, for someone so promising."

I remained still; the coffee and sandwich grew colder. The crowd of phantoms around us continued to unknowingly walk between the shafts of bright sun interspersing the buildings, alongside the alien-green vapour.

"It is clear from your work, that you have adopted classic archetypes as self-coping mechanisms; interpretive lenses, if you will," the old man offered, peering at me over his tortoiseshell spectacles. "You have the strong, masculine figure of Jon-Paul – being the typical male representation of capability, vigour and strength... the protector. To balance this, you created Meili – the feminine epitome of sensitivity, wellbeing and nurture... the caregiver. Between them, you have fashioned the ideal of the Father and Mother figure."

"In addition, you formulated John, as the scholastic archetype of the wise old man, of seasoned thought and insight. John was the Grampa-sage. Accompanying him, was the doting grandmother-jester – or old crone, with her gnostic-understanding – figure of Teresa; being earthy and humorously-engaging."

The old man avidly described how I even constructed the irresponsible figures of Josephina and Elizabeth, in order to project my own less sophisticated psychic components onto. They were the archetypes to express my more immature and embarrassing processes, allowing me to more safely explore unrefined impulse-gratification issues.

"And of course," he sounded like he was reluctant to recognise the next point, "there was the character of Florinda." He paused, examining me as though frightened he would trigger a psychotic episode. "The model witch and shaman-figure – of advanced age, spiritual wisdom and insight; the perfect archetype of the teacher."

"You must recognise that these are delusions – splintered sections of your overwhelmed mind; which has created alternative constructs to soothe and protect your... understandably troubled... psycho-emotive terrain. You even created a range of counter-archetypes in the form of the so-called *Omega Assembly*, to represent the more threatening and unacceptable shadow elements to your psyche."

"Just think about it for a moment," he pleaded of me. "My character of Henrick... Hen-Rick... Henry Richardson... is cast as the leader of the adversarial counter-organisation group. He stands as the biggest threat to your new magical reality; just as I posed an intolerable threat to your delusions."

For a split-second, I desperately wanted to believe the refined old man. I wanted to wrap myself in the warm, comforting narrative of being *somebody*. More potently, there was a sharp momentary temptation to give myself over to him and his story, where there lived a weirdly soothing allure, to the possibility of allowing myself to be mentally unwell.

The act of letting someone else house, feed and provide structure and support for me.... for medication to control my very mood and thoughts. Well, there was so much temptation in that – in alleviating myself of *personal responsibility*. For a blinding second of white-hot doubt, it caused Robert to come dangerously close to finding his way back.

As the psychiatrist talked, I could only stare out at the passing phantoms before me. From a place of *seeing*, I could detect their luminosity with ease. Yet, I could also *see* that alien forms of awareness simultaneously dominating the same environment.

The amber-golden glow of luminous *balloons of awareness*, was clearly evident to *see*, as the abundant human presence dominating the landscape. Yet, pockets of intrusive colours – of greens, blues, violets and whites – infiltrated in-between the golden waves.

Some of these alien forms of awareness were round. Others, looked like twisted honeycomb. Others still, appeared to live on the surface of the amber cocoons of human awareness, like parasitic mould. Yet different foreign luminosity, hovered around in spikier forms, like giant seedpods.

There was an unhealthy connection between the invasive species of alien luminosity, and the native amber-yellowish forms they had attached to. Yet, the individual people living within the *allies'* tethers, were wholly unaware of the energetic transaction.

Non-human alien sentience was manifest right within the bustle of the modern city itself – and yet not a soul was privy to the invasion. Particularly unnerving to me, was that as Dr. Richardson continued to appeal to a forgotten memory, I only perceived more-and-more of the alien invaders, at a staggeringly bountiful and diverse range.

The whisps of sulphurous swamp-vapour fought with the chemical tendril of the meatball panini, the combined touch of both bringing me to a deep *knowing:* that the drastic and unprecedented urbanisation of modern humankind, had opened a previously-inaccessible doorway into the *unknown*. The density of modern awareness, had warped the core substance of the human-dimensions of reality, into something that the *ancient seers* had neither experienced or even conceived of.

Now, an invite to previously-inaccessible layers of foreign *assemblage* had been cast-out to the universe. New *allies* – uncharted realms, of alternative conduits of awareness – had responded to humanity's unwitting beacon. They occupied our unprecedented reality, at cost and without recognition. Modern movies portrayed alien invasions as loud, explosive, and world-shattering. None of us had the foresight... insight... to consider we may already be under occupation, of a much more soothingly seductive servitude.

"The devil's way in, is through kindness, flattery and a smile," Robert had once been told by an old pipe-smoking old hippy. Or... had he?

A finger of dark-green smoke tapped me, and someone else's memory jumped forcibly into my struggling mind-state... a complete memory of Robert's.

He had studied under a professor of clinical psychology, when reading at university. The young Robert had idolised his mentor, and followed him everywhere, in order to satisfy his insatiable greed for understanding.

Whether they attended to patients, undertook research, assisted with transcripts, or drank fine-wine at the mentor's home – the professor loved to talk, and Robert loved to soak it all in. Just how long had Robert tried to emulate the role of 'dutiful student'?

Despite being outwardly liberal, Robert's professor had repeatedly demonstrated a surprisingly conservative undercurrent on life. If a person matured, dedicated themselves to rewarding work, married into a monogamous two-person attachment, ideally raised some children, developed meaningful social bonds, and actively contributed to society – these were the in-born genetic hallmarks that would result in good health and mental stability, being the actualisations of the evolutionary template of humanity. The professor maintained that it was when people strayed away from these core human milestones, that psychological illness and dissatisfaction arose.

Robert had never been entirely comfortable with his professor's leanings towards tradition and conservatism. Overlooking Robert's life-spawned, knee-jerk, reactionary rejections of 'the norm', the basic math had just not made sense to him.

For the vast majority of human history (including pre-history, concerning the modern physical emergence of homo sapiens) the manifest population of humans on the earth, had totalled roughly under the two-million mark. Modern-man, was predominantly evolved to be a harmonious creature within relatively isolated living – co-existing in much smaller 'tribal' communities.

Even as relatively recently as fifty-thousand B.C.E, the entirety of the collective human population had only ever reached short of the two-million mark. Now, the current population of many individual cities alone, is more than had ever been collectively alive across the entire globe.

Only in the eighteen-hundreds did the collective span of humankind total a billion concurrently manifest. In the space of merely two-hundred years – a mere fraction of a blink in geo-evolutionary terms – mankind then metastasised by eight-hundred percent, to eight-billion inhabitants.

This factor alone – the raw, unprecedented numbers – is what Robert's professor had routinely overlooked. It is what he found many classic academic disciplines, religions and politics routinely overlooked too. Looking back to past models of idealised human existence – of traditional templates and classic biological drives – was made painfully redundant in view of the new figures. There were no pre-existing societal, communal, psychological, familial or religious frameworks with which to adequately compare the current human condition.

Yes, there were likely to be very real and very contributary core, biological mechanisms hard-wired into the psycho-biology of every human – the meeting of such conditions would historically result in greater wellbeing, fulfilment and accomplishment. Yet Robert had never been fully convinced these classic milestones were any longer allowed to be applicable.

The stress and strain of super-dense, hyper-communal living, forced new frontiers onto modern humankind ('neo-sapiens'?), the likes of which not a single one of our ancestors had ever had to confront. The current manifestation of humanity was – for better or worse, knowingly or otherwise – living in a real-time, and wholly-unprecedented, experiment. They stood on the knife-edge of an abyss, with violent actualisation and the doom of ignorance on either side.

Considered through a zoological approach, certain problems of manifest modern living could be explained. After all, it has been well-documented how neurotic animals become, when forced into captivity. Confined bears pace agitatedly back-and-forth, engaging in repetitive nonsense-behaviours as a form of self-stimulation. The chimp flings its own excrement, in order to vent its frustrations at being denied its natural nomadic lifestyle. When forced into artificially-dense environments like zoos, even once-sociable 'herd-like' animals of inborn genetic collectivity, will become aggressive, eating their young, fighting with mates and parents, and turning to all manner of anti-social behaviours.

In this view, modern human cities are merely glorified zoos ('mega zoos') – with the equivalent manifestations of neurotic expression from artificial captivity. I wondered as to just who our curious guests were, watching us perform the equivalent of public-masturbation in order to promote a response from our strange visitors, beyond our ape-like comprehension. We likely saw their shadows tapping at the glass of our enclosure; but did we truly comprehend the so-different forms on the other side of the pane?

When considered from an evolutionary perspective, the current explosion of the human population also makes sense. Rates of so-called 'deviant' ('abnormal' in the exceptionally restricted biological sense, of not promoting reproduction) traits like homosexuality can be explained. Studies have shown across various species, that instances of homosexuality rise in-line with an increase in population; the increased rate of manifestation in itself, being quite natural. One could argue it as nature's built-in counter-mechanism to account for rampant, unchecked over-population.

Even on the abstract level of the sorcerer's explanation, having so many *luminous balloons* being knotted into the underlying material of *awareness*, naturally results in the waywardness of modern humanity – twisting the raw substance of awareness into tumour-like formations. The strain-of-tension across the collective awareness, would be unprecedented and unthinkable to the *seers of antiquity*.

Looking out across the duality of the urban-luminous environment, I could *see* the perils of modern humanity. In one perception, the likes of exhaust emissions, the sea of dominating and interlacing electromagnetic waves, the micro-plastics, the synthetic oestrogens, the social hyper-complexities, and the conflux of semantic tsunamis all saturated mankind's new environment.

Now, the young of such a cognisant species were subjected to a global onslaught of ceaseless communication – being exposed to a deluge of information within a single month, than their ancestors typically faced in an entire lifetime.

Even the colouring, preservatives, abundance of salt and sugar, and the processed ingredients of the meatball panini before me – assembled and partly cooked hundreds of miles away, flown at perversely-inflated cost to carbon-footprint, to be warmed in the city's café – glowed with threads of damaging luminous substance. As tiny and insubstantial as such malicious strands of luminosity were, they only served as yet another vulnerability to coax alien *assemblage points*, when interwoven with the modern human matrix.

Thousands-upon-countless-thousands of such tiny hostile hooks of luminosity spanned the great tapestry of modern human existence. They were not native to this particular realm of energetic reality, thus serving to undermine the collective luminosity. They made its surface more appealingly tenderised to alien conglomerations of awareness.

Going deeper into *seeing*, it was the attachments to the new wave of *allies* that partly-accounted for the manifest suffering of contemporary humanity: of their insatiable craving, the rape of their very own home, their unshakable depression, their hunger and greed, their chronic anxiety and collective delusion.

Above all, the stench of *self-importance* permeated the human landscape. The descriptive force had a choke-hold on modern humanity. Their ability to *see* was almost gone. Doom lay in even the simplest meatball panini; and until then, the instability of their own perceptual cohesion was exacerbated, as humanity relayed a universe-wide invitation to all sorts of unknown foreign life.

The fox-ally had been right. *The sorcerers of antiquity* had explored relatively adjacent bands of awareness – courting the spirits housed within the nearby realms of the *tonal* and *nagual*. However perverse the co-dependant relationship of *ally* and sorcerer had been, it had been handed-down for countless generations, across countless cultures, as a set of stable practices – termed 'sorcery'.

The worst cases of the *old seers*, had been those examples who left their humanity behind entirely. They split from the human *sheet of awareness*, and shot-off to explore the *great unknown*. As incomprehensible as their experiences would have been, they no longer had organic connections to tether or taint themselves with humanity.

But now – thanks to the unprecedented distortion of modern man's awareness – whole new frontiers of sorceric exploration had been opened. Yet in the blind state of their descriptive self-delusion, modern humanity suspected not its new opportunity, nor the new threats.

Wholly alien *allies* flooded in – unknown to even the most daring of old sorcerers. Sitting there listening to the psychiatrist detail my psychotic break, I could *see* the new forms moving right within the city's crowds all around us.

As always, the city provided in abundance. I could *see* the living demonstrations, shining out amongst the throngs of luminous cocoons.

A lone confident young woman strode passed, talking animatedly away. I could not tell if she was talking to herself, to voices in her head, someone on a mobile device, or if she conversed with the mosquito-like, pig-sized, glowing *ally* hovering right over her head, attached via a thick bundle of hair-like tentacles. Once upon a time, it would have been quite easy to determine who she was talking to. Not any more.

Of course, the old *allies* were present. A well-dressed civil-servant walked by, thinking himself savvy for charging personal indulgences at cost to the taxpayer. A compact, donut-shaped ring of greenish light had burrowed within the lower regions of his luminosity. Blinded by his own cleverness, he utterly failed to perceive how his own greed chiefly weakened himself.

The street-preacher across the road, vented his sermons with an anger of passion, which betrayed not the teachings of his gospels. A rather satiated *ally* floated next to him, its red-like aura glistening as it suckled on something else than truth.

Some of the ancient *allies* manifested in astoundingly-banal human form. Gaunt men and women of shaggy dry skin, empty eye sockets and protruding spines walked amongst the shoppers. The most frightening observation, was watching how the *tonals* of so many individuals worked tirelessly to actively blind them to the intrusion of the grotesque wraiths, right there within the crowds.

Yet, there were new *allies* too.

A young university student sat on the bench across the road, in front of a dilapidated old church. I could see the nervous activation of so many of her luminous strands, causing her to feel an unwarranted and inexplicable daily onslaught of anxiety. She was barely on the verge of keeping it all together. The luminous tendrils attached to her mid-section went entirely unnoticed, as the *cluster-ally* tapped-and-agitated her luminosity for sensational sustenance. It fuelled her inexplicable and delectable vibrations of fear, by drip-feeding her whispers of the *great unknown*.

A living parade of Tourette's, ADHD, social disorders, neuroticism, sexual addiction, self-harm, substance abuse, and physical, emotional, mental and sexual trauma spawned amidst the city's luminosity, as would mould from dampness. The reach of the new *allies* extended throughout the golden glow of humanity.

Yet, it was not only the effect on individuals that was evident. The very intrusion of these alien *assemblage points*, was warping the fabric of our own layer of reality. The population aged at a rate never before witnessed in human (pre)history. Increased cases of dementia and loneliness only bloomed as a result of the luminous intervention, with the counter-effect of humanity considering itself so clever. The *wraith-allies* simultaneously propagated in response to our self-congratulatory corruption.

Infant life daily blossomed into the world at a staggering rate. The *Great Mother* strained with malnutrition, in her exhaustion being unable to provide the nutrients needed to suckle her insatiable children. The myth of humanity's self-aggrandisement blinded itself to the unsustainability of the endeavour.

War, extremism, alienation, self-importance, profound loneliness, arbitrary racial divides, (self)hatred, infantilism, polarisation, narcissism, warped political idolisation, where just a handful of the magnified effects rippling through the *sheet of awareness*. The distorted underlying awareness, affected the position of so many individual *assemblage points*. It was just as much so, as being tethered to an office cubicle, policed by a statistical-monitoring software, and having one's performance broken-down into increasingly unrealistic, sterile and power-sapping increments, for exploit. That, was never part of our ancient heritage. And, the new *allies* thrived for it.

The world was breaking down. Gone were old, known communities and nations. Now, one had the instantaneous means in their pocket, to communicate with the other side of the planet. Such a thing would have been incomprehensible to even our recent ancestors.

Yet now, the immediate and overwhelming demand-of-expectation and aggression-of-communication this burdened upon the average person, was not even recognised.

People now travelled on a daily basis, commuting via great migration patterns, far further than their ancestors traditionally lived, or even traversed in one lifetime. The soul-sucking demands – the hours robbed of each day of lived experience – went unperceived in pursuit of narrative and endless consumption, way beyond the chronic depression that infested their being. As vital luminosity dulled to the hours wasted of waiting for delayed trains, new *allies* snuck in to nurse.

A quick pill was all it felt was needed to alleviate the feelings of unnatural kink within awareness. More *false-allies* flooded in, their tethers dripping false promises, whilst suckling at our most vulnerable places.

And there, amongst it all, the new *allies* had masterfully responded to – and tapped – the most profitable mine of all, pre-laid by their alien forebearers: the bounty of *self-importance*. In our depravity of plague-like infestation, we lapped-up the sweetened-yet-bitter lie of separation.

Across the street, an ambitious, young internet wannabe held up a group of children with learning disabilities, in order that they could self-record in front of a well-known store-front. A group of mothers paraded their toddlers in high-end fashion, and even more fashionable boasts of anti-vaccination propaganda – their pedigree dogs snorting and struggling to breathe besides them with their bastardised faces, decorated in more expensive attire than the city's homeless.

The café's young-adult supervisor, screamed to berate a younger waiter – and bolster their own brittle sense of authority – to appease the older customer, who had in-fact made the mistake. A young, over-preened woman aggressively rebuked a man in a wheelchair, because she secretly had to reinforce her own fragile self-worth inherited from a weak, absent father.

A middle-aged man strode aggressively out of the gym, his chemically-swollen muscles barely containing his exaggerated physical form within his showcasing attire. He pushed passed people within the crowd, crossing the road and forcing the cars to stop for his presence. In the brittle security of his rigid self-assuredness, he did not perceive the swarm of tiny, glow-fly-like *allies*, quietly nursing upon the strands describing his pineal gland, testes, adrenal medulla and liver.

A lone elderly gentleman, silently wet himself on a bench, as the pigeons pecked at his expanding stream. So many citizens strode passed, completely unaware to his silent plea for death. The armoured manifestation of an oversized woodlouse-like creature, went unseen attached to the rear of his cocoon. It sucked at the unravelling remnants of narrative cohesion, of the old man's *tonal*. Soon, he would even forget his own desire for release.

A young child sat underneath a neighbouring table, as his mother conversed with a companion over lunch – criticising their mutual friends. I could not help but laugh, at the sheer abandoned delight the child expressed, when playing with his new-found snail-friend. The potent joy he experienced at squidging its slimy body, was a raw pleasure his mother had long forgotten. His unapologetic delight of direct experience, had been miraculous!

Suddenly, the mother smacked the stunned creature out of the child's hand, berating, "No! Dirty! Nasty!" Another spell of the *Black Magicians* hooked itself within the child's pliant luminosity. Another anchor-point crystalised within his brilliant luminous cocoon, making another weakness for the *allies* to attach on to. The toddler wailed in distress, as another untethered *ally* moved closer.

Looking across the road, I could see a huge lady traversing the sidewalk on an electric mobility scooter. The sheer strain of the weight she carried – being of a size that no ancestor would have recognised merely a few generations ago – rendered her unable to walk. Her knees, back, shoulders and hips hurt as far back as she could now remember. Unforgiving discomfort, was bodily woven into her entire reality. The raw sores inside her thighs gave her constant irritation and no relief. Her living daily experience was of relentlessly unforgiving discomfort. That, alongside embarrassment, self-loathing and bitterness.

She was sweating profusely, even though it was not warm outside. Her breathing was short and strained, robbing her very life-force of vitality. The burden of her own breathing was yet something else to endure. The fact that she could not afford a suitable scooter able to properly support her weight, only exacerbated her suffering.

I could hear the inner thoughts of the mobility-impaired woman, as she navigated the crowds of people snorting in derision at her clumsy presence. She was miserable. Her life was miserable. She felt deeply unattractive, even on a base social level. She repulsed even herself, to the point that she had not seen her own naked body in years.

As the morbidly-obese rider trundled off with her protesting scooter, both she and the crowds failed to see her companion – a luminous cocoon unlike any I had seen. It was something like a glowing ball of cable, or a steel-wire sponge. Whereas most other forms of awareness resembled variations on an egg or ball-like theme, the uniqueness of this particular *ally*, came from the abundance of spaces between the entangled structure. Those spaces somehow determined how energy-hungry this particular constitution of alien life was.

I did not like the feeling surrounding this particular *ally*. Its *assemblage point* was a diffused film across multiple tubules of awareness. Whilst relatively small compared to some of the other luminous forms, it gave off a much greater feeling of density – albeit, this had nothing to do with normal thoughts of weight or gravity.

This 'jumbled' *ally* was uniquely attached to the very bottom of the lady's own luminous cocoon. The mere presence of its unique structure, demanded disproportionately greater energy consumption. Rather than directly attach itself to the woman's own luminous fibres, it created something like a concave dent in reality, that allowed the sufferer's luminosity to 'sink' into – something akin to the immense gravitational pull surrounding a black hole, which sucks the light from neighbouring stars with destructive consequences. The trick of this *ally*, was in the insidiousness of its gentle coaxing method, as opposed to some of the more outright aggressive tactics that betrayed the presence of other *allies*. This particular *inorganic* being allowed you to stumble into its trap day-by-day, rather than approach and ensnare you directly. *You*, did the disproportionately-taxing work for *it*.

The woman in the scooter suffered a more inexhaustible fatigue than those around her understood, or that her own weight dictated. Yet, she no more perceived the foreign *assemblage point*, which had drawn her into its energetic gravity well, than she did the children making pig-impressions behind her.

Modern humanity's unprecedented proximity to the new forms of alien life bleeding-in from hitherto-unexplored realms, was now their biggest challenge. The multi-dimensional position of their *assemblage points*, served as a gateway and beacon – ushering in the new luminous matrices. Their accompanying vibrational frequencies echoed out across humanity's layer as unexplainable, exaggerated psycho-emotional disturbance. The emotional clamour betraying the *allies'* presence, was infinitely louder than the din of the city.

Sat amongst the crowds, it was clear that modern humanity had become possessed – not by ghosts or aliens or spirits. They were affected by the new proximity of *inorganic* awareness, bleeding-over from unperceived realms wrapped up within the very folds of reality itself, right in front of them.

Yet, this was not entirely the fault of the alien awareness. Humanity had done this to itself – bred to unsustainable levels, which only forced us out of our natural luminous habitat and harmony. The subsequent strain on our own layer of awareness, had served as an irresistible food-source to the alien life-forms. They were as tethered and addicted to us – to the unique balance of form and experience – as we were unwitting victims of their unperceived influence. Even the luminous matrix of the *Great Mother* had been distorted by mankind's ignorant and unchecked manipulations of awareness.

Robert's professor had been quite wrong. Humanity could no longer look back to the old ways of being. Our ancestors would have been horrified and confounded by the contemporary challenges we had created. They would have been immediately defeated by the mere prospect.

Humanity's only hope was in unorthodox, unprecedented and creative solutions – of pushing itself forward. Exploration of genetics or outer space were a fool's errand – heralding the doom of the species, via even greater servitude to the *tonal*. Only more *allies* would follow down that path.

Discipline, will, and exploration of the creative realm of the *nagual*, were humanity's only true lifeline. The way of sorcerers was the only avenue left open to save modern man, in seeking to establish a new, previously uncharted breed of new sorcerers: of *Meta Seers*, or *Pioneer Seers*.

"… please, you must come with me," the old man's voice intruded into my direct *knowing*. He appeared exhausted, as if utterly desperate to bridge the gulf between perceptual realities, and hook his former patient back into the security of his world. Only a table sat between us, yet it appeared an insurmountable distance.

As the pregnant thread of coffee caressed my nostrils, another alien memory of Robert's came to me. How was he so easily possessing me?

A fundamental and life-changing experience had once happened, when Robert had accompanied his professor on his clinical rounds. There, they had chatted with a schizophrenic patient, who had deteriorated, suffering delusions and hallucinations, yet who still refused to take her medication. The thing that had immediately struck Robert, was just how drastically tired such a young woman could look. The thought had occurred to him, that she was battling something much more exhausting than mere living.

Robert's professor had tried to reason with the patient as to the need for pharmaceutical support. Yet, the young lady had come back with a retort, that deeply shocked Robert, and left him utterly without counter-reason – leaving him feeling he was 'on the wrong side'.

The young patient had calmly retorted that when she was medicated, life was hard – the endless and exhausting responsibility to face-up to the harsh realities of holding down a steady job, paying rent and bills, and meeting social expectations. It was unrelenting and exhausting, providing little relief or promise of reward. On medication, she felt incomplete – a hollowed and spent version of whom she was meant to be, under constant gravity to be something else. Yet, when she forewent the drugs – as much as she knew she could not as readily rely on her grasp of her reality – the undeniable truth of it, was that life was much easier.

"So, why on earth would I go back on my medication?" she had calmly asked of Robert's professor. To Robert's shock, his mentor could provide no sufficient reply – only skirting about a vague reply that she, "should." In that moment, the young schizophrenic patient had made eye contact with Robert, exchanging an intensely brief moment of deep, mutual understanding, whereby they both recognised the awful truth of the situation.

It was then that an intriguing thought occurred to me: had in fact, Robert mentored under a university professor, walking with the aid of a cane? Or, was that so-called memory, a delusional schism stolen of his psychiatrist, and projected as a construction of a psychotic mind?

"You have to hear me, Robert! You are ill. You need help. Come with me; please permit me to help you!" the old man appeared uniquely desperate amongst his finery. "You cannot carry on living on the streets…"

With that, a curious thing occurred to me: how did he know I was homeless?

My appearance was perhaps a little less highly-maintained than Robert's. My clothing was a little more worn, my nails a little longer, and I had the beard that Robert had never had the confidence-in-vanity to grow. Yet, I had purposefully maintained a socially-acceptable… or socially-vague… appearance. At best, I could be described as shabby or unfashionable, but not assumed to be homeless.

The old man seemed to pick-up on the suspicion, without my need to verbalise.

"I mean," he stumbled, "I saw you sleeping in a doorway not so long ago. It was evident you were on the streets. I have been looking for you ever since," he justified.

Again, this did not satisfy me. I had been exceptionally careful to remain unseen throughout the city. This included not sleeping in public spaces, such as shop fronts or throughfares. It was just safer that way, both on a bodily and energetic level.

"There are no *allies*, no alien forms of awareness!" he appeared to be almost getting angry. "There is no grand conspiracy of sorcerers! You... are... unwell. Let me take you..."

He appeared to deliberate for a moment, trying to muster his best argument. "You were doing so well. And, that is still not beyond you. We can still work together to get you homed, cleaned-up and find you a nice little job again. You can have a partner and friends... a family even. But, you must commit to being well. You have to take your medications and attend our sessions."

"You can still have a normal, worthwhile life of meaningful connections," he offered as a closing plea.

Across the street, a taxi driver honked at a decrepit old lady shuffling over the cross-walk, screaming obscenities at her to hurry. Further along, a market stall trader doubled the cost of his candy, as he realised his customer had learning difficulties. Elsewhere, a businesswoman angrily shouted down her phone, whilst a hard-up street musician got trash thrown at him by a group of laughing teenagers. A young waitress got yelled at by a customer, for not selling something that was not on the menu.

On-and-on the din of the city raged – the living expression of now-normal modern life.

Next to us, the young child was being soothed to the loss of his snail-friend, by being allowed to drink his mother's coffee – with its extra double-shot of caffeine and sugar-rich syrup. His mother ignored the child, in favour of gleefully swapping stories as to her best friend's marital infidelities.

I could see the faint green-pink hue of the coffee's flimsy light of awareness. It had been an old crutch and pseudo-ally of Robert's – as equally disabling as it was motivating. It had helped him to write a book, whispering recollections in his ear like a muse.

There was clearly an attraction to alleviating myself of *personal responsibility* – of consenting to giving myself over to the care of the psychotherapeutic machine. There was a weird – almost hilarious – desirability to allowing myself to be quite mentally unwell. After all, I held no sense of *self-importance* anymore, that could feel offended at the possibility. It would all be quite neat and easy really.

Yet, where the old ghost had lost me, was not in his skirting around the subject of mental health – but in his appeals of the so-called real world, as representing it as a worthwhile goal to work towards. He had failed to grasp that everyday life no longer held any attraction to me. In fact, quite the opposite.

In conforming, taking on-board the collective narrative, and working over decades to suppress my true nature in favour of society's expectations, I could be rewarded with the chains of an apartment and bills, a soul-sapping job of agonising routine, and the opportunity to pay taxes and accrue debt. If I were lucky, I could drag a new expression of life into that endless struggle too.

In reaching for good mental health, I could live a life of quiet, medicated desperation. The principal reward would be of a slow, exhausting death from drowning within the spells of the *Black Magicians*.

Both my own coffee and sandwich remained untouched as I silently stood, wholly disconnected to the old ghost's final pleas. He stood with his cane, but I was already immersed within the crowds, being swept away into oblivion, like a drop within the ocean.

Maybe I was quite mad, like the young patient of Robert's professor. Yet, living between the competing descriptions – of over-populated urban zoo, and the luminous swamp with its alien invasion – remained the most vastly appealing option. The normative world of reason held absolutely no promise or appeal. There could be no liberation that way.

The second enemy of man had presented itself to me: clarity. I could *see* so much of the nature of realities now. The world of fog and lighting and alien awareness was indeed, very real. It was impregnated with *knowledge* and *power*, and the promise of *infinity*.

Yet, the everyday world flaunted by the old man, also contained a clear path – one of comfort, stories and responsibility-absolving attachments. Neither one was more unreal or unworthy as the next. That path offered a cold, clinical clarity of neatly condensed thought and experience.

But like the young patient of Robert's old professor, there was no obvious answer as to why the so-called 'normal' world was worth the effort. I could admittedly walk that oh-so-difficult path. I could commit to normative wellbeing. I could seek the opiate-like comfort of civilisation and collective living.

"But, why should I?" the patient's pertinent question echoed into my mind, still embarrassingly unresolved after decades. Like Robert, I also could not provide a worthwhile answer.

All that was required, was for me to make a choice – to fully commit myself to either the 'real' everyday world, or the 'real' world of sorcery. There would finally be a cohesion-of-thought, and refreshing clarity-of-perception, once I made a choice… either choice.

Walking away between the alien-spectres haranguing the bustle of people, I stepped between their deep unrest and chronic unease – traversing the emanations of sadness, natural to any mutually-unhappy co-dependant relationship. I disappeared between the city-stimulus and the light-fractures of the ghost-swamp, residing myself to be utterly at peace between neither.

Disappearing within the unresolved haziness of duality, I realised I was picking the hardest route of all… of creative self-reliance, untouchable *non-being*, and of endless unresolved contradiction. And yet, I was quite at peace doing so, finally recognising the insubstantiality of both worlds.

10

The Mirrored Wings of the Eagle.

(aka: Passing the Three Gates of Dissolution.)

It had been just as my *fox-ally* had predicted. Yet passing through the three gates – the last strands of Robert's infection – was no less taxing for the pre-warning.

The first passage occurred one overcast night. I had been dumpster-diving in the back alley of the city's commercial district. One of the stores was being aggressively renovated, and I had come across a veritable treasure trove tossed in the trash.

There was discarded wall-insulation, which whilst a little dusty, would at least serve as comfortable bedding at the likes of the nearby roof-top sanctuary. My biggest find, was a load of torn and bent cardboard – albeit, which had metallic foil partially glued to one side. When pulled off the mouldy card, the silver material would serve as an excellent insulator to line my clothing (replacing the long-tattered newspaper currently stuffed within my jacket as a thermal lining). Furthermore, the foil was waterproof.

I do not know whether the Aladdin's-cave of vagrant treasures had drawn the other two men, but it was all-too-obvious they were also homeless... yet hostile. They swore and threatened me with an immediacy of violence, if I did not leave.

I felt confused. I could not tell if it were my lack of strategic mindfulness, in not noticing their approach, or not understanding their presence and words. I heard them; I understood their language. However, it may as well have been an ancient demon speaking to me, in a long-forgotten archaic dialect.

The shorter man appeared as though personally offended by my silence. I felt sorry for him; that in his destitution he still clung to so much.

His response was to pull out a flick-knife on me. Lunging, he made contact only with air.

I moved almost as if in slow-motion – in a disconnected realm of time, pattern and momentum. The attacker's actions were obvious to me, as though his intentions were being transmitted ahead of his crude gestures of physical movement.

He lunged. He slashed. He swore in frustration, and called me names. The more I dodged, the angrier he became. Sympathy flooded in response to him missing his opportunity to be free.

Robert had been specifically trained in martial arts to account for weapon's attack. His bear-of-an-instructor – Jon-Paul – had advised him to consider a knife or gun akin to a feather-duster or hair brush. Putting too-much fear and focus on the weapon itself – merely an inanimate object – would cripple anyone defending themselves. It would, "fuck with their ability to truly listen," the hulking instructor had advised.

Instead, Robert had been instructed to concentrate on the attacker's own limbs as the offensive weapon – being the transmitter of *intention*, and the true means to disable the opponent.

As with most of the teachings Robert was exposed to, it had been accepted on a shallow, academic level. It made logical sense to him, but he had never truly 'owned' the knowledge, as his ex-forces instructor frequently admonished.

Yet in that back alley, I danced and twirled as though courting the wind. The knife was of absolutely no concern to me. Within my intrigued detachment, I gave it no opportunity to make contact – the sharpness of its narrow blade being made wholly impotent by the clumsy intentions of its wielder. Within that weirdly-slowed expression of time – where form was grotesquely slower than *intent* – I was curious about my attacker's mind-state. I could almost hear his *internal dialogue* of frustration and desperation – flowing from a much older and profoundly persistent place, than my simple refusal to engage. His lashing-out, had absolutely nothing to do with me. So, how could I possibly be offended by his trying to take my life?

To my attacker, I represented a lifetime of frustration. My refusal to be acquiesce to his will, only reminded him as to his recurrent lack of *power*.

Despite my detachment, I could still sense risk permeating the situation. This was not of bodily harm, but the risk of interference... of human intervention. By far, the biggest threat to my unique situation, was for this scenario to require the attention of the likes of the police or ambulance personnel. That, would draw too many questions. And, no blade was as to that same magnitude of risk.

Whilst I had doubts as to the ability of anyone to physically constrain me in my new found state-of-being, there remained much darker dangers – which I felt were almost too unbearable to even consider.

The police would ask questions of identity. The hospital would insist on discourse, and checking social security details. The authorities would bring expectation, imposition and suffocating discourse. To someone on *the path of knowledge*, the spells of the *Black Magicians* were deadly.

No, the risk of the *tonal* being forcibly imposed from the outside – of potentially being forced to engage – was too overwhelming to contemplate. I could palpably feel description, structure, narrative and meaning leaching into the immediacy of the situation, like a fatal wound that was already haemorrhaging.

Knowing I had to act fast, I identified an opportunity. Forcing the attacker's hand to bend into a painful position towards his own wrist, the weapon dropped with a yelp. My own hand stole the falling knife – something Robert had been taught never to try; yet in my new perceptual-speed, focussing in on the momentum (rather than the narrational threat of the blade) felt like child's play.

Barging into the attacker, I span, dropped, and unexpectedly forced the knife through the Achilles tendon of his companion – stabbing and wrenching at the flesh. He sank screaming, as I span away.

The shorter antagonist, released a barrage of frantic obscenities in my direction. A genuine chuckle escaped me, as I thought how odd it was that he was demanding to know *why* I had done such a thing. "What a perverse creature the *tonal* is!" I mused to myself. But, my holding his own bloodied knife up to his nose, soon calmed his agitated diatribe.

One of the attacker's was physically incapacitated, bleeding-out and in pain. I had left his companion with a decision to make: to either continue in his dubious chances of fighting me for scraps, or to attend to his friend, who increasingly needed assistance, if the level of blood was anything to go by.

"No matter how cruel or saintly you may be," Florinda had once advised Robert, "you are obliged as an *impeccable warrior*, to always award the other person a choice."

Only now, did I understand those words. You could promote change to manifest within a situation; but only in leaving another the agency of *choice*, could you grant them the most magnificent gift in the universe: the chance to refine their own mastery of *intent*.

Sensing the decision made of the standing vagrant, I quickly patted both men down – retrieving the only mobile phone they had amongst them. Smashing the phone beneath my heel (I did not have the time, light or advantage to be able to remove the SIM card), I only further confounded their vulnerability. My intention was to guide them to rationally act in self-preservation, over the choice to react from belligerent *self-importance*.

I motioned the standing antagonist to leave. He helped his companion up, whilst throwing curses at my silent form. He called me, "weird," and a, "freak," for my lack of speech. As I saw the glowing-orange, barnacle-like *ally* suckle at the base of his spine, I pondered if he were right.

Robert would have felt bad. He would have indulged in his 'civilised' sensibilities, and fretted and over-analysed his own actions.

Robert had never pierced human flesh before. He had never truly immobilised a man with a weapon. Worse, being the marionette of ever-modern urban civility, Robert would have been mortified to have mutilated a homeless person. After all, not only did infection present a risk to someone without dedicated healthcare, but adversely impacting on a vagrant's ability to move around, was one of the most disadvantageous things to be done to someone on the streets.

In the same respect, destroying a homeless person's mobile phone was disproportionately damaging. They likely depended on that tool to claim financial aid or state benefits (many modern outlets did not provide free food or goods, without first registering with the local authorities, to queue-and-claim, with pre-authorised vouchers and electronic codes. Even being homeless had been electronically-bureaucratised).

Goodness, Robert would have morosely indulged over the consequences of those actions. He would have sought out his teachers, and bored them with endless hours of gibbering moral quandary. Like an addict, he would have medicated himself with his self-masturbatory *inner dialogue* – perversely reassuring himself of being 'sophisticated' and 'kind', from his fretting over such matters. He would have completely failed to *see* how that would still only be his *self-importance* manifesting.

Yet, as I stood detachedly gazing at the two retreating men, I felt... nothing. In my new worldview, it was a simple transaction. They had been fully within their rights as fellow individuals, to try to take advantage of me. But in doing so, they entered into an energetic contract of sorts – whereby I had the equal right to defend myself. They had no grounds to argue grievance, when they had willingly entered into the inherent transaction of the situation, bringing the risk of the return of their own underlying *intent*. In their aggrieved curses, their *self-importance* leaked-out much more so than their blood.

Power. It was simply an interplay of *power* – being the constant phenomena of 'cost-and-reward'. It was the endless back-and-forth, which a white-haired witch had so often said was inherent within every fibre of the inter-lacing luminous landscape. I understood that from my silent *place of no pity* – where no anger or divisive feelings of retribution extended towards the men, and no useless guilt or second-guessing indulged towards myself. It simply, *was*.

Discarding the knife within a sewer-grate, I felt the wings of the *Eagle* as more than an intellectual musing. Similar to the idea of karma, Robert had been taught how the *intent* of man was reflected by the wings of the *Eagle* – each feather of its encompassing wings, formed of a perfectly polished mirror-like substance. The *intent* cast-out from each *balloon of awareness*, was reflected back towards that same anchored structure at some point – not as a moralistic value-judgment of 'right' or 'wrong', and certainly not from am omni-present and judgemental god-figure.

Florinda had been quite right – the *Eagle* was utterly impartial and uncaring to the petty whims of such tiny globules of awareness. It was enough to let such forms construct their own fates, to tenderise themselves as foodstuff.

Whereas many comfortingly attribute the idea of such karmic-like consequences to outside influence, the reality remained that it is merely the natural energetic fruition of the *intent* each person transmits – this being what is behind an act, a behaviour, a complex thought, a word, or even a fleeting impulse. Thus, each *balloon of awareness*, was ultimately responsible for their own destiny – in how much they had mastered the command of *intent*, and set-up the pre-conditions for its return manifestation to the point-of-origin.

This, was ultimately the natural extension and crux of sorcery – not to develop 'magic' and 'otherworldly' phenomena, but simply to hone the handling of perception, through the refinement of *intent*, towards personal liberation. The reflection of *intent*, was mere natural energetic exchange within the *Great Flux* – and how currents of *intent* moved and echoed over short and long distances, with delayed or accelerated impetus.

It was no romantic metaphor, as Robert had taken it on-board as.

Robert had heard *intent* more poetically called, *the active side of infinity*. A diminutive Chinese instructor had elsewhere said it was, *the agent of spirit*.

As my attackers retreated with ego-fuelled promises of retribution, I could see the great ripples of their *intent* from how they illuminated specific bands of awareness, that stretched-out to *infinity*. I coldly watched as I *saw* how the fibres of their luminosity re-wove themselves in different connection to the universe – like conductive cables – to allow the later return transmission of their most valuable asset.

I wanted to feel sorry for them. Yet, compared to the chock-full form of Robert, I was hollow. He would have been disgusted and guilt-ridden at the night's events. He would have been repulsed by my response, or lack thereof. I was entirely empty – devoid of any human concern for either myself, or my fellow man. I had simply responded, and moved as though an antennae in-tune with the broadcasts of *intent*.

Power, was all that mattered now.

That realisation caused me to shudder, and for a distant motor to roar. I realised I had passed the first gate, signifying the end of my current existence. It was like a death-knell of cold shivering. My lack of morality – my need to simply move in-line with the dictates of *power* – came with the realisation that I was losing my human form.

The second gate, manifested in the sun-dappled courtyard of academia.

Sat within a university campus, I watched how many of the students did not have the funds to dress expensively (or many, the impetus towards self-grooming). Some of the more affluent students even felt it quite rebellious and bougey, to purposefully dress-down. So I had figured-out that I could go relatively unseen amongst the students, as I waited for the abundance of leftovers that they habitually wasted.

It was as I was enjoying the chirping disagreement of two bold chaffinches, quarrelling over some discarded crumbs, that someone caught my eye. A pretty, young woman, sat alone at one of the tables – absorbed in reading. She appeared utterly captivated.

I experienced a wistful momentary indulgence, revelling in her bursting energy of optimistic youth and focused investigation. The world still remained at her feet, at the mercy of that amazing and keen mind of hers. She was bursting with potential.

The spells of the *Black Magicians* had very clearly taken hold of her years earlier, as they do with the best of people. And, whilst the strength of her young beliefs was aggressively bolstered by the *tonal* of her youth, she still yet possessed some of the energy of curiosity. Her *tonal* was a good one, still allowing for the slim possibility that she may find an alternative way. No matter how remote, magic remained open to this studious young woman, and it was heartening to observe.

The young woman looked to have experienced an uncharacteristic chill in the sunny air. As she read, a shiver ran up her spine. The student absently pulled her shawl closer around her shoulders, still engrossed in her book.

This prompted me to look at the object of her focus. There were glyphs or crude markings on the cover. A vague suspicion plagued me, that I used to be able to decipher such designs. Or, maybe it was another contamination bleeding over from Robert's memories?

Yet, it was the imagery on the cover that finally forced a jolt of recognition. She was reading a printed copy of Robert's book! Even Robert himself had never seen anyone own a printed copy. That would have pleased a monstrously vain part of him. It would have bolstered his *personal history*, with something as stupidly inane as, "I'm a real-life author now!"

For me, it only spooked me. The world became chill and dark, without the sun ever changing.

I wanted to run over to the young woman, yank the book from her hands, and tell her to run! "Death, only awaits within that book!" I wanted to scream at her.

There was a great, inexplicable urge for me to tell that eager student, that what the book represented was so painfully statistically-remote, in view of the *tonal's* tyranny; that her life-force and attention would be much better spent elsewhere! I desperately wanted to reach-out in compassion, and warn her of the failed author who did a terrible thing, and suffered as a result.

I wanted nothing more than to pay back to the *spirit of man*, as an old white-haired witch had once advised the author. That meant warning the naïve student, to get her to take her tentative foot off the *path of knowledge*.

Yet, I could only sit; frozen in petrifying understanding.

Almost in sympathetic reaction, an icy shiver ran up my own spine, scaring the chaffinches away. I had passed the second gate, as the *ally* had foretold.

Crossing the third gate came shortly after the second. It felt like the two were related. Yet, the third and final impasse was heralded by a simple – but crucial – mistake.

Whilst I had been avoiding social interactions, the real threats were not from people, but rather what came with them: the constant threat of the *tonal* to bring back discourse, narrative, description, labels and meaning. That, was the real risk… always the danger of bringing *him* back.

A cohort of the *Coyote Nagual*, Taisha Abelar had described in her own work how she had faced recommendations that sorcerers should forego looking at reflective surfaces, like mirrors. The risk was the bolstering of self-reflection, the grooming of *self-importance*, and ultimately, the continued obsession with the *personal myth* of *self*.

Robert, had always considered such practices as too idolised and impractical – almost cult-like in their sterility of sanction. Yet now, I had a more practical, direct real-world knowledge of the sound reasoning behind such recommendations.

Mirrors and reflective services, were magical tools that pulled *intent* to manifest in the realm of the *tonal*. The problem now, was that the likes of high-gloss surfaces, self-facing cameras and video-calls were increasingly rife throughout modern living. Now, such magical snares were normalised and wholly unseen, as a result of the enchantments of an entire civilisation. Skyscrapers of huge mirrored-glass, now stood as monuments to the spell-casting of the new ways.

"Ironically, old chap," a pipe-smoking aged hippy had once told Robert, "the one thing the *tonal* can never do, is to look squarely at itself – to court disaster by bringing the *ego-myth* under the light of genuine attention. And to achieve this deceptive slight-of-hand, it turns the individual's focus outwards, to become obsessed and distracted with the abundant reflections of *self!"*

"Stroke the pussy of *self*, in order to forget within the rapture of climax, that there was never was such a thing to begin with!" his wife had added, cackling with laughter, as she pantomimed a grimacing face of over-strained self-pleasure. She had then gone on to search the entire kitchen, as though having genuinely lost something important, calling, "Here pussy, puss, pussy!…" into the pots and pans, oven; even calling inside Robert's satchel.

Since I had left Robert at the airport, I had not looked into any reflective service with any great inspection. Of course, I would occasionally catch a vague shape or shadow pass a car window or store front. Sometimes, I would even detect the dual presence of a *double* figure in the reflection too. However, I had not focussed on such images, being as ghost-like and illusionary as the people around me.

It was as though such mirrors and shiny surfaces were portals to another realm – one whereby I would be attacked by introspection and the *internal dialogue*. There, I would be transported to place I was not sure I harboured enough *personal power* to withstand.

Yet shortly after seeing the young student with Robert's book, an unusual event had occurred – one both utterly banal in its commonality, yet profound in its magical consequences. I had been rooting through a trash-pile of old clothing, that a charity shop had tossed-out – with the items not being of good enough quality to even accept as donations.

In searching amongst the tattered sweaters and broken crockery, I had not expected to suddenly pull aside a strip of canvas, to reveal an old spotted mirror. It was the first time I had been confronted with a clear image of myself – and it stopped me dead in my tracks, almost mesmerising me.

Whilst I did not fully recognise the thinner face staring back at me, the remaining remnant of rationality knew it had to be 'me'. What was truly shocking, was that my hair – once a traditional family colour – was now stark white!

Robert would have assumed that his hair going white would make him look older. Yet, as I indulged in examining myself in the discarded mirror – almost for the first time in a year – the complete absence of colour curiously made me look significantly younger.

When had my hair turned snow-white? Was it shock or trauma? Was it that, which separated myself and Robert – the colouration the mere depth of a strand of hair? As I walked away panicked, I felt like I should know those answers. The questions only burned within me with a ferocity that denied understanding.

I realised that I should have recognised an *omen* – a manifestation of the *Great Flux*, in sympathetic communion with my own luminous cocoon. The self-reflection indicated of the student's book, had been more of a warning to me, than to the young woman. I should never have ventured into the temple of worship for intellectualisation and narrative.

It was the same night after seeing my image for the first time, that I started to come down with a mysterious sickness. Its onset came with an unusual aggressiveness.

For twenty-four-hours after looking at myself, I experienced an intense – yet isolated – patch of heat on my face. It was as though someone were shining a heat-lamp from above the left side of my head – intensely and externally heating only one isolated portion of my face. But equally, it was as though sensing the heat a foot or two away from my skin, on the tangible boundary of a larger surface area.

At first, it was considered as merely an intriguing curiosity. After all, my new life was full of such unique sensations.

Yet, bodily illness quickly consumed me. I was weak, exhausted, and a strange fever ravaged me. Even laying outside on the store-top roof, I could not get cool or rested enough. Every inch of my body hurt with a physical tenderness – every turn of my non-existent sleep, felt as an agonising pressure. It was though my skin were trying to reject the outside world of physical form.

The shadow of my own death sat mere feet away at a nearby skylight. It was silent, having long since stopped its conversation with me.

I knew this was no ordinary illness. Whether it was some trick of the occult from my encounter the psychiatrist-sorcerer, the psycho-somatic manifestation of guilt from injuring the homeless attacker, the reaction to confronting the reflection of *him*, or the final unravelling of the last vestiges of my civilised mind… I knew I had reached an impasse.

"Change comes regardless," was the last thing my death had spoken to me, almost with *her* voice.

Forcing description and cohesion on myself via a hospital visit, was automatically accepted as a foregone disaster. I simply would not survive that. Yet, I also knew that burying myself, or speaking with the little plants, would now be as insufficient.

Florinda had once undertaken – what Robert considered to be – a set of meditative practices with him. It had revealed the location of his *last battle on earth* – the place to make a gesture of his *last dance of power*, when death finally came for him at the end of his life.

It was alleged to be a collection of movements (of assemblage?) that a warrior gains throughout their trials and experiences of life. The more *personal power* they gather around themselves, the greater the final gesture allowed by death.

For any practitioner who had successfully undertaken the *recapitulation*, Florinda had once advised that there was no need for such a gesture with death – as there would be nothing left to express from such a formless being. "Such a warrior would already be prepared at a moment's notice for death!" she had claimed. "They live their lives already as their last dance."

Being quite full, Robert had been surprised (and quietly disappointed) to discover the *place of power* for his *last battle*, was a little raised mound within a swamp. There was none of the glorious mountain-scape or lush foliage he had wished for; no grand views, and no spiritual presence. Just cold, stinking bogland as far as the eye could see.

That, was where I now knew I had to go. Yet, I just did not have the *command of power* remaining to me, to pull off any abstract perceptual feat to get there. The purple-ish discolouration within a patch of my luminosity, prevented me from folding inwards. The reality of *the first ring of power*, was mercilessly hooked into my flesh and bones.

Equally, I had no linear sense of geography to guide me, not knowing where my last stand was to be performed. After all, Florinda had never bodily taken Robert there; and even if she had, Robert was hardly on speaking terms with me anymore.

No – to make my last gesture before death, I would have to get there the old-fashioned way... setting off on foot, for one last explorative adventure. Despite my physically agonising state, I knew it was what *power* demanded of me. And, I was resolute that I was not going to undertake my last living experience of this magical life, on a dirty, noise-infested rooftop, amidst the bustle of city clamour and pigeon droppings.

Slowly, I set off to the outskirts of the city. By now, I knew which isolated train stations I could hop on-and-off, with reduced chance of being caught. I rode the local train all the way out to the last isolated stop, making use of the toilet facilities to accommodate my diarrhoea. My being felt intent on rejecting everything with each step.

Once back on foot, I moved step-by-painful-step further away from the city. I had taken no belongings, and no food. Too painful and exhausted to feel hungry, I maintained no pretences about needing worldly possessions by the end of my journey.

As I passed-through dwindling villages, along country paths, and through less defined fields, the first enemy of man increasingly threatened me: fear.

After everything, I was certainly not afraid of dying. Robert himself had always been afraid of the circumstances immediately prior to his death – that of his last experiential circumstances of life. But even that was not the fear I now carried with me.

My shadow kept apace immediately behind me, kindly stopping to accompany every deliriously painful twinge I endured. It patiently waited, as the entire world shook in reaction to my death-spasms.

The fear I experienced, was death's quiet, cold breath behind my left ear, simply reminding me that my time was up. Only death's kindness was permitting me to make this one final trip, as a gesture towards our shared history. The pilgrimage itself, was the final dance allowed by a lifetime's acquisition of *personal power*.

In my obscured state, I just could not tell how long that lifetime had been – decades, or only a year? So, I did not know how much time I had left to make my gesture in the end.

The fear that gripped me, was that I would be too late. For what, I did not know. But every ounce of my feverish being was increasingly scared I would not arrive in time.

I walked. I searched. I hoped for *affirmations* and *omens*. I forced myself on. To where or what, I was not quite sure – other than, "the last place to make a stand, as only befits a warrior," as a white-haired witch had once told a ghost.

I felt wet. Whether that was from urine, diarrhoea, or my excessive sweating, I could not tell. It did not matter anymore. Pushing on, my body trembled with agony and effort, the very earth itself seeming to shake with each painful step.

The only thing that kept me going, was the sound of an electric-buzzing, like a motor boat or scooter engine. I knew it was the call of my *ally*. It was the little fox guiding me, to wrestle with it on the outskirts of perceptual reality. What else was there to do, when all else falls away? I had been resistant to the *ally* all along, yet now – when everything had been stripped from me, there felt an antidote to the fear: giving in completely.

The electric-buzz increased with each step. It would be nice to have some company at the end, I thought. With that weakening indulgence, my body doubled in excruciating spasm – like I had been tasered with the cumulative current of the *great unknown*.

Eventually, I found the swamp. Or more accurately, it may have found me. I could not have told you how many hours or days I had walked.

There was an old gnarled tree, atop a springy mound of green-blue grasses. Trudging to settle myself against its trunk, I no longer prioritised the first rule of homelessness – not caring how my boots and socks became waterlogged as I splashed through the swamp channels.

I would have been mindful of the noise too, lest I disturb the spirits of the area. But it is curious that at the end-of-life, how liberation proportionately flows from the cares left behind. There was freedom found in finally letting go of a lifetime's tension. I was exhausted.

I was now shaking with something more than cold and fever. Burying myself to re-align within the matrix of the *Great Mother*, would have once been a consideration. But, I now had no energy for that.

All I could do, was relax, allow, and let go – to give into the experience.

The swamp was misty, allowing no grand final view. I thought for a moment that my eyes were failing me. Murky patterns of blue-white floated past, like wraiths searching for the lost souls of the departed. Only the shadows of a few trees spoke of veiled earthly secrets nearby – my final companions to act as witness; the last clues to the presence of a world.

And yet, for all the bog's lack of wished-for majesty, I did experience a profound peace there. The earth was primordial and untilled. The tree was stunted, yet primeval, and spoke not of the hand of man. A beautiful hovering dragonfly told of the ancient lineage of life.

In fact, as desolate and deserted as the swamp first appeared, I could *see* it was teeming with life. Beetles, worms, flies, leeches and even bacteria, all thrived within the grey-green landscape. The simple existence and abundance of life, was beautiful.

Robert had felt naïve and foolish, for having secretly wished that his own *last battleground* to *dance for death*, would be something visually stunning and magnificent. He had hoped for a majestic plateau, or fairy-tale forest. Deep down, he had hoped it had been the stunning vista of 'don Juan's abode', which John and Teresa had built for him.

Yet, as I sat in the unremarkable drudgery of the swamp, I realised it was utterly perfect! The environment was impregnated with an ancient, unearthly stillness, the likes of which the city never knew.

The swamp held ancient knowledge. Its energy was a slow tempo of untouched time. The very air itself felt as though paused – the landscape holding its breath in respect of a profound secret just about to be revealed. Who would have guessed it – that at the end of all things, it was nothing but profound silence and stillness that I needed. Despite my worsening physical condition, I felt nothing but gratitude emanate from within my bones.

The crooked tree whispered something silent and soothing to me – it let me know my death would be of benefit to it, and so much else. I was not alone. I never had been. The *Great Mother* was soft, springy and comforting underneath. The nutrient-rich bog-waters teemed with endless life. The little tree held me up, supportive until my last breath. I could think of nothing more peaceful, than that moment right there in the swamp – the damp air infinitely still, the sounds muted, and the cruel harshness of form relaxing into nebulousness.

There had been no worse prospect for my last living experience of life (within perceptually-collapsed form), than the possibility of the fuss of people, the weight of expectation, the drone of dialogue, the imposition of strangers, the whir of machines, the clatter of hospice or hospital, the stink of awareness-numbing medication, and worse – the spectatorship of strangers.

Silence. It was such a simple and miraculous gift! There was power in silence!

I wanted to laugh. I was grateful at the end! I was just supremely thankful for every last crummy experience, of the harsh, tiresome battle of existence. It had all been… quite glorious!

I had finally passed-through the three gates I had been warned about: the gate of people, the gate of mind, and the gate of body. It was finally time to let go. I only fleetingly wished that my next reconstitution on the *great sheet of awareness*, somehow find more peace… somehow make it, where I had not.

I wanted to shift into *seeing*. I wanted it to be my last living experience – to *see* a living universe erupt with the golden luminosity of home. I assumed it would be the only proper gesture worthy of a warrior's last stand on earth.

I shifted my *assemblage point* with a final gesture of *intent*. Yet, the world did not explode into one final, glorious sight of an infinity of iridescent light threads.

As I lost cohesion, the last experience I had was of a little animal curling up in my lap – almost fox-sized. Despite the immense pain its gentle physical touch caused, I was grateful for its companionship.

Then, the world became black.

- 11 -

The Path of Knowledge.

(aka: Communion with the Four Directions.)

I was surprised to find myself waking. Or was it, disappointed?

It was still a misty day, albeit the sun was evidently beaming high above – trying its hardest to penetrate the thick mists. Columns of light meandered in-and-out of focus across the swamp, as though a great prison casting searchlights for an escaped convict. It gave the fog an unusual beauty of depth.

Despite the daytime, I had no idea just which day it was.

Tentatively easing myself up, I realised that all of my physical symptoms had passed. In fact, I felt surprisingly energised and alert, as though released of a burden.

As I straightened myself up, I saw something by my feet, next to a tumble of earth and rock. It was the corpse of a fox, which by look of the hallow ribcage, empty eye-sockets and leathery skin, had been there for considerable time.

Something had changed. What that was though, eluded me. There was a distinct energetic shift in my luminosity, as though bands of highlighted fibres were rapidly re-organising themselves. I had no idea what that meant, but it felt as the beginning of a wider process. Time, was ticking away.

Was I too late?

I opted to wash myself and my soiled clothes in the bog-water. It was not ideal, yet the thick curtains of vapour surrounding me through 360-degrees, created an ideal opportunity. The pools were icy-yet-refreshing. Even the mineral-rich, peaty smell of the grainy water felt comfortingly homely.

My wet clothes were freezing to the touch when I put them back on. However, it only left me feeling invigorated after my experiences of the previous day or two. Setting off at a brisk pace, I reasoned movement was the best way to keep myself warm – even if I had no idea which direction I was setting off towards.

The terrain rose sharply underfoot, becoming rockier and harder. Just as suddenly, I began a steep decline, having to remain wary of the increased foliage and slimy mosses underfoot.

The fog began to ease-up a little as I descended. It was clear I was making my way down towards an ancient forest. When the scattered mists allowed, the spooky shadows of stunted trees came into view, their branches twisted and bent with harsh centuries of enduring the wild exposure to the winds.

Robert had known a woodland like this once – of ancient trees purposefully left uncultivated by man, older than any city or town. It was a strange place, where the light itself looked to be tinged green. The mangled little trees had been ancient, draped in centuries of lichen and various epiphytes. That wood had the impossible flooring, covered in an endless and uneven array of giant boulders, of which the old trees twisted out of the cracks.

If I had found myself in the same place, I would know where I was. Yet, I felt as though I was progressing further into a deeper valley than Robert had. When the fogs momentarily receded, the sight of the forest expanded for many more considerable miles than the enclosed woodland Robert had encountered.

The latter-part of twilight was encroaching, whereby the world is lent a wash of infinite shades of blue-grey. The once-white fog was now a watercolour blend of shifting blues and blacks, and the trees became haunting shadow-figures diffused by vapour.

For an indulgent moment, I wished Robert were with me. As idiotic as he was, he had more of a clearly defined worldly orientation, and – with his love of labels and identification – may have known precisely where I was. Feeling a little confused, I briefly wondered what had ever happened to Robert, as though I should know the outcome to his story.

Figuring I had reached the bottom of the valley, the floor flattened out and the mists receded a little. There was a clear path underfoot, that ran straight north-to-south.

I thought that it may be a better – less exposed – place to stay for the night, reasoning the fog may have lifted in the morning. However, I noticed something curious in the darkness.

The trees on my right side, to the west, were an unexpected dark mass of oak, chestnut and silvery ash. This starkly contrasted to the trees on the left-hand-side of the path, being of much taller, and much darker, pine, fir and hemlock. The two seeming eco-systems should not have stood in such contrasting existence, merely opposite sides of a path.

Examining this curiosity more closely, it was then that I first saw the figure, stood like a sentinel just under the dark shadows of the edge of the western treeline. Reflexively, I jumped, though I did not call out.

It was unnerving, as the silhouette of the woman appeared to be watching me. However, she made no motion to engage or move. My first suspicion, was that perhaps the lady was lost.

There was something elusive-yet-felt familiar about the tiny woman. I took a step off the path, into the springy ferns and bracken, in order to get a better look.

The thought came to me that I should call out. However, I could not consciously recall how to do so.

As my eyes adjusted to the night-time hues, I realised with a greater jolt that it was Robert's mother! Yet, it was how he would have remembered her as a small child. His mother watched me, with a calmness in her eyes that she had never shown in life. But still, she made no move.

With increasing inspection, I realised that what I had taken for the silhouette of tree trunks behind her, where the remainder of Robert's family – set out in an ever-expansive triangle of ancestors.

Robert's father – again younger than should have been possible – stood only a step behind his former wife. A clear step behind the pair, where the recognisable figures of Robert's grandparents. Behind them standing silent, where eight adults who Robert had been shown from photographs, to be his great-grandparents. Their clothing was charmingly antiquated and threadbare.

Standing tall and chivalrous in the line behind the great-grandparents, was a man that I initially mistook to be Robert himself. He even emanated the same righteous air of feigned civility. Yet, the realisation came to me that this was merely a distant relative; albeit the transmission of genetic heritage was remarkably evident. The pair could have been mistaken as twins, had their manifestation not been separated by nearly two centuries.

The line of people within the trees, was clearly Robert's biological ancestry – countless individuals stretching out amongst the shadows, to merge with the blackness beneath the canopy. Each family member stood silent amongst the trunks, peering at me with an unspoken expectation.

A noise – or probably more accurately, a gentle tug at my mid-section – made me step back onto the path, and turn to the left. As my eyes turned in-line with my body, it was just as unnerving to find a host of similarly-paraded shadow-figures standing deathly still underneath the eastern trees.

I did not need to examine the foremost person standing just at the edge of the evergreen tree-line. The powerfully-built frame. The white hair. And those deeply amber eyes, almost glowing like a feline in the inky blues that appeared to blot the entirety of the scene. The warm glow of those old eyes, felt like the only colour possible of existing amongst the dark.

It was don Juan.

Behind the enigmatic old Indian sorcerer-figure, stood his teachers: the tall, dark-haired, burly figure of the Nagual Elias, and the smaller-yet-spry Nagual Julian, with his mischievous eyes. Behind them stood the Naguals Rosendo, Lujan, Santisteban, Sebastian, Miguel, Anam, Santiago, Jacinta, Tanok, Yaotl, Itzcali…

Standing alone on the path, I turned left-and-right to examine the generations on either side of me – each line fanning out into incalculable numbers into an old darkness beneath the trees. I could feel a choice looming – offered to me via the collective stares from either side. Without a single word ever being said, the weight of expectation felt almost tangible, being thicker than the dense whisps of fog gliding between us.

Robert, had always stubbornly and frustratingly reacted-out to being forced into making any sort of unsolicited choice. Myself… I was calm and clear, realising a choice must simply be made. It was the dictates of *power*; and who was I, to argue with the *Eagle's emanations?*

I was about to move, to commit myself – without ever knowing what that would actually entail. But something behind distracted me.

It was the faintest of light, casting a long, delicate shadow of myself ahead on the path. At first impulse, the faint glow could easily have been mistaken as the effect of moonlight. Yet, the moon was no-where near as bright that evening, being a mere clipping in the sky. Similarly, the shadow was so long, as to tell me the light-source was almost at ground-level. More telling, was that the light had a distinct blue-green luminosity to it.

Turning, I found the little fox-ally sitting patiently behind me. His coat glowed with a semi-iridescent shine, as though the fur fibres were hollow, and struggling to contain an inner ethereal radiance. I realised he was trying his best to represent himself as a fox.

"Choose neither," the *ally* offered as carefully as he could, without moving his black lips. "Shackle yourself to neither realm of human bondage. Come with me, to the edge of the forest, and there we can finally wrestle. Tether your luminosity to mine, and I can show you dazzling accomplishments of *power!* I have so many secrets of the earth to share with you, as to make you a *man of knowledge* unparalleled in the world of men! I can make you a living *Nagual*, the likes of which the world has never seen... even the old *Crow Nagual*," the fox tilted his head to his left, to indicate don Juan.

"You can lead your own lineage." The fox offered a little more quietly, in response to my silence of deliberation, adding with a careful whisper, "*Nagual Roberto.*"

"I can give you so much more, beyond the ways of *old seers* and kingfishers. I could lead you to *allies*, who know the secrets of *five-pronged Naguals*... who could make you the head of a new, modern line of *seers*. You would be a fierce Nagual, of which neither the old or new worlds have ever known!" the little canine promised.

"Or, I can take you to *him*..."

It had almost been inaudible. Yet, I knew exactly of whom he spoke: *The Death Defier* – the unique sorcerer-beyond-age, who had transcended known experience. *The Death Defier* was an energetic rupture disguised as a human, who had affected the lines of a thousand ancient sorcery lineages. *The Abomination*, as others called him, was the unique luminous-phenomenon who offered perceptual gifts as payment, in exchange for an offering of energy.

For a split-second, it was more tempting than I dared to admit.

The fox's light had been semi-encased and ethereal; delicate somehow. As such, I was a little unnerved when a sudden, bright-white star-burst exploded from behind me – casting a shadow as dark as the void, to the north. Encasing the little fox in complete obscurity, his own light was forced into shadow within the overpowering brilliance.

Turning, I held my hand up to shield my eyes from the intense radiance. Yet, this was not a light of electromagnetic waves, or experienced of the eyes. It could not be shielded with the mere contours of flesh.

My luminous body adjusted and re-aligned to the intrusion, and the harsh-whiteness shrunk back a little, to retreat back within form. A tiny butterfly flitted delicately to the south of the path. It struggled to contain the pure brilliance of the blinding white light – casting little dancing star-rays as its wings slowly flapped.

Suddenly, the butterfly-form exploded back outwards, as if struggling to maintain form in this world. A great supernova of intense-white light shot outwards in all directions.

Once again readjusting to the change in luminosity, I could *see* a perfectly round luminous cocoon of pure white light in front of me. It hovered a few feet above the path, and its surface-area was smoother than I had any right or framework to judge. Yet, within that impossibly-smooth surface light, rested a great attraction.

Turning, I could *see* the fox-ally was a blue-green *luminous egg*, floating behind me. However, unlike the completely balanced and self-contained white cocoon to my south, the fox's luminous form was a little elongated, with softer tendril-like fibres attaching it to the ground.

"Ignore him," came a reverberating voice from within the white form, almost like choral singing. "Forgo the world of people, leave behind brood and magician. Only with me, can you achieve true freedom. I will take you to boundless realms, beyond age, time, form, struggle and concern. As my companion within eternity, I will show you wonders your human form cannot hope to comprehend."

"With me," the mind-voice of the white cocoon promised, "you will know true release. You need never suffer human concerns ever again."

There was even more temptation in that possibility, than I had thought possible.

The white cocoon appeared to unravel one of its own white luminous fibres, taking care to unspin within the four-dimensions of reality, of which it was trying hard to contain itself.

As the infinitely-delicate white line – of a clarity, purity and intensity beyond what any concept of white is understood – uncurled within the air, what I could best describe as a portal opened. Behind the southern *ally*, a vortex of pure energy and speed opened – a promise of a scope of creativity and eternal existence, wrapped into immediate all-knowing comprehension. I understood that the dimension of time was unknown for such an alien assemblage. I only had to let go, and step forward with the butterfly *ally* – the being calling from the realm of the *nagual*.

The fox-form of blue-green luminosity repeated its offer of sorceric prestige and *power*. It sounded a little desperate, as though struggling to make a sufficient counter-proposal.

Robert's mother and ancestors looked on, with grounded, maternal eyes offering a level of earthly belonging Robert would have been unable to recognise. Don Juan examined me, with reassuring golden-copper eyes, yet which offered no sign of guarantee.

Something made me look down at my hands. They were physical: of weight, mass, length and tactile substance. Yet, they glowed a deep, translucent green – almost as though made of a cloudy gel.

There, on the left thumb, was a tiny scar, which Robert had procured as a child. He had gotten into a fight with one of his older brothers, having been thrown through a glass door.

The tiniest mark – but one of the earth, of history, of having belonged and existed. How had I come to bear Robert's mark?

I realised that I was in a *dreaming* state. Yet, I also knew it was no less real for that.

What a common man may consider as delusional, fanciful or unreal, I intrinsically knew had just as much substance as the ghosts-of-description that Robert had lived within. It was all only a matter of alignment.

In my stillness, I allowed the *Great Flux* to flow in, through, about and around me. The manifestations of *power*, were all part of the same fractal-dimensional medium of the *Eagle*; all on equal footing, all offering equally-empty promises.

With that, something about my own energetic existence imperceptibly shifted. The dream-image of the dark tree-world came to me, with its shifting golden light, its organic winds of intent, looked over by that one distinct star. There was a memory or hidden promise I was supposed to remember. It was woolly and indistinct, as the silhouette-shadows of the tree-ancestors.

The decision had already been made... a long time ago.

As if in acknowledgement of that realisation, the white light of the butterfly-ally retreated. The green-blue of the fox-ally began to recede. Darkness began to swallow the forms of Robert's family. And, the copper glow of don Juan's eyes began to diminish.

Power, was pulling away from me, like the tide retreats before the great wave of a tsunami. None of these paths held true *power*, only false promise.

"There are only four paths before you," the fox dared to offer, as a last desperate manoeuvre. "You must choose north, east, south or west!"

"No," I flatly replied from within the centredness of my mind. "There is an infinitude of ways... at least three-hundred-and-sixty degrees of choice, as far as I can *see*."

"So, which do you choose?" the now-dark fox asked, with genuine curiosity. For the first time, the vibration of fear emanated from his own realm.

"The only way I ever really could..." I said, heading out towards the diffused artificial orange-glow the distant city forced upon the night sky, "... I choose the *path with heart*."

- 12 -

Return.

(aka: Acquiescing to the Flow of Power)

I had returned to the familiar din and bustle of the city. Washing and eating, I chose to rest at the central location of the deconsecrated church.

I could feel the *designs of the Eagle* moving about me, manoeuvring me into place. I was merely a pawn in the endless breathing of the universe. And with that understanding – with a clear new wind blowing a cleansing current through the matrix of the *Great Flux* – the slightest cinder of regret threatened to consume me, as I went about getting my affairs in order.

Change. That one great rule of the *flow of power*, which can never be unbroken until the end of all things – when the *tonal* and *nagual* finally stop vying with each-other through the *sheet of awareness*. Until then, the two sides forming existence endlessly danced, imbuing the universe with a force of perpetual exchange.

Change… comes… regardless.

I almost heard her voice, as Robert once had. He had been such a fool to take her teachings so superficially, on a cheap cognitive level.

Sitting in the transept of the ruined church, I easily shifted into a balanced state of expanded luminosity. From there, I calmed the shine of my *assemblage point* from the side of the *tonal*, relaxing my focus, allowing my *intent* to shift a little out and inwards.

The glowing conduit – which encased such a minuscule part of my overall energetic being – followed and shifted, with a magnetic ease. It had a feel of inherent liquid reactivity. Its position, radius and movement were the simplest dictates of *intent* – even if that was largely unconscious and habitual to most people.

I knew I would lose that soon myself.

As my *assemblage point* sunk and expanded a little, a sense of gratitude rippled out as resonance. There had been relief in being released from forced imprisonment, of the habitual place of collapsed perception, anchored to the great banal view across the descriptive ocean of the *tonal*.

Too soon. All too soon.

There were a delicate band of fibres within my luminous cocoon, towards my mid-

151

left side – not that any perception of luminous reality had anything to do with three-dimensional tangible orientation. The tiny cluster of dormant bands – *seen* as asleep, due to the dulled nature of their shine – had not been permitted to run through the lens of the *assemblage point* for a year. The currency of *intent* they had been invested with, had been miniscule. Now, I allowed them to flow through the eight-dimensional conduit of perception; to be activated by the glowing caress of its attention.

The cluster of isolated luminous fibres lit-up almost excitedly, humming with a delicate amber inner radiance. I could *see* the lines running through and out of my form, off into the great wash of the boundless luminous landscape. I knew where they ended… or at the least, who they ran-through on their wider journey to *infinity*. At the end of those delicate lines of luminosity lay the *Eagle* itself; yet I had to stop much sooner in that journey.

A tug of feeling from the seat of my *will*, exploded as a point-of-brilliance that shot-off down the small cluster of fibres. They gently danced in newly-activated excitement.

I took a moment to consider the underlying vibration of luminous-awareness itself – to consider its 'energetic signature', as the fox-ally would have put it. It was simply, potently, radiantly and beautifully… *compassion*. It flooded me. It linked me. It was something I had been aware of – to varying degrees – all along. Compassion, was the fundamental resonance of awareness itself.

A dying *knowing* came to me: my luminous manoeuvre was the *sorcerer's beacon*. It was pure magic – being the intentional manipulation of perception; an energetic undertaking that even the *sorcerers of antiquity* seldom used. After all, the *old seers* were solitary and sombre creatures – preferring the dazzling delights of the *unknown*, and the petrifying exhilaration of the *unknowable*. They had secretly hoarded their *knowledge* like dragons, not sharing their gold.

How could any fellow human compare to such treasures? No; the *sorcerers of old* had instead chosen *infinity*. They shied-away from their fellow men. Whilst easily retaining the means, there had been seldom any need to send such a signal. Yet, in the end, their isolation had cost them dearly.

Climbing the tumble-down remains of the city-facing tower, I pulled myself up into the beloved first-floor room. Sitting at the stone windowsill watching the hub-bub outside, I ate a little piece of cheese, which I had found when passing a children's play area. Some infant's drool-ridden leftovers. But, it was enough for me. Its taste and potency were utterly delightful and satiating! The vibration of its taste, was experienced almost as singing.

I laughed. Robert would have been grossed-out by the idea of eating left-over scraps found in public. Yet now, I accepted that it would not kill me. My ancient body born of a collective species, had evolved to be rather efficient at handling the awareness of bacteria and microbes. I had a new faith in my immune system to look after me – not requiring the hand-sanitisers, gels and anti-bacterial sprays that modern man had become so obsessed with. Nowadays, entire industries were based on profiteering from perpetuating the fear of the unclean. What *old seer* could have conceptualised such dark magic, cast of such a monstrous scale?

No; it would not be the little germs of an infant that killed me. I knew it would one day be *power*, my command of *personal power* – my position within the *Great Flux* – would be what finally did me in, moving me into a direct relationship with my death. Yet, that was not going to be today, it seemed.

I settled down for the night. The din and bustle of the city noises lulled me into sleep, alongside the coos of the pigeons above in their own slumber – their tiny forms like little grey-purple gargoyles looking down from above.

That dream again. The one of the vast, dark horizon of the beautiful world of shadow-trees. The mellow copper globe of the sun; the ripples of warm amber light, flitting through an infinitude of unseen individual leaves far down below, like golden waves surfing a vast ocean.

Collectivity. Connectivity. Something else…

The same sense of familiarity. The feeling I should recall *something*. I just had to let the same light flow through me. *Allow it*. It was right on the tip of my tongue!

That dark world was not the earth as I knew it. It was a representation. It was the collective awareness of all of humanity.

Each of the individual dark leaves represented a thought, impulse, feeling or construct – attached and blooming form of the singular being, of each individual tree making up the darker continental forest mass. The boundless dark world of the impossibly-infinite tree-scape, was humanity itself – the same, great growing organism with its interconnected roots deeply hidden within the earth.

As the invisible winds of *intent* blew across the canopy of the massive forest, the individual leaves lit from within, as the breeze caressed over them. At that gentle whisper of life's touch, a brief golden luminosity revealed the beauty of inner structure within each leaf, as it passed through. The wind ran across the black mass of human collective form, with beautifully delicate ripples of luminosity surfing over the treelines in response.

As the light flourished within each individual leaf, thought, perception and form came into being. But just as magically as life glowed to existence, so too did it as easily dissipate back into a state of quiet darkness – of subdued potentiality – as the winds moved on to massage the wider contours of mankind's forest-mind.

Thought, form and perception were all too fleeting and precious. They were mere blooming echoes – beautiful, infinitely-delicate and oh-so-transient in their fleeting unrealness. They were so truly magical in their manifest form of structured emptiness.

At last – with a briefly-painful burst of radiance from my own leaves – I recognised the solitary lilac star shining out amongst the radiance of the celestial infinitude. It asked me to look up at the dazzling heavens, rather than to the warm appeal of the forest below. The guiding bright star looked back at me.

I awoke, sitting in the full-lotus position as usual. Despite my ordeal of the preceding few days, I came to, feeling rested and whole… ready. I would miss this *power spot*. I would miss so much… of which, I would only later forget. I knew I would lose so much… or rather, gain too much. Yet, I *saw* how the *Eagle's emanations* now receded, wholly immune to my wants. My own leaves were becoming dark once more.

Someone else's wave would manifest here at some time-and-place. My own was waning.

There was a noise from down below; from within the main section of the church. The scrape of wood on stone felt jarring, and I momentarily struggled to recall the other erratic and jerky sounds. They were harsh on the ears, almost artificially generated.

Voices! They were the sounds of human conversation! I almost laughed to myself. How long had it been?

I lowered myself down from the hole in the ceiling without making a sound. Once upon a time, Robert would have been pleased with that simple grace-of-acrobatic achievement. Now, I merely moved like a shadow, thinking nothing of it, yet grateful for the last moments of peace it allowed.

"... your fault!" the taller young lady with the nest of glossy, curly hair accused the old man. "He did what he did, because of your stupid games!"

She was angrily pointing at the old man, seated upon what remained of a graffitied pew. Yet, the doe-eyed woman kept a distance from him, as though scared he could physically harm her, despite the gulf of age and his use of a cane.

Indeed, it was curious to note how the young woman had manoeuvred her dourer companion between them. More curious, was how unconcerned for her own welfare the more dishevelled woman seemed. Instead, she merely spoke unheard words to an unseen companion. Smiling, I could well understand the appeal of that.

An old, disused feeling flitted awake inside me.

"You foolish girl!" the old man retorted. He looked worn by more than her youthful accusations. "Maria Elena... your own founder... deliberately pitted our lines against each other! What else was I supposed to do, but act *impeccably* in-line with the rule of the *three-pronged Nagual?* If you were any sort of legacy to *her*, you would realise that!"

I knew that last painful reference, was not to the former Native American cohort of the infamous author-anthropologist. The old man sunk into himself a little, as though referencing the white-haired witch was too painful for him. He was clearly struggling to maintain himself.

"You've cost us everything!" the young lady screamed at him, holding back her tears amidst the ruins of the church. Empty spray cans, drug paraphernalia and dirty magazines littered about the three visitors. They appeared just as out-of-place in the squalor, as did the remains of the saints carved into the walls.

"No..." my voice croaked, feeling alien for not having been used for a year, "he hasn't."

The three of them stopped dead in their argument, staring wide-eyed at my unexpected intrusion. They looked as if having seen someone rise from the grave.

"In fact," I said, getting used to the sound of Robert's voice again, "we should be grateful, as he given us everything."

"You!" Josephina gasped. "Where?... How?... I mean..."

Elizabeth merely ran over to me, giving me a great squeeze of a hug.

"You stink... and you're grubby," she released me with a smile. "But, I like your new look!"

"You're… you're back?" Josephina hesitatingly queried, understandably hesitant to look to me for reliability. "It was actually you who called us? I never thought we would see you again. I… I mean, we…"

"… we thought you were too far gone," Elizabeth finished for her, with a frankness-of-fact as she examined my uncharacteristic appearance. She impulsively offered me a lint-covered candy found from inside her sleeve.

Catching Henrick's look of incredulity, I offered, "What? No psychiatric advice this time?"

He only shrugged his shoulders in response, as though to say, "You can't blame a guy for trying."

As the impeccably-dressed old man rose from the bench, I saw how he was fiddling with something in his pocket. I got the distinct impression that he was deliberating whether it was wise to risk a sorcerer's attack.

"Don't' bother Henrick," I stopped him in his tracks. "Your line is done. It's over."

"You cannot *know* this," he accused, although his voice betrayed that he actually did.

I did not need to argue with the *Paladin of Intent*. *Seeing*, let me *know* that he was haemorrhaging *personal power*. It was abandoning him in favour of those around him. It was clearly intertwining me, and re-constituting the two women, even if they currently could not *see* it. Yet, I knew I too was rapidly losing the ability to *see* it too.

I recognised the irony, that the head of the current *three-pronged lineage* was bleeding-out *personal power* to three lesser wayfarers. He would be furious by that, as well as made impotent.

The *Omega Assembly* could try. They could continue to hunt *The Death Defier* and the re-constituted manifestation of the anthropologist's awareness. But, they were now finished. Even if successful in finding *The Death Defier*, that being could but *see* the dregs of their *power*, and only offer them gifts of destruction.

The fallen members of the *Omega Assembly*, would be best pursuing lives of happiness, personal contentment and dedicated-purpose. Yet, I knew they would not. It was their damning legacy that they could not. The anthropologist had seen to that so long ago, in the Mexican desert. *Power*, was a funny thing. The return of *intent* was a cruel joke of the universe.

A strange sensation of empathy washed over me. It was a shadow of Robert's. I could feel its fingers working its way back in under my skin.

Striding behind Henrick, I moved to a fallen stone basin that had collected fresh rain water. Stooping, I delighted in the vibration of refreshing coldness. I would miss such simple truths of direct experience. More than dirt was being rinsed away.

Running my wet hands through my longer hair, I immediately knew that the whiteness was washing out. It was reverting back to Robert's old colour… *my* old colour.

Josephina and Elizabeth jointly gasped at my theatrics.

"How… how did you do that?!" Josephina held her chest in amazement, almost as though she had been struck.

"It was a sorcerer's manoeuvre," I flatly offered, knowing it would explain nothing to their stubbornly reasonable and linearly descriptive minds. Was this the gentle amusement Florinda had so often taken in Robert's... no, *my*... company?

"A mere act of *intent*. My *assemblage point* is shifting back, and I am on borrowed time to perform such trickeries."

"You've been playing all of this goddamn time?!" Josephina indignantly shrieked. "After all you've put us through... it was all an act?!"

"No," Henrick quietly offered, peering intensely at me with his sharp emerald eyes. "He pulled off a true act of *stalking*, the likes of which the Nagual Julian himself would have been proud."

He had not meant it as a compliment. The old man was suddenly pale with the dawning realisation of his own folly.

Josephina appeared adamant in her determination to be offended. Holding my hand up, I cut-off her verbal onslaught.

"This past year was no mere deception," I explained. I was hesitant, but only because it felt like I was rapidly losing something precious – taking a step further away from true *knowledge*, with every word I spoke. "I truly was homeless. I truly was... no-one."

"You weren't just pretending?" Elizabeth quietly asked, desperate for confirmation that I had not intentionally deceived her. Of the two women, I had always felt most like a protective sibling towards Elizabeth.

There was that growing feeling again.

"Not at all. I finally took Florinda's teachings on-board..." I tried my best to explain, knowing it would be insufficient.

"How dare you say her name?!" Henrick spat, with barely-contained rage.

"... I finally got out of my own way, and owned the name *Abelar*," I continued, oblivious to the fury within the old man's watering eyes. "I *stalked* myself... ironically, by dropping such labels entirely."

"What you did to achieve that," the old man snarled. "That woman was more than you could ever dare to dream!"

"Very true," I calmly admitted, becoming familiar to the sound of Robert's voice occupying my throat. "Yet, the point of my *stalking*, was something you and your line have not yet conceived. And that, was to your detriment old man."

His green eyes flared and flittered. Comprehension was slowly coming to him, just ahead of my words.

Explaining how Florinda had visited me amidst the trials of Amsterdam, she had momentarily taken me aside from the chaos to explain the situation – how the joint-lineage leader, Maria Elena, established the two lines in respect of the *rule of four* and the *rule of three*. In her *impeccability*, Maria Elena had wanted the designs of the *Eagle* to manifest as they naturally should, thus granting each lineage proper opportunity to thrive.

After decades of co-existence, Amsterdam represented a crucial divergence in the mutual running of both lines. It centred on a schism surrounding the mysterious thirteenth member... myself. The juncture had apparently been foretold years earlier, by two oracles, partly resulting in the misidentification of another thirteenth practitioner – the mistake in itself an inheritance of the *Coyote Nagual.*

What I had not told my cohorts... or even been able to admit or perceive for myself... until then, was that when Florinda had taken me aside, forcibly dislodging my *assemblage point* from its habitual position. She had given me her equivalent of the *Nagual's blow*, shifting me into a state of *altered awareness.*

This, is an alternative state of perceptual acuity and cohesion, within which the likes of temporal speed and cohesion flow differently. There – in the *left side of awareness*, with the *assemblage point* shifted over more towards the *nagual* – Florinda offered additional teachings.

The difficulty with left-side transmission, is that not only is the student vulnerable, but they subsequently forget the experiences and details. This is due to their inevitably shifting back to their *right-side* state of 'normal' being, under the *tonal's* customary dominance – being party secured by the wider influence of *collective intent.*

Such lessons may manifest as niggling half-memories (at best). They may appear as dreams, requiring decoding. They can even surface as problem behaviours or physical illness – desperately trying to manifest into right-side awareness, without destroying the protective mechanisms of the descriptive *tonal*, with its addiction to a singular continued narrative, familiarity, *personal history* and everything 'explainable'.

Teachings to both the right side (normal) and left-side (magical) perceptual realms has both its benefits and drawbacks. Within *altered awareness*, the student can be more open to direct demonstration, the handling of *will*, and less reactionary to what can be called 'magical' states of reality.

The immediate down side to such dualistic teachings, is that the student typically loses all conscious memory, when their perceptual reality inevitably shifts back to their usual position of cohesion. The profound lessons and bizarre experiences are repressed, or explained away. The magic, is forgotten.

Engaging in left-side teachings can ultimately be damaging to an apprentice, especially if their right-side awareness is already given to neuroticism, moroseness, or unhealthy habits. The re-surfacing or semi-surfacing quasi-memories can cause the student to go quite mad – itself still a protective mechanism of the *tonal*, in desperate attempt to safeguard's its usual dominance over the wider being. After all, it is still better to be reassuringly stark raving mad, than recognise mankind's infinitesimally-small understanding of the *great unknown!* The former merely strings together a different (socially-fractured) narrative; the latter, offends the central-pin of *self-importance* which holds together the entire *myth of self.*

The savvy sorcerer can utilise left-side teachings for a more impactful transmission – as a bolstering tool, but not a full alternative. Left-side teachings allow the student to archive luminous *knowledge,* encoded within the fibres of awareness outside of their usual perceptual positioning. Then, with timing or accumulated self-ownership of *personal power,* the teacher can ensure the lesson manifests and is properly understood – representing true *knowledge*, outside of right-side limitation alone (including temporal limitation) – just when it has the most fortuitous impact.

Part of the budding student's efforts thus focus towards *cleaning the island of their tonal* – insomuch as reorganising their lives around the concept of *impeccability*, and re-aligning their archived luminous fibres, to bring them under the halo (attentional recognition) of the *assemblage point*. Thus, the apprentice regains conscious awareness, and a command-of-being, that was seemingly implanted in another time and place – yet which now possesses them with an uncharacteristic strength of self-ownership and dualistic counter-existence. The sum becomes greater than either part.

In some respects, such a sorceric phenomenon can be considered alongside classic psychology memory recall – whereby human memory is recognised as a rather fragile and generalised, active and on-going retrospective reconstruction. In cognitive understanding, the mind can only recall certain memories or information, based on the co-existing conditions of (contextual) 'cues'. If the external prompt (cue) – such as a specific study environment, chemical ingestion or emotional mind-state etc – is absent, the memories remain vague or forgotten.

The act of recalling left-side luminous teachings are similar, insomuch that they rely on the conditions of developing enough self-discipline and *impeccability*, as to dislodge the *assemblage point* enough, in order to move it back to the same luminous position of the original teachings. With sorcery, one is essentially dealing with 'assemblage cues'.

Thus, it becomes a rather taxing and infuriating – and indeed, actually quite dangerous – affair for the sorcery apprentice to recall fundamental teachings and experiences. With modern humankind being predominantly dominated by the rational and narrative-obsessed side of the linear consistency of the *tonal's* dominance, there is massive resistance to even recognising left-side teachings (altered awareness), let alone utilising them. Much like a petulant toddler, the *tonal* would much rather break the mind, than concede dominion to alternative influence.

As I explained, Josephina looked outraged, as to not feeling subject to Florinda's equal investment. She looked at me, the same way I must have looked at her so many times.

I wanted to appease Josephina… comfort her. Robert would be back in full possession soon enough. At any moment, I would be the petty fool quarrelling with her once again.

Whilst time allowed, I continued to explain. In Amsterdam, the *Omega Assembly* had forced me into an impossible choice: to join them, fully relinquishing myself in their warped efforts to obtain unfathomable levels of *power*, or for Florinda, Josephina and Elizabeth to be injured… or worse.

In taking me aside, Florinda had told me in advance of the awful choice that would be forced upon me. Being a peerless practitioner, she could clearly *see* it, as an unmistakable manifestation of *power*. Events were cumulating just as the *Eagle's* design. The old lady had said between wide, smiling cherry lips, that she could *see* more clearly as *will* manifested. It all felt quite inevitable to her, and I had been in awe of her lack of resistance.

Yet, I had fretted. I had pleaded. I had argued with her. Florinda had only laughed, as she so often did in my presence.

"What have I taught you dear boy," she had prompted through smiling blue-purple eyes, "when life presents you with two implacable options?"

"To always seek the third option," I had begrudgingly admitted in that cosy Amsterdam parlour. "We find the unexpected possibility... the path born of creativity... the *warrior's way.*"

Nursing my tea in front of that fire, Florinda's final teachings to me, had been to explain *the shadows of personal history*: twelve inter-related *tales of power*, of defining moments of our lineage.

Yet, there was another ghost of a memory running parallel to that too. She had also taken the time to relay the tale of *The Death Defier* – the immortal, all-powerful rupture-of-a-being, inherent to the human layer of awareness. Whereas the *Omega Assembly* coveted the ancient deathless sorcerer as a fountain of secrets and *power*, Florinda's line – the true energetic heirs of the Nagual Juan – found *The Death Defier's* existence to be abhorrent.

For the *Omega Assembly*, Florinda's second tales would have been hugely profitable. For her, they were an anomaly and teaching tool. For myself, they had been provided as a warning.

The two co-existing narratives – of *the shadows of personal history*, and the tale of *The Death Defier* – sat impossibly within the memories reclaiming my mind. Yet, I understood it as more than the transmission of words or ideas. It had been the *simultaneous* telling of both sets of stories – one to my *left-side awareness*, whilst the other was concurrently relayed to my *right-side awareness* – which the old lady had artfully utilised as a tool in itself. In transmitting two stories simultaneously, it had been enough to dislodge my *assemblage point* from its usual position. For Florinda, the art of storytelling had been a legitimate sorcerer's manoeuvre in itself.

As I explained, a green flash of greed crossed the old man's hungry eyes. He wanted to know what Florinda had revealed to me. To Henrick, I represented a final flare of desperate hope.

"You still don't get it do you?" I gently guided him to realisation. Josephina and Elizabeth watched engrossed, as if their moving would break a spell. "Florinda's teachings within the *second attention* were merely a tool. Interesting stories. *Tales of power...*"

"Her name is sullied in your mouth!"

Despite everything... after all of this time... I could see the decades of painful love the old man still carried for her. In that moment, I saw the art of Maria Elena's masterful manoeuvre – in setting this perfect pair up against each other with competing lineages. Mutually-running hate and love had been the impetus the lineages had needed. They had been bound and pre-destined all along, by the simple commands of their entwined *intent*.

"Now Maestro Henrick; it is you that do not *see* the awesomeness of your love's *impeccability*," I offered slowly, aware to his hand on the grip of his cane, that contained a blade. "It is you, that do Florinda a disservice, in underestimating her."

I knew I was on dangerous ground. At any moment I could prompt the cobra to strike. Yet, in order to finish what was started – in order to seal *power* shut over the abomination of the *three-pronged line* – I must finish Florinda's work.

"I know what you did," he growled in trembling rage. "I watched you kill her!"

"You saw no such thing." I casually waived a hand, as if swatting away an irksome fly.

"But Rob... we also saw..." Josephina interjected, seemingly surprised at herself for taking Henrick's side. I could detect the machinations churning in her head: *what if he really is mentally ill?*

"When Florinda took me aside in Amsterdam, she pushed me into *altered awareness*. From there, she used the tales as an energetic framework, within which to anchor her true instruction – to be activated at just the right time, when my *tonal* should be challenged just enough, and shrink back, to action her plans from within an uninterrupted and unimpeded *nagual-state*."

"Of course, she relied upon you shrinking my *tonal* in the first place, to act as a trigger to activate me," I offered to an insulted Henrick. "To which, you played your part brilliantly."

Josephina and Elizabeth exchanged uncomprehending looks with each other.

Leaning forward, as if revealing a secret, I continued, "Florinda made you *see*, exactly what she wanted you to *see*. In that sense, you too helped her," I smiled, more at the memory of the old woman's astounding *impeccability*. "As a peerless *seer*, Florinda knew precisely the cheap power-play the *Omega Assembly* would attempt to manipulate. As such, she played your group like the self-blinded fools you were."

Henrick's eyes searched my own, for signs of deceit or mistake. He only found devastating resolve.

I explained that Florinda had – via masterful command of her own *intent* – manipulated the *assemblage points* of all present in that Amsterdam basement. It had not been too hard, given the agitated state everyone had been within, in the tense stand-off. The instability-of-assemblage, had only been exacerbated by the close proximity to the *ancient seer's* burial site.

The result – or rather, the only rational interpretation left open to the linear constructs of the *assemblage points*, as anchored firmly in-place by Florinda on the side of the *tonal* – was that I had outwardly kicked the old lady hard in the chest. To them, I had broken her ribs and neck with the brute force of my blow, forcing her over the lip of the abyss, into the cold darkness below. Their eyes had watched full of description; yet none of them had truly *seen*.

From the solidity of their perspective, I had killed Florinda. Even afterwards, to my own unreliable recollection – to the inevitably stubborn re-orientation of my own *tonal-influenced assemblage position* – I had done such an evil and unthinkable thing.

With Florinda's assistance gone, my *tonal* had immediately tried to force my *assemblage point* back to its habitual spot, of cohesive reality... and failed. Yet, there was greater reason for the failure.

Florinda's teachings in *left-side awareness*, had also implanted a temporal schism – a timer of sorts – within my luminosity. Given the unavoidable cognitive and emotional dissonance such an act would cause within my usual self-narrative, it was clear the habitual cohesion of my *tonal* would suffer. It would be challenged. It would be nudged out of a place of comfort and reliability.

It would cause a release of luminous energy.

"Are you saying…" Josephina's large brown eyes were wet with hesitancy. "Are you saying she is… alive?"

It was in revealing what happened, that I felt truly remorseful towards Josephina – compassionate as to how much pain I would cause. She had idolised the old woman, as we all had.

"She knew what she was doing," I attempted to reassure. "In fact, it was her brilliance that constructed the energetic manoeuvre. But I'm afraid not Jo."

Elizabeth grabbed her stumbling cohort, almost as though she had been struck from a blow.

"She's… she's really gone then?" Elizabeth looked at me with pleading eyes.

I smiled.

"I'm afraid… also, no."

Incomprehension furrowed Josephina's usually-pretty face. The women even exchanged confused looks with Henrick – who appeared not to know whether to hope or hate.

"Like all things on this annoyingly-confusing path we have chosen to walk on, consider the old lady un-alive," I offered, smiling at how I now sounded just like her in my annoyingly confusing terms. Once, I would have hated that. "Or, perhaps un-dead; or non-dead-yet-not-alive. She is both and neither – beyond our realm of maddening duality."

The pained looks of the two struggling women prompted me to explain further.

"Florinda knew the *designs of the Eagle* were drawing a long-due schism within the jointly-running lineages, untangling the threads of *intent*. The unique time of the *mysterious thirteenth* was rising. Decades of confusion, starting from the time of the Nagual Carlos' misidentification, were soon to be remedied."

"Naturally, Florinda wanted her line – don Juan's true heirs – to flourish," I was watching Henrick closely. "To this end, she sacrificed herself, but not in the bodily way your *tonals* could only interpret."

"No! No! No…" Henrick was shaking his head, as if trying to dislodged a painfully unwelcome thought.

It was then that I realised he had been having the same recurrent dream – of the dark tree-world of *collective intent*, and the lilac star looking down from the cosmos. And it was only now, like myself, that I saw he was finally understanding its significance.

"The wily ol' girl enabled me to pull off a cheeky manoeuvre. I did not kick her with my foot; rather, I gave her a massive infusion of my own luminosity, helping launch her energy body far out into *infinity*."

"But… but, just where is that?" Josephina trembled.

"Right here," I opened my arms, knowing the explanation – as real and accurate as it was – would be wholly insufficient for her.

"That awful cracking sound we all heard, and were traumatised by," I clarified, "was actually the product of my *double* coming out of the top of my head. Your *tonals* could only interpret it one way though; especially as Florinda anchored them in that place."

I held up my hand to block Josephina's inevitable questions. "Don't ask me how I did it, as Florinda had placed me in a rather unique perceptual state. Even now, as I take back on-board the old disguise of Robert, everything is becoming annoyingly hazy... like several concurrent dreams I have just had, but which are all too quickly fading in the cold harshness of so-called reality."

"So you *have* been acting all along, this past year?" Josephina insisted, as if she needed it to be true.

I explained that the force of Florinda's input in Amsterdam – and my subsequent actions – had been so tremendously inconsistent with my typical idea of 'self', that it had caused a splintering in the *internal dialogue* as usually maintained by my *tonal*. Subsequently, I had not been capable of holding together the previous description of 'Robert' as a cohesive self-myth. He... I... had needed time to regather our resources.

Simultaneously, the raw energetic cost of pulling my *double* ('*luminous body*', or '*other*') out, had taken a year to reconcile. It had been a strange, disjointed year of profound insight, painful inconsistency, and what would ultimately be irreconcilable loss.

Essentially, that rupture-in-self, had been the effect of my energetic investment to Florinda's luminous body – the cost of my aiding her to reach the border of *the third attention*. It had taken all of that time, bathing myself within the collective luminous field of the city's inhabitants – with its template of structuring *tonal* – to help re-energise me, and coax my *assemblage point* back to its former position.

In response to Elizabeth's equal hope that she too may be right, I also had to explain that I was not mentally ill either. Somewhat strangely, it seemed to disappoint her.

"You're trying to reason things out," I explained to the women; "trying to push things neatly into this or that. That's only your *tonal's* machinations; and they are wholly insufficient for the sheer mastery of Florinda's luminous achievement."

"You have been *stalking* all this time," Henrick offered, not as a compliment, but as begrudging proof that he still comprehended. "Like the Nagual Julian of old, you pushed your *assemblage point* to the wholly unique place it needed to be. You became the perceptual reality you needed to be..."

"I was truly homeless. Truly no-one," I conceded. "In view of what I had done, it was the only way I could be. It was the only possibility of ever coming back."

Josephina doggedly insisted it had to have been a pretence – maybe an elaborate act, but an intentional deceit none-the-less. A great swathe of sympathy flooded over me for her, for how she was struggling. I could feel her *tonal* aggressively rallying to smooth-out the luminous fibres of a narrative that only extended so far.

Explaining that the last year had been unique for me, I tried to clarify how it was a truly unprecedented learning period – surpassing anything I had ever experienced. It had been a true act of *stalking*, as worthy of the *old seers*. The *assemblage point* had been pushed to cover wholly new bands of reality. That was as close to being someone else, as anyone could get.

What I did not reveal to my cohorts, was how quickly I already felt dumb and coldly-disconnected. The tell-tale sign was that whilst I could still remember quasi-memories of turning into the likes of a kingfisher, I was unable to recall any procedural framework for doing so. Worse, was that I was experiencing a growing point-of-angst at being unable to sufficiently explain the inconsistent memories – or were they now dreams? That dissonance, was the hallmark that Robert's old worldview was quickly descending on me, reclaiming its old dominion.

Henrick laughed cruelly, "Then you have gone and ruined your own life in the process! You have nothing! No *power!* And now..." he peered at me intensely beneath his white brow, "now the old foolish ghost of Robert possesses you once again. You're losing even your new found freedom!"

I felt his taunt more keenly than I cared to admit. There was a weight... a cloud... an engulfing landslide of narrative... and a loss of something pure and precious... with every second the memory of 'Robert' solidified within the old empty space of my mind.

"I've lost nothing," I lied to Henrick. "All along, Florinda... John... Teresa... Jon-Paul... Meili... they all warned me from the beginning, that I would be a fool to face the *path of knowledge* without a back-up plan."

A tell-tale judgement of Robert's had re-possessed me, as I reflexively glanced to Elizabeth and Josephina. I knew the women would have little appreciation of a back-up plan... a 'plan-B' or 'safety net'. For better or worse, they had always had other people there to look after them, to save and bolster them when required.

Smiling, I realised that my own parent's ineptitude and indifference – their very inability to look after me – had been one of their truly greatest gifts. I had unwittingly grown into an adult who always went into every situation having pre-prepared an alternative. It was a sign of a natural *stalker*, Florinda had told me.

I briefly indulged in a curious thought: was a *stalker* made, or born? I figured it made as much sense as asking, whether people were the cause or effect of *intent*. Meili would appreciate my new *mind mine*.

A strange pang of gratitude washed over me, finally extending out to my parent's. They had each tried their best, in truly taxing circumstances. And the failure of their best, truly had been a gift to me all along. It had taken years of grooming from my teachers – and a year of something else entirely – for me to fully recognise the true sacrifice my parents had made. A lifetime of their own misery and suffering had been the cost, in order to bring to fruition a child with the proper intentional heritage of detachment.

Only now, did I finally recognise the beauty of the gift they had inadvertently provided me with all along. They... my childhood... really could have been no different, if I were not to manifest right here-and-now. It was they, who had set me on *the path of knowledge*, since before my conception. With my dying eyes, I could *see* the threads of *intent* floating back across generations and lifetimes, being much wider and connective my own solitary cocoon.

Responding to the blank expressions on the women's faces, I explained that once Florinda had finished talking with me in Amsterdam – and I was back within typical *right-side awareness* – I had made one simple phone call.

For several years, I had lived in the house of a woman, Isabella. She had witnessed my growing association with Florinda and the group. And, despite her own unorthodox practices under the vague guise of 'spiritualism', Isabella had worried – or more, made accusatory threats – that I had joined a cult of sorts.

Her judgement of my new lifestyle had finally forced her to provide an ultimatum: to cut all ties with the group, or to leave her house. I had left. Isabella had been furious – not because I had abandoned her, but simply because I had refused to acknowledge that she had been 'right'.

Yet, even with the bitterness between us, I knew Isabella and the flavour of her judgements very well. Whilst still angry at me, if she thought for a moment that she could 'save' me from the 'cult', she would not hesitate. Her own *self-importance* – disguised as more self-aggrandising, spiritually-lacquered altruism – was easy to play.

Thus, I made Isabella my unwitting back-up plan.

I had apologised to her, speaking directly to the *self-importance* of her *internal dialogue*. Confessing with acted embarrassment that I may have gotten involved with a nefarious cult after all, I pantomimed just how frightened I was. I played on my upbringings, cursing myself for being foolish enough, not to see how my weak identity and isolation had left me vulnerable to brainwashing!

I also made a point to perform this ritualistic appeasement in-front of her 'spiritual' friend-group. That way, I knew lay a far more soothing courtship of her *self-importance*. After all, John had taught me that the (re)enforcement of *ego* – of the *personal myth* of *'self'* – was achieved in principal relation to other people. He had maintained, that there could be no sense of 'self', without external reference to the 'other' – without validation of the story via other reference points of awareness. Thus, to bolster anyone's *internal dialogue*, John had advised it was always most effective to do so in a social setting, as befits a true *stalker*.

Florinda had claimed that I had hooked Isabella's group – using my *intent* to influence their *assemblage points*, so that they could in-turn rally Isabella's *tonal*. The old lady claimed that it had been a worthy act of a true sorcerer.

Isabella had lapped it up. She was practically salivating in self-congratulatory narrative.

It was as such, that with Isabella cast in the role of my 'saviour', that she agreed to become my power of attorney. I granted her a level of personal access to my life, which I had thus far not extended to the most intimate of people, even former romantic relationships. It had been a hard lesson in itself, for me to let go of my own *self-importance*, and allow someone the possibility of controlling my life.

I signed legal papers over to Isabella. I got important documents and detailed agreements drafted and notarised. She was witnessed-in as the go-to person within all important aspects of my life, should something ever happen to me. Being alone in the world, she merely assumed I was acting responsibly. I was, but not in everyday terms.

Despite her own evolved claims of spiritual enlightenment, Isabella adopted the role of my 'saviour' with a vigour. She could tell all of her friends how she was selflessly rescuing me. She could tell them she had been 'right' all along. And, I was happy to allow that, in fruition of my own plans.

The strategy was, that should I ever contact Isabella with a pre-agreed codeword – that she already had immediate access to all of the important aspects of my life. My financial outgoings had already been covered for several forthcoming years. So, she would only need to tidy up loose-ends – such as sealing-off the water, electric and gas to my home – acting as caretaker until my hoped-for return.

Normally, I would have felt uncomfortable imposing on anyone with such a level of responsibility. Yet, I knew Isabella was doing it for selfish reasons, of bolstering her own personal narrative. The *tonal* truly is insidious in the best of us.

After speaking with Florinda, I had gone on to make that one telephone call from Amsterdam.

'Osorio,' I had clicked the phone down on her. One word, had been enough for Isabella to put the plan into motion. One word, was enough to ripple out and change a lineage.

Thus, I had been prepared to do the unthinkable. And, as my mind finally unravelled when I touched home soil in the airport, all my affairs… or more accurately by that point… all of Robert's affairs, had already been put into order. I could let go.

"You see Henrick," I offered to his growing realisation, "I now only need to make another phone call, and I can pick-up right where Robert left off."

"Of course," I mused, stroking my beard, "getting used to social considerations again, may take a while." I had offered it in jest; yet there was a greater sting of truth behind the sentiment.

"But, what *really* happened to Florinda?!" Josephina asked, almost as if afraid for the answer.

I felt for Josephina especially. I could almost see the frantic efforts of her *tonal* to explain and soundly rationalise my story – and suffering and failing, as a result of being inadequately able to. I momentarily wished that Florinda was present. She would have been able to explain it much better than I.

"She's waiting on the edge of *infinity*," Henrick spoke as a whisper with his *knowing*. There was both anger and awe in his voice. "She collaborated with you, in order to shoot off to the very boundless edge between the *second* and *third attention!*"

He was right. The two women listened as I confirmed that my injection of luminosity to Florinda, had helped her ignite almost the entirety of her luminous cocoon… but not quite. That had been the mastery of her art – in not fully letting go into the temptation of the *great unknown*, but in holding back just a little… just enough for the rest of us.

Florinda had leaped to the very fringes of the *unknown*, whereby she was to wait as guide for the rest of her line. She had made the ultimate sacrifice of not only self, but also of pure liberation itself. She was hovering as a guiding light – a beacon – until such a time as the rest of her fellow sorcerers could join her on the final journey.

"That star," was all Henrick could muster, in response to the final decimation of his own line. "That lilac star…"

He would never see his beloved again. The realisation was the final blow that destroyed him. Until then – as a true member of the *Omega Assembly* – he had held out hope that death was not as final as most perceived. This realisation, was something much more devastating to him. If Florinda were not dead, but not of this earth either, then she was utterly beyond his reach.

The *Omega Assembly* would go on. The remaining members would try. They would scheme and plot and truly give it their best. But any *seer* would know, they now were energetically castrated. The *Omega Assembly* were now of no threat to the *four-pronged lineage*. As per Maria Elena's original intentions born of the *Coyote Nagual*, we had used the *three-pronged line*, as a catapult to *freedom* for ourselves.

As though it had all finally been too much, Josephina exploded in a barrage of accusations. "It's all been nice and neat for you!... You've been pretending all this time, whilst we've been struggling!... You're Florinda's favourite pet – privy to all her little secrets!... It's all soooo easy for the great Roberto!"

Finally, she appeared to exhaust herself of whatever she needed to get off her chest.

"You really don't get it, do you?" I asked, with muted concern. "You really don't understand what the true cost of all this is for me?"

Her wet, soulful eyes blinked at me without comprehension.

"The cost to me of this past year, was never convenience, or comfort, or some caricature of pretending; it was not even in forgetting who I was..." My voice quavered, but this time not through a lack of use, but the emotion of what I myself was realising. "The cost to me – which is almost unbearable – is that I have to put *his* skin back on... I have to be *him* again! I've lost..."

I could not go on. I could not admit to everything that I had experienced, which was already fast becoming foreign and hazy to my everyday recollection.

I simply grieved, feeling as though I was about to engulfed from within, and join the old lady. The feeling threatened everything.

"How do we find her?" Josephina meekly asked, trying to disguise hope amidst a new tone of sensitivity. I knew she had a thousand questions. I knew I was going to be nothing but a disappointment to her, for my insufficient answers.

Robert was clawing his way back in. I was not entirely convinced I wanted that. So much pain and strife lay ahead for everyone.

I laughed ironically to myself. That annoying conflict-of-thought. The uncertainty. The mental masturbation. The wearisome self-indulgence. It was a sure sign that Robert was almost back to his old position of *assemblage*.

"What do we do?" Elizabeth flatly asked, with a pragmatism that reminded me of my old wartime-educated grandmother. The three of us turned our backs, wholly indifferent to the defeated old man left sobbing amongst the deconsecrated ruins of the church.

"We do our best," I offered. "We try, and figure it out together. We go on, and attempt to be *impeccable warriors*, as she taught. Only then, does it give us a shot at finding Florinda, hovering out in the vastness of *infinity*. Only in living up to the one chance her sacrifice gave us, do we get to join her, and perhaps one day go home."

- 13 -

The Mysterious Thirteenth.

(aka: Never·Reaching Ixtlan)

A year had passed, before I resurfaced on Isabella's doorstep. I needed to reclaim the spare key to my own property, letting myself in like a visiting guest.

As predicted, she squealed in delight at seeing my dishevelled form. Or more accurately, Isabella was delighted to have felt proven right all along. She had 'saved' me.

"Look at you," she judged, handing me a cup of 'immune-boosting' tea – having supplemented it with homeopathic essence of 'Bison-spirit'. "I shouldn't have let you go. What those ghastly people did to you!..."

In reality, she had no idea what the group had actually done for me. Yet, I endured her predicted onslaught of judgements in silence. Thanking her for her invaluable help, I proceeded to my apartment... hesitant to even considering the word 'home'.

Showered, shaved, my hair cut and in fashionable clothing, I stood at the mirror. It had been several days since my resurfacing in civilisation, and it felt stranger than I had predicated.

Just who was that guy in the mirror, looking back at me? Obviously it was me... yet, something elusive had changed. I could only stare at the lines of his face, the familiar contours, and those eyes.

It still felt like I did not fully know just who was looking back at me from those eyes. Had all of me returned, I wondered.

I busied myself within a list of practical chores, from re-connecting the utilities of my apartment, shopping for food, getting my hair cut, getting the car out of the compound, and removing Isabella as power of attorney. Yet, something nagged at the corners of my quickly-congealing mind – a lingering feeling of obligation.

I searched the streets, visiting all of the old haunts looking for Nameless and his nameless companion. Trying to think like I had for the past year, it was with growing dismay that I realised I could not. My thinking was shallow, harsh, cold – of form and petty reason.

The winds did not speak to me anymore. The little plants had become silent.

The wholly insufficient limitations of my mind had violently taken hold again. I felt like I was drowning.

Eventually I did find Nameless – stooped over a park trash can, cheerily humming away to himself. At first approach, it broke my heart that he appeared startled and afraid, with his immediately backing away. He had always been nervous of those who had not understood him – and of that, there were many. Even his nameless canine barked in defensive anxiety at me, trying its best to defend her master on only three legs. I did not think the dog could outwardly see me through its milky eyes; more that it was reacting to its master's emotional frequency. She growled in entirely the wrong direction.

"Toy solider," I offered in a calming tone, holding out the most expensive meatball panini sandwich I could find on the way. "Toy solider."

Nameless peered at me, hesitant. His wordless eyes scanned me over, and a smile broke out on his face, at the dawning comprehension that it was me. His dirty, stinky and scabbed form hugged me tightly, and I was all the more grateful for it than he could ever realise.

I moved quickly and intensely to home and advocate for Nameless. Florinda had always said it was proper for a warrior to make suitable gestures of reimbursement, as token for *paying back to the spirit of man*.

Even with my benefactorship, what I had not anticipated was just how difficult it would be to get Nameless back into society – to find him the basics of shelter, safety and sustenance. I fought too many times with representatives of the local state services, with receptionists, doctors, social workers and financial aid providers.

Without a history, social security number, family connections, medical records or even a name – none of the official services were eager to help. Nameless was truly no-one to them, and for that, society rejected him. Society desperately… almost aggressively… needed him to be someone – to have the solidity and comforting predictability of narrative, before they would consent to allowing themselves to be called 'helpers'.

The *Black Magicians* commanded their rituals be enacted. They demanded the sacrifices be made at the altar of conformity. Yet the acolytes of civilisation never understood, that they were necromancers conjuring the insubstantiality of phantoms only.

I did eventually manage to find Nameless some token of security. It was mainly via the more genuine good-hearted efforts of local charities, staffed by volunteers who had experienced the unique challenges of homelessness themselves at some point. I heard too many stories of loved ones who just disappeared without any trace – and how state bureaucracy was too inflexibly-sterile to care, the police too overstretched to search, and society too willingly blind to those without solid stories.

I was truly shocked how many people could disappear in contemporary, western so-called 'civilised' society. Despite the privilege of living within the 'inner circle', the cohorts of the *Coyote Nagual* had been no exception to this. *Taisha Abelar* and *Florinda Donner (Grau)* had also disappeared without a trace, at the time of their Nagual's departure. Now, the *Omega Assembly's* Aidan, Katrina and Marta – and their even less fortunate preceding cohorts Philomena and Carl – were victim to that… inevitable?… legacy.

Witnessing the pain of those intent on using their hurt to help others, I felt a pang of guilt at what I had done to my own family years early, before ever having met the group. At least, I had left my family with the gift of a comforting story, to soothe themselves.

But with the kindness of volunteers, and a little financial investment of my own, I was eventually able to house Nameless. The compassion of such aid-workers reached beyond the requirement for *personal history*.

I saw Nameless settled into his own place. It was small and sparse, but it was sheltered and safe.

Yet, the first time I went to visit him, I was deeply shocked. His attendant support worker explained that the first thing the state had done, was to remove his nameless companion and have the dog euthanised. The three-legged companion of so many years, had been considered a luxury the state would have no part in sustaining. It had been deemed easier to have the dog put down, than to even call myself. After all, I was not legally recognised as any next to kin to Nameless.

My heart shattered at what I had done.

Nameless sat in his armchair staring at a blank wall. His eyes were vacant, focused on somewhere distant I could not see. A thick string of drool fastened his chin to his collar.

"He doesn't really do much else," his kind-hearted support worker offered, by way of some sort of explanation. "He doesn't get any visitors, doesn't say anything, and doesn't go out. Only the visiting psychiatric nurse deals with him. It's probably the medication they make him take."

"Do… do you actually know him? Do you know his name?" she asked, placing her jacket on to leave. I felt she was truly interested to know him, as a person. She had heart.

"I wouldn't do that to him," I quietly offered to her confused expression, as she left.

"I'm so sorry," was all I could offer him. His now-dull eyes appeared not to recognise me. "Daddy shouter."

In my re-merging civilised mindset, I had taken Florinda's teachings too directly… to linearly. In my ego and obligation, I had done Nameless a huge disservice, and injured his spirit. It was not the proper payment befitting of a sorcerer – not honouring his own true warrior spirit, in the beautifully unique and innocent form he had once been his best.

Florinda had been right, as always. Robert… I… was a stubbornly violent fool.

Coming back one night (I had taken Nameless' own front door key, knowing he would not have used it), I brought supplies. A waterproof rucksack full of necessities – food, toiletries, clothing, sleeping bag, matches, good socks, and zip-lock bags etc. I did think of leaving cash with him, but ultimately decided against it. I did not want to make him a target. And, I had previously seen Nameless overlook discarded notes in favour of the likes of plastic bags, appearing to have little idea as to the social construction of monetary value.

Taking him out as far into the quietude of the industrial district, I lay him down beneath the warmth of the overhead humming conduit. I stayed with him until the next evening, when I saw something of his former self emerge.

"Toy solider!" he chirped, eagerly taking the hot drink and sandwich I offered him, smiling for the first time since I had 'helped' him.

I sat silently by, lost to my thoughts next to my thoughtless companion. A jarring shiver ran up my spine, to the tune of *thrum-thrum-thrum*. Now as Robert, that sound felt as though taunting me to remember something – something elusive, nestling within the darker recesses of my now reconstituted mind. I figured I would recall it in time, if it were important.

"Be well, my friend," I offered Nameless, with genuine well-wishes of his success, as I stood to leave him. "Toy Solider."

Arriving back at the stark, white-washed, sterile confines of my apartment, I experienced the sudden need to cry. It was all too hard... much harder than it should be. A part of me had the sudden urge to go back out, and join Nameless.

Instead, I splashed cold water on my face, and got the coffee machine going. As I waited for the pressure to build and the water to heat, I found myself at my writing desk. There, I absently opened the draw for the first time since returning.

A finely-crafted gold pocket timepiece gleamed alongside a sleek, touch-screen watch. Various expensive pens and trinkets were scattered next to my designer glasses. All of it, a draw of empty vibrations.

It all felt sickening somehow. I experienced it as a great wave of nausea, caused by the endless clamour of description shouting out from the silence of my apartment.

But there, amongst the din, was an old notepad and chewed pencil I had never seen before. I recognised the fine scrawl of John's handwriting. He had started the draft with the title, '*Lineage: The Art of Stalking... part one, by Robert Abelar.*'

I had not seen the group since my return. I had instead tried to solidify myself in the various necessities of re-organising Robert's... no, *my*... life. Yet, the truth of it was that I was not sure how to approach my old cohorts.

I knew they would not reject or judge me. Josephina, Elizabeth, Sam and Chris would likely have a hundred questions. But, that was to be expected.

Rather, I felt like Robert was there, already present with the group. It was him, who I was truly reluctant to encounter... the final nail that would secure a lid on the previous year. It had been a year that Robert would never have thought even possible. And now, I too struggled with trying to reconcile some sort of cohesion and understanding onto the experiences.

What I had done to Nameless, was stupid, self-centred and full of self-importance. I realised that habitual stink of personality had descended on me already. I was no better than Isabella, after all.

I resolved to return to the group. I still had commitments to honour; and there were fellow warriors on the *path of freedom* I was bound to. Moreso, I still clearly had work to do on myself.

Strolling through the city to the old town quarter, it was a bright, cheerful day.

Meili opened the door, ushering me in through the narrow hallway full of paintings, treating me as though she had only seen me yesterday.

"Come in silly monkey!" she chirped in her carefree manner. "You late. We have been waiting for you!"

Jon-Paul, Michael, Vince, Hui, Josephina, Elizabeth, Sam and Chris were all huddled around the kitchen table, animatedly chatting. Even the usually-reclusive Anouska was present, smiling at me from beneath her thick glasses. John placed the old milking stool down next to him, patting it as invitation to join them. The twins appeared almost bursting to hound me with questions.

"What do you think old chap?" John offered, between blue puffs of his pipe. "We were just discussing the benefits of psychotropic pharmacology, within the trends of modern psychotherapeutic industry..."

Teresa placed a misshapen earthen mug of sweetened nettle tea into my hands, whispering into my ear, "welcome back poppet."

"I think..." I momentarily hesitated, struggling with something. "I think that the models of western psycho-medical interventions are predominantly structured around the unchallenged – and too often unrecognised – assumption of ego-enforcement. As such, there are obstacles inherent to not recognising the limitations of such a biased approach, when presuming pharmaceutical support..."

I was an intellectual buffoon. I was espousing academic diarrhoea. I was mentally-masturbating with crude form and narrow descriptions. I was the idiot that had done the brilliant spirit of a nameless companion an utter disservice. I was the man-child who still craved the companionship and guidance of his old white-haired teacher, who he had unwittingly helped to push beyond his own reach.

I was Robert Abelar once again.

The Eagle.
('The central axis of reality, consisting of 48-demensional fractal awareness)

The 48-bands ('refractions' or dimensions) of Reality

1	2	3	4	5	6	7	8
21	22	23	24	25	26	27	28

The 8-layers able to sustain stable Assemblage Points.

('The 'Goldilocks Zone' of awareness)

+5	+4	+3	+2	+1		-1	-2	-3	-4	-5
16	17	18	19	20		29	30	31	32	33

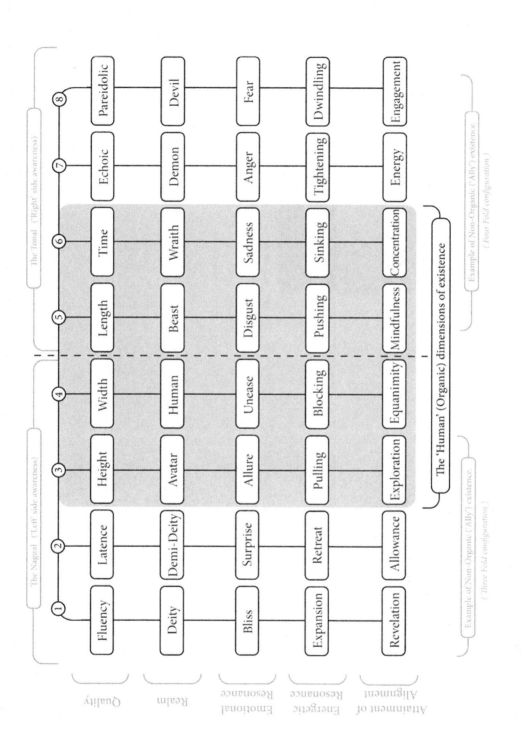

The Nagual ('Left side awareness')

The Tonal ('Right side awareness')

	1	2	3	4	5	6	7	8
Quality	Fluency	Latence	Height	Width	Length	Time	Echoic	Pareidolic
Realm	Deity	Demi-Deity	Avatar	Human	Beast	Wraith	Demon	Devil
Emotional Resonance	Bliss	Surprise	Allure	Unease	Disgust	Sadness	Anger	Fear
Energetic Resonance	Expansion	Retreat	Pulling	Blocking	Pushing	Sinking	Tightening	Dwindling
Attainment of Alignment	Revelation	Allowance	Exploration	Equanimity	Mindfulness	Concentration	Energy	Engagement

The 'Human' (Organic) dimensions of existence

Example of Non-Organic ('Ally') existence
(Four Fold configuration)

Example of Non-Organic ('Ally') existence
(Three Fold configuration)

175

1.c. 'The 'multi-phasic' nature of the Assemblage Point.

1.a. The traditional 4 dimensions have a smaller overlap, collapsing less luminosity under the 'halo of assemblage', and thus reduced ('lower-resolution' or shallow-'depth') perceptual cohesion. The remaining dimensions of the total 8, remain wholly outside of perceptual range. Overall, the Assemblage Point is more diffused and less focused, granting less control and manoeuvrability across the total 'balloon of awareness'.

1.b. The typical orientation of a 'sorcerer' or 'seer'. The traditional 4-dimensions have greater overlap, resulting in more luminosity being brought under the 'halo of awareness' (increased perceptual range). Likewise, there is slight overlap in the remaining dimensions, as all realms are 'sunken' (brought into focus) towards a more complete totality of being (i.e. a move towards greater perceptual cohesion).

1.c. The 'multi-phasic' (diffused) existance of the 8-dimensional Assemblage Point on the 'balloon of awarness'. Essentially, the Assemblage Point is a perceptual conduit and lens focusing and collapsing the luminious fibres of awareness into perceptual cohesion.

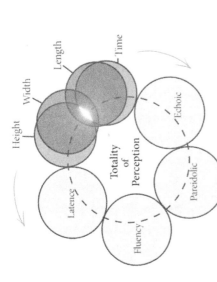

1.a. Orientation of the **Assemblage Point** of an Everyday Person.

Height *Width* *Length*

Time

Echoic

Pareidolic

Fluency

Latence

Totality of Perception

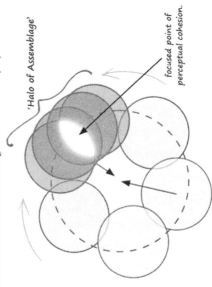

'Halo of Assemblage'

focused point of perceptual cohesion.

1.b. Orientation of the **Assemblage Point** of a Seer.

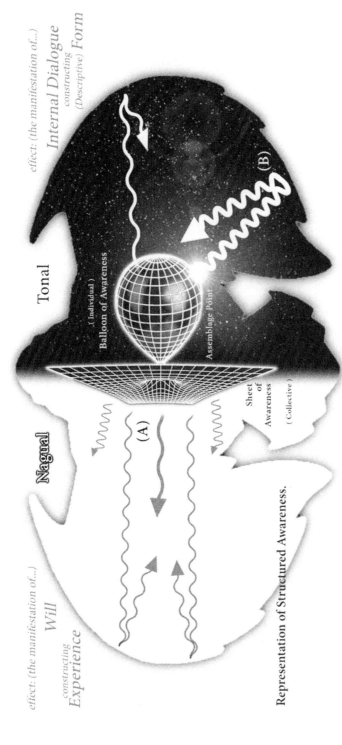

effect: (the manifestation of...)
Internal Dialogue
constructing
(Descriptive) Form

Tonal

(Individual)
Balloon of Awareness

Assemblage Point

(B)

effect: (the manifestation of...)
Will
constructing
Experience

Nagual

(A)

Sheet
of
Awareness

(Collective)

Representation of Structured Awareness.

Intent moves as the only active force, throughout the fluidic mediums of the 'nagual' ('left side awareness') and 'tonal' ('right side awareness').

Intent, can either be *collective* (A), emanating from the wider 'sheet of awareness' (the collective of multiple balloons - akin to 'background radiation'). Intent can also emanate from an individual 'balloon of awareness' as a more localised force (B).

The return ('speed' or 'manifest effect') of intent - as reflected by the mirrored wings of the Eagle - depends on i) its 'wavelength' (i.e. the original force of transmission) and ii) its 'latency' (i.e. how much it originally came under the 'halo' of *cohesive* awareness of the individual *assemblage point*). Collective and Individual intent, can equally manifest on both sides of the nagual and tonal.

Depending on these factors, intent can manifest ('complete its return journey') either in more immediate effect, or even manifest in a longer 'delayed' journey of 'recycled manifestations' (other lifetimes).

If you enjoyed this book, then please take a moment to leave positive feedback on Amazon

After all, there is much more to this story… more to the Lineage… and only as a collective effort – as a magical force of shared intent – will we arrive there together.

Robert.

Other titles to watch out for in the LINEAGE series:

also within the Eagle's emanations:

LINEAGE: Further Tales of Power.

LINEAGE: A Parallel Reality - Conversations with doña Florinda.

LINEAGE: The Naguals of Time.

LINEAGE: The Art of Dreaming (part two).

LINEAGE: The Eagle's Flight.

LINEAGE: The First Ring of Power.

LINEAGE: The Expression of Emptiness.

LINEAGE: The Sorcerer's Manoeuvre.

LINEAGE: The Search for Ixtlan.

LINEAGE: The Art of Stalking (epilogue / part three).

Printed in Great Britain
by Amazon

40201713R00106